Westward Expansion Almanac

Westward Expansion Almanac

Tom Pendergast
and Sara Pendergast
Christine Slovey, Editor

AN IMPRINT OF THE GALE GROUP

DETROIT · SAN FRANCISCO · LONDON
BOSTON · WOODBRIDGE, CT

Westward Expansion: Almanac

Tom Pendergast and Sara Pendergast

Staff

Christine Slovey, *U•X•L Editor*
Carol DeKane Nagel, *U•X•L Managing Editor*
Tom Romig, *U•X•L Publisher*

Rita Wimberley, *Senior Buyer*
Dorothy Maki, *Manufacturing Manager*
Evi Seoud, *Assistant Production Manager*
Mary Beth Trimper, *Production Director*

Shalice Shah-Caldwell, *Permissions Specialist*
Michelle DiMercurio, *Cover Art Director*
Pamela A.E. Galbreath, *Page Art Director*
Kenn Zorn, *Product Design Manager*

Kelly A. Quin, *Image Editor*
Pamela A. Reed, *Imaging Coordinator*
Robert Duncan and Dan Newell, *Imaging Specialists*
Randy Bassett, *Image Database Supervisor*
Barbara J. Yarrow, *Graphic Services Supervisor*

Marco DiVita, Graphix Group, *Typesetting*

Library of Congress Card Number: 00–036375

Contents

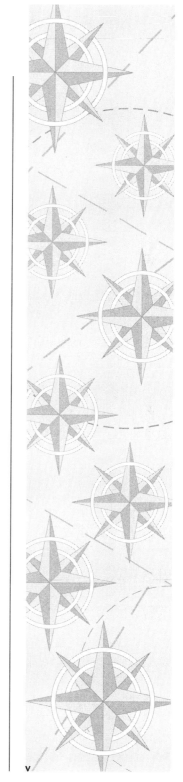

Introduction xi

Reader's Guide xv

Timeline xvii

Words to Know xxxv

Research and Activity Ideas xliii

Chapter 1: Claiming the Near West:
Territorial Expansion to 1812 1

    Disrupting the Balance of Power 2

    The French and Indian War (1754–63) 3

    Opening the West 4

    The Revolutionary War (1776–83) 5

    The Ordinance of 1785 7

    Excerpt from the Land Ordinance of 1785 (box) . . 7

    The Northwest Ordinance 8

    Taking Indian Land 9

    Land Sales 10

Meriwether Lewis.
*(© Bettmann/Corbis.
Reproduced by permission.)*

Carving Farms from the Forest 10

Obstacles to Expansion 12

The Louisiana Purchase 14

The Coming of the War of 1812 16

Tecumseh and Indian Resistance 16

The Battle of New Orleans (box) 17

Chapter 2: Opening the West **21**

The Fur Trade 22

Claiming the Land 23

Discovering the Land's Riches: Lewis and Clark . . 24

Sacajawea (box) 28

The Inhabited West 29

Founding Astoria 33

Trappers Map the West 34

Topographical Engineers 35

The Mountain Man Rendezvous (box) 36

John Frémont, Promoter of the West 37

Mapping the Inland Territories 40

**Chapter 3: Driving the Indians Westward:
Indian Removal to 1840** **43**

First Encounters 44

Following God's Plan 44

The White Tide 45

Early Hostilities 46

Dividing the Land 46

Fighting for the Old Northwest 48

Little Turtle's War 49

Defeating Tecumseh 49

Driving Native Americans Westward 52

Andrew Jackson, Indian Fighter 52

The Seminole Wars 52

Indian Removal 53

The Trail of Tears 54

Manifest Destiny and the
Plight of Native Americans 55

Chapter 4: Claiming the Far West: Territorial Expansion after 1812 . . . . **59**

The Dreams of a President 60
The Drive for Expansion 62
Manifest Destiny (box) 63
Texas 64
Acquiring the Oregon Territory 66
War with Mexico. 68
The Gadsden Purchase (box) 70
Populating the West 70
Land and Gold. 70
Farmers and Ranchers 72
The End of the Frontier. 74

Chapter 5: Trails West **77**

The First Expeditions 77
The Father of the Santa Fe Trail 79
Susan Shelby Magoffin:
A Woman on the Santa Fe Trail (box) 80
Near Death at the Cimarron Cutoff 80
Danger on the Trail. 82
The Oregon Trail 84
The Great Migration 86
The Routes West 88
Stocking a Wagon 92
The Donner Party (box). 94
Indians on the Trail 96
Death on the Trail 97
Other Dreams, Other Trails 98
Trails' End 102

Chapter 6: The Gold Rush. **105**

California before the Gold Rush 106
The Discovery of Gold. 110
John Sutter (box) 113
Gold Fever 114
Getting There. 115
Levi Strauss (box) 118
In the Goldfields 120
The Mining Camps 122

Vigilante Justice. 123
A Diverse Country 124
Modern Robin Hood: Joaquin Murieta 126
Gold Rush Legacy 126

A sheep corral doubles as a hotel in California during the gold rush.
(© Bettmann/Corbis. Reproduced by permission.)

Chapter 7: Winning the West:
Indian Wars after 1840 . . . . **131**

Indians of the Southwest 132
Navajo Resistance. 133
The Apache. 135
Cochise 136
Blood on the Plains 137
The Sand Creek Massacre 139
Geronimo (box). 139
The War Escalates 140
Black Hills Battles 141
The Battle of Little Bighorn 142
The End of the Indian Wars 143

Chapter 8: Westward Expansion and Indian Culture . . **149**

The Common Culture of Trade. 149
The End of Native American Power. 151
The Iroquois 152
The Navajo 155
The Plains Indians 159
Using the Buffalo (box) 162

Chapter 9: The Wild West **169**

Guns and Lawlessness 170
The Gold Rush 170
The Cowboy Frontier 172
The Cattle Boom 174
The Cattle Drive (box). 176
The Wild Life of a Cattle Town 178
Dancing Cowboys (box) 180
Cowboys and Killers. 181
The Fence Cutter's War 183
The End of the Wild West 184

Chapter 10: Religion and the West **187**

    The First Missionaries 187
    Native American Religious Traditions. 188
    Protestant Missionaries 193
    Mormons. 196
    Peter Cartwright, Methodist Preacher (box) . . . 197
    Some Must Push and Some Must Pull (box) 200

Chapter 11: Technology and the
Making of the West **205**

    Canals. 206
    The Stagecoach 209
    Black Bart (box). 212
    Railroads 213
    Mary Fields (box) 214
    Guns. 217
    The Pony Express 221
    The Telegraph 223
    Barbed Wire 225
    The Barbed Wire Industry (box) 226

The Frontier and American Character **231**

    Defining the Frontier 232
    The Call of the West. 233
    The Difficulties of Moving West (box) 234
    Manifest Destiny 235
    The American Character. 236
    Democracy and the Frontier 237
    Spreading the Myth 240
    James Fenimore Cooper (box) 241

Where to Learn More. **247**

Index **249**

Deadwood stagecoach traveling to South Dakota.
(© CORBIS. Reproduced by permission.)

Introduction

In the years between 1763 and 1890, what began as thirteen British colonies clinging to the eastern seaboard of North America expanded into a sprawling independent nation that stretched 3,000 miles from the Atlantic to the Pacific Ocean. The story of the westward expansion of the United States is at once a romantic saga of human accomplishment and a tragic account of human cruelty. The steady march of American settlement into the West created national heroes and helped define the national character. Mountain men, miners, explorers, pioneers, cowboys, and outlaws lived such colorful and independent lives that their exploits continue to be celebrated in fiction and in film into the twentieth-first century. Many historians maintain that the process of settling the West—carving farms and communities out of the wilderness, surmounting tremendous odds to move whole families across the sprawling continent—made this nation's inhabitants more resourceful, independent, and rugged than their European forebears. In the romantic version of the settling of the West, stalwart pioneers carved their chosen land from a howling wilderness, building the most powerful nation in the world in the process.

However, from the perspective of the Native Americans who inhabited North America for thousands of years prior to white settlement, the westward expansion of the United States looks decidedly unromantic. Though there were wide variations among American Indian cultures, they shared a bond with the natural world and a sense that land could be used but not owned. The Indians were ill-prepared—culturally and biologically—to deal with the impact that Europeans would have on their lives. Diseases carried to the continent by Europeans took a terrible toll on Indian populations even before colonial British settlers began encroaching on Indian lands. As the colonies freed themselves from British rule and settlers pressed farther west, clashes with the Native Americans occurred more frequently. Indians were depicted as hostile and ignorant savages and whites did not hesitate to take Indian land and kill Native Americans who resisted. By the 1830s it had become official government policy to drive the Indians from land desired by white settlers. For more than a century, Americans waged relentless war on Indian populations, killing men, women, and children in their quest to rid themselves of what they called "the Indian menace." By the end of the nineteenth century, Native Americans who had survived the Indian Wars were no longer free to roam the land but were confined to reservations. To the native inhabitants of the continent, westward expansion was an utter disaster.

In this book we have tried to acknowledge the validity of different perspectives of westward expansion. Some chapters tell the story of the steady movement of settlers into the wilderness, and of the efforts of soldiers and diplomats to claim land for American control. Other chapters tell the story of the century-long conflict between whites and Indians. The book covers the gold strikes, wagon trains, and cattle drives that made westward expansion such a colorful and interesting era of American history. It also discusses the effects that westward expansion had on Native American cultures. Because this book is concerned with explaining the westward expansion of a growing nation, we have emphasized the role played by the colonial British and the Americans. But we have tried throughout to acknowledge the shaping influences exerted by American Indians as well as by the Spanish, Mexicans, French, and British.

In the chapters that follow we have tried to cover the major events and themes in the westward expansion of the

United States. Our account begins with the conflict between French, British, Indian, and colonial forces in the 1750s and 1760s for control of the area just west of the Appalachian Mountains. It extends through the nineteenth century to the final defeat of the American Indians and the closing of the frontier in 1890. We have tried to present objective accounts of the romantic events that are so closely associated with westward expansion—the California gold rush, the wagon trains, railway construction, and the cowboys—but also to account for the small and mundane events that made westward expansion possible. Westward expansion was the work of an entire nation: for every dramatic leader like Andrew Jackson or Daniel Boone, there were hundreds of settlers who were equally brave and determined to claim their place in a new land. Many of the most dramatic westward movements were started not as part of the grand vision of an influential leader but as the result of independent pioneers striking out and pulling civilization along behind them. Our goal throughout has been to present an accurate portrayal of the complex, difficult, and violent process through which a young nation slowly pushed its boundaries westward.

—Tom Pendergast and Sara Pendergast

Reader's Guide

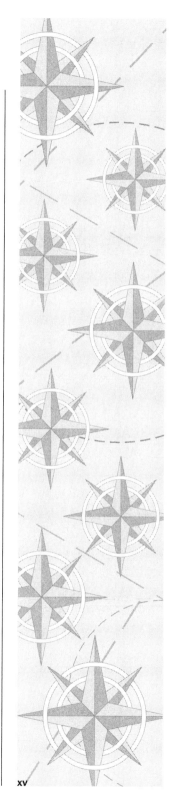

Westward Expansion: Almanac presents a comprehensive overview of the frontier period in American history, covering the years between 1763 and 1890 when the United States expanded from the original thirteen British colonies to a nation of forty-eight states stretching across the North American continent. The volume covers all the major wars (the Revolutionary War, the War of 1812, the Mexican-American War, and the many battles between whites and Indians); the land purchases (including the Louisiana Purchase); the important trails linking wilderness to civilization; life on the frontier; how Native Americans were affected by westward expansion; and technological advances that made expansion easier.

Format

Westward Expansion: Almanac is divided into twelve subject chapters, each focusing on a particular topic, such as the diplomatic negotiations and military conquests that made western lands available, the gold rush that launched the settlement of the Far West, the Wild West, and religion in the West. The chapters contain sidebars that highlight people and events of special interest, and each chapter offers a list of additional sources students can go to for more information as well as a list of any other sources used in writing the chapter. More than sixty-five black-and-white photographs and maps help illustrate the material covered in the text. The volume begins with a timeline of important events in the history of westward expansion; a "Words to Know" section that introduces students to difficult or unfamiliar terms (terms are also defined within the text); and a "Research and Activity Ideas" section. The volume concludes with a general bibliography and a subject index so students can easily find the people, places, and events discussed throughout *Westward Expansion: Almanac.*

Dedication

To our children, Conrad and Louisa, who have journeyed with us on our own westward trek.

Special Thanks

Special thanks are due to Lynne E. Heckman, teacher of American history at Valley View Middle School in Snohomish, Washington, for helping us understand the needs and interests of middle school students and teachers, and to the many historians and writers whose work on the West we filtered through our minds as we prepared this collection.

Comments and Suggestions

We welcome your comments on *Westward Expansion: Almanac* and suggestions for other topics to consider. Please write: Editors, *Westward Expansion: Almanac,* U•X•L, 27500 Drake Rd., Farmington Hills, Michigan 48331-3535; call toll-free: 1-800-877-4253; fax to (248) 414-5043; or send e-mail via http://www.galegroup.com.

Timeline of Events in Westward Expansion

1622   Indian chief Powhatan's younger brother, Opecha-
nough, starts the first Indian war by attacking
colonists in Jamestown, Virginia, to protest white use
of Indian land.

1754   The French defeat George Washington and his men at
the Battle of Fort Necessity on July 3–4, beginning the
French and Indian War.

1763   The first Treaty of Paris is signed, ending the French
and Indian War. Under the treaty, France relinquishes
its claim to Canada and the Ohio Valley to England
and hands over its holdings west of the Mississippi
River to Spain.

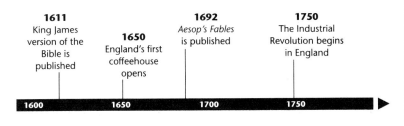

1611
King James
version of the
Bible is
published

1650
England's first
coffeehouse
opens

1692
Aesop's Fables
is published

1750
The Industrial
Revolution begins
in England

1600   1650   1700   1750

1763 Hoping to end Indian attacks in the Ohio Valley, the British issue the Proclamation of 1763, which recalls all settlers from west of the Appalachian crest and forbids further emigration into the area.

1769 Catholic missionary Father Junipero Serra and the Spanish army establish the first of twenty-one missions along the coast of California. Serra directs soldiers to round up the Native North Americans and bring them, by force if necessary, to the missions.

1775 After years of hunting in and exploring the rich forests of Kentucky, Daniel Boone cuts the first road over the Cumberland Gap to found Boonesborough in Kentucky.

1776 The Revolutionary War begins. Among the many factors contributing to the war are clashes between colonists and the British over access to land west of the Appalachians.

1783 The Revolutionary War ends. The second Treaty of Paris grants the newly formed United States of America its independence. The United States gains all of the territory from the Great Lakes south to the Gulf of Mexico and from the Appalachian Mountains west to the Mississippi River.

1783 To raise revenues, the newly formed U.S. government claims all of the Indian lands east of the Mississippi River (consisting of present-day Indiana, Kentucky, Ohio, and Tennessee) to sell to settlers. The Chippewa, Delaware, Kickapoo, Miami, Ottawa, Potawatomi, Shawnee, and Wyandot nations and some Iroquois warriors join together to oppose the invasion of U.S. settlers into their territory.

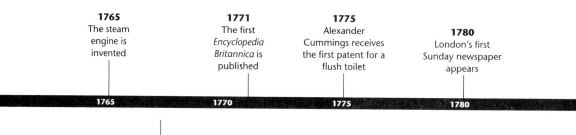

1765
The steam engine is invented

1771
The first *Encyclopedia Britannica* is published

1775
Alexander Cummings receives the first patent for a flush toilet

1780
London's first Sunday newspaper appears

1765   1770   1775   1780

1785 The Ordinance of 1785 establishes a pattern for surveying and dividing all territories westward from the point where the Ohio River leaves the state of Pennsylvania.

1787 The Northwest Ordinance, also known as the Ordinance of 1787, provides for the orderly creation of future states, establishes a system of laws in the territories, forbids slavery, and guarantees certain civil rights.

August 20, 1794 The Battle of Fallen Timbers takes place near present-day Fort Wayne, Indiana. Bands of Shawnee and Miami Indians led by Little Turtle (Miami), Blue Jacket (Shawnee), and others go into battle against General Anthony Wayne, known to the Indians as "Blacksnake." The Indians are forced to retreat when British support disappears.

November 19, 1794 The Treaty of Amity, Commerce, and Navigation between England and the United States (also called Jay's Treaty) is signed, reestablishing trade between Great Britain and its former colonies. In late 1794 the British agree to withdraw from fur trading and military posts they occupy in U.S. territory. With the withdrawal of the English, Indian nations lose an important ally against the United States.

May 1803 The United States purchases from France more than 800,000 square miles of land west of the Mississippi River for $15 million. The Louisiana Purchase doubles the size of the United States. This territory today makes up the states of Arkansas, Iowa, Kansas, Louisiana, Missouri, Montana, Nebraska, North Dakota, Oklahoma, South Dakota, and parts of Colorado, Minnesota, and Wyoming.

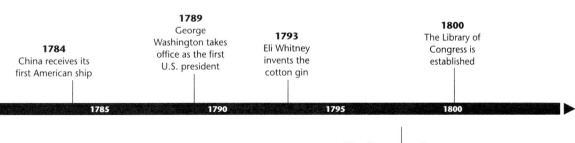

1784 China receives its first American ship

1789 George Washington takes office as the first U.S. president

1793 Eli Whitney invents the cotton gin

1800 The Library of Congress is established

1785   1790   1795   1800

Sacajawea helped guide the Lewis and Clark expedition.
(Drawing by Alfred Russel. Reproduced by permission of Corbis-Bettmann.)

Shawnee chief Tecumseh.
(Reproduced by permission of the Granger Collection, New York.)

May 14, 1804 Meriwether Lewis, William Clark, and their entourage set out from St. Louis, Missouri to determine whether the Gulf of Mexico and the Pacific Ocean are linked by a river system. Finding no such water connection, they pioneer an overland route across the Rocky Mountains.

1805 Tenskwatawa becomes known as the "Shawnee Prophet." The Prophet travels widely among the western tribes, urging Native Americans to reject European ways and renew Indian traditions. Tenskwatawa's brother, Tecumseh, uses these teachings to create a military and political confederacy of Indian tribes.

September 23, 1806 The Lewis and Clark expedition returns to St. Louis after nearly twenty-eight months of exploration. The expedition had been given up for lost, and its return is celebrated throughout the country.

November 7, 1811 Battle of Tippecanoe takes place in the Indian village of Prophetstown in present-day northwestern Indiana. Governor William Henry Harrison of Indiana attacks the Indian village with one thousand soldiers and defeats the Shawnee in the absence of their chief, Tecumseh.

1812 The War of 1812 begins. In a war that is often called the Second War for Independence, Americans seek to finally eliminate the British presence in the Old Northwest and to end British attacks on American ships carrying goods to France.

October 5, 1813 The Battle of the Thames takes place along the banks of the Thames River north of Lake Erie in present-day Ontario, Canada. Indian leader Tecumseh hungers for a final showdown that will once and for all drive the Americans from Indian lands. The British

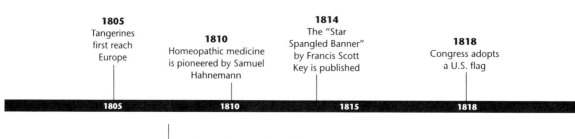

1805
Tangerines first reach Europe

1810
Homeopathic medicine is pioneered by Samuel Hahnemann

1814
The "Star Spangled Banner" by Francis Scott Key is published

1818
Congress adopts a U.S. flag

1805   1810   1815   1818

troops fighting alongside Tecumseh retreat after a powerful charge by mounted U.S. soldiers. Surrounded and out-manned, Tecumseh and his men fight on in bloody, hand-to-hand combat. Many Native Americans are killed, including Tecumseh.

The Battle of Tippecanoe. *(Reproduced by permission of CORBIS/Bettmann.)*

1814   The Treaty of Ghent ends the War of 1812. The British agree that all the territory south of the Great Lakes to the Gulf of Mexico belongs to the United States. The British also agree not to give any help to their Indian allies in this territory.

1817   Work begins on the 363-mile-long Erie Canal, which will link Rome, New York, and Buffalo, New York.

1820   The U.S. Congress approves the Missouri Compromise, which outlaws slavery within the Louisiana Purchase territory north of 36°30' latitude. Missouri enters the Union as a slave state, while Maine enters as a free state.

1821   Mexico gains its independence from Spain and opens its borders with the United States.

1821   William Becknell leads a small caravan from Franklin, Missouri, to Santa Fe, in present-day New Mexico, becoming the first American to travel on what is known as the Santa Fe Trail.

1823   William Ashley begins the annual rendezvous for American fur trappers in the Rocky Mountains. Trappers gather at the annual mountain man Rendezvous to sell their pelts and gather a year's worth of supplies.

1824   A Cherokee language alphabet with eighty-five letters is perfected by Cherokee scholar Sequoya. The letters are borrowed from the Roman alphabet but they bear no relation to their sounds in English. Along with other letters they represent all the vowel and conso-

1820
The *Venus de Milo* is discovered

1822
J. N. Niepce creates the first permanent photograph

1825
The world's first wire-suspension bridge opens

1820   1822   1824   1826

The Erie Canal.
(Reproduced by permission of Archive Photos, Inc.)

nant sounds in the Cherokee language. Sequoya's alphabet makes the Cherokee the first literate Indian tribe.

1825   The Erie Canal is completed and within one year it collects $750,000 in tolls.

1825   James Ohio Pattie leaves Santa Fe in what is now New Mexico and travels into present-day Arizona on what becomes the Gila Trail.

1827   The Cherokee Indians, in an attempt to prevent the U.S. government from forcing them off their land, form the Cherokee Republic. The Cherokee establish a capital in New Echota, in present-day Georgia. They write a constitution that calls for three branches of government, similar to the U.S. Constitution.

1828   The first Native American newspaper, the *Cherokee Phoenix,* begins publication.

1828   The Georgia state legislature passes a series of laws that abolish the Cherokee government making it easier to claim Cherokee territory.

1829   Gold is discovered on Cherokee land in present-day Georgia. Gold seekers arrive in overwhelming numbers and lawlessness begins. Georgia increases its efforts to relocate the Cherokee to lands west of the Mississippi River.

May 28, 1830 The U.S. Congress votes in favor of the Indian Removal Act, calling for the removal—voluntary or forced—of all Indians to lands west of the Mississippi.

1834   Congress establishes Indian Territory, which covers parts of the present-day states of Oklahoma, Nebraska, and Kansas, far smaller than the "all lands west of the Mississippi" that whites had once promised.

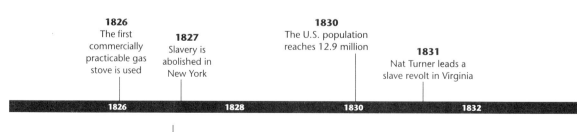

1826 The first commercially practicable gas stove is used

1827 Slavery is abolished in New York

1830 The U.S. population reaches 12.9 million

1831 Nat Turner leads a slave revolt in Virginia

1826   1828   1830   1832

December 29, 1835 A small group of Cherokee sign the Treaty of New Echota, selling all remaining Cherokee land east of the Mississippi River to the United States. The majority of Cherokee oppose the treaty.

1835–42 The Seminole Wars begin in the winter of 1835. After Seminole Indians refuse to leave their land in Florida, they are led by war chief Osceola in a fight against U.S. army troops in the swamps of Florida. The war costs the U.S. government more than $20 million and the lives of fifteen hundred troops. Osceola is captured during a truce and dies in prison in 1838. The war continues until 1842, at which time most Seminole are moved west of the Mississippi River.

April 21, 1836 Mexican president Antonio López de Santa Anna and a large army lay siege to a band of Texans holed up at the Alamo Mission. After a ten-day battle, every American man is killed. "Remember the Alamo" becomes the battle cry of Texans who fight back against Santa Anna and win independence for the Republic of Texas on May 14, 1836.

October 22, 1836 The Republic of Texas claims all land between the Rio Grande and Nueces rivers. Sam Houston is sworn in as president.

1836 The Spanish mission system in California collapses. Native Americans leave the missions to find that the land has been changed forever. Animals and crops introduced to the area by the Spanish make it virtually impossible for California Indians to live off the land in the way they had before the Spanish came.

1836 American inventor Samuel Colt patents the revolver or repeating pistol.

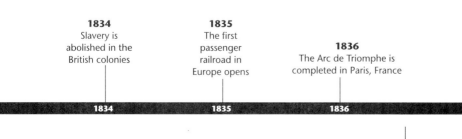

1834
Slavery is abolished in the British colonies

1835
The first passenger railroad in Europe opens

1836
The Arc de Triomphe is completed in Paris, France

1834　　1835　　1836

1836 Narcissa Prentiss Whitman and Eliza Spalding, two Protestant missionaries, become the first white women to cross the Rocky Mountains when they travel westward with their husbands.

1836 U.S. settlers move in on Creek Indian land in Alabama and purchase all available food. Drought and famine make life impossible for the Creek. Facing starvation, the Creek agree to go to Indian Territory.

1838 The U.S. Army forms the Corps of Topographical Engineers to look at western lands with an eye toward settlement. The Corps of Engineers makes maps and surveys of the frontier until the 1860s.

October 1838–March 1839 The removal of the Cherokee Indians from Georgia to Indian Territory (present-day Oklahoma) begins when General Winfield Scott and seven thousand federal troops are sent to the Cherokee's homeland to insist that the Cherokee leave. Scott's troops imprison any Cherokee who resist and burn their homes and crops. The Cherokee remember the trek as the "Trail Where They Cried," while U.S. historians call it the "Trail of Tears." More than four thousand Cherokee die on the forced march before they reach their destination in March 1839.

1843 The Oregon Trail is opened from Idaho to the Grande Ronde Valley in Oregon. The Great Migration, the name given to the first major exodus of emigrants westward, draws one thousand settlers onto the Oregon Trail.

1844–45 The U.S. Congress passes laws to build military posts to protect settlers moving from the East to California and Oregon. These forts cause conflict with Indian tribes along the route.

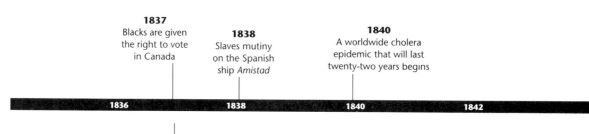

Eagle Rock at Scotts Bluff on the Oregon Trail in Nebraska.
(© Dave G. Houser/CORBIS. Reproduced by permission.)

1837
Blacks are given the right to vote in Canada

1838
Slaves mutiny on the Spanish ship *Amistad*

1840
A worldwide cholera epidemic that will last twenty-two years begins

1836   1838   1840   1842

March 1845 President John Tyler signs a resolution to bring Texas into the Union. Because the border of Texas is still contested, Tyler's action angers the Mexican government and it breaks off diplomatic relations with the United States. A conflict soon arises between the two countries over the official border. Texas and the United States claim the Rio Grande as the southern border. Mexico argues that the Nueces River, a few hundred miles to the north, is the actual border.

1845 Mormon leader Brigham Young leads his followers from Nauvoo, Illinois, more than 1,000 miles to the Salt Lake valley in present-day Utah.

January 1846 President James Polk orders General Zachary Taylor to advance a force of thirty-five hundred U.S. troops to the Rio Grande River.

May 11, 1846 President Polk sends a war message to Congress declaring that Mexico "has invaded our territory and shed American blood upon American soil." On May 13 Congress declares that a state of war exists by act of Mexico, votes a war appropriation of $10 million, and approves the enlistment of fifty thousand soldiers.

June 14, 1846 California's Bear Flag Revolt begins when settlers claim their independence from Mexico and raise a flag bearing a black bear and a star at Sonoma.

June 15, 1846 Britain and the United States sign the Oregon Treaty, granting the territory south of the 49th parallel to the United States. Though Britain had occupied this territory first, by 1845 American settlers significantly outnumbered British settlers in the area.

1846 Trade along the Santa Fe trail reaches an estimated $1,000,000 from a traffic flow of 363 wagons and 750 men; by 1860 trade tops $3,500,000.

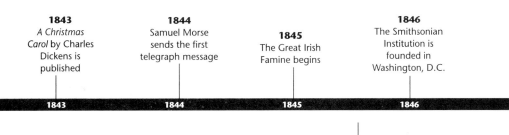

1843
A Christmas Carol by Charles Dickens is published

1844
Samuel Morse sends the first telegraph message

1845
The Great Irish Famine begins

1846
The Smithsonian Institution is founded in Washington, D.C.

1843　1844　1845　1846

1846   The Donner Party, a group of eighty-one men, women, and children, sets off on the Oregon Trail, heading toward California. Unable to cross the snow-covered mountains, members of the Donner Party eat dead members of their party in order to survive the long winter. Of the original party only forty-two survive.

November 1847   Members of the Whitman mission in Washington territory are massacred by Cayuse Indians, who believe the missionaries have started a devastating measles epidemic.

January 24, 1848   James Marshall discovers gold at Sutter's Mill in California, thus beginning the California Gold Rush.

February 2, 1848   The Treaty of Guadalupe Hidalgo is signed ending the Mexican-American War. The treaty grants the United States all or part of the present-day states of Arizona, California, Colorado, New Mexico, Utah, and Wyoming. It is a territorial addition second only to the Louisiana Purchase and virtually doubles the size of the country.

1848   By the end of 1848, five thousand Mormon settlers have traveled to Salt Lake City.

1849   An estimated thirty-two thousand people take the overland routes to California in 1849, most in pursuit of gold.

1850   The U.S. Congress passes a series of laws to address the growing divisions over the slavery issue and disputes over the land acquired in the Mexican-American War. The famous Compromise of 1850 addresses the problem of slavery in the new territories of New Mexico and California. It outlaws the slave trade in Washington, D.C., but allows it everywhere else throughout

Gold rush miners in California.
(Reproduced by permission of The Granger Collection, New York.)

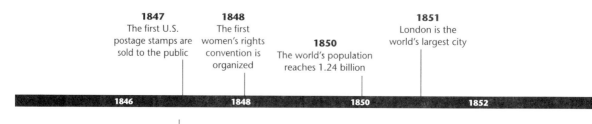

1847
The first U.S. postage stamps are sold to the public

1848
The first women's rights convention is organized

1850
The world's population reaches 1.24 billion

1851
London is the world's largest city

1846   1848   1850   1852

the South. In addition, California is admitted to the Union as a free state, and a new and tougher fugitive slave law replaces the poorly enforced Fugitive Slave Act of 1793.

1851   Tensions between the army and the Navajo Indians escalate quickly after the army constructs Fort Defiance in present-day eastern Arizona.

1856   The first of the Mormon handcart companies (settlers carrying their belongings in carts they push by hand) leave Iowa City in June, arriving in Salt Lake City four months later.

1858   John Butterfield's Overland Mail Company opens for service September 16. The company transports mail from St. Louis to Tipton, Missouri, by train and then transfers it to stagecoaches for the trip to San Francisco, California.

1859   Miners flock to Nevada to exploit the so-called Comstock Lode of gold and silver and later that year to Colorado when gold is discovered near Pike's Peak.

April 3, 1860 The Pony Express opens, providing the first rapid overland mail service to the Pacific coast.

April 30, 1860 A force of one thousand warriors led by Navajo chiefs Manuelito and Barboncito attacks Fort Defiance in present-day eastern Arizona, killing a number of soldiers before being driven from the fort. No longer able to overlook isolated Indian raids, after 1860 the army is determined to destroy the Navajo.

October 24, 1861 Telegraphers send the first message from San Francisco to Washington.

1861   General James H. Carleton of the U.S. Army forms Indian reservations in New Mexico. Carleton plans to

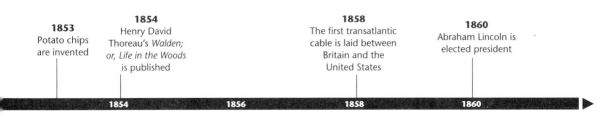

1853
Potato chips
are invented

1854
Henry David
Thoreau's *Walden;
or, Life in the Woods*
is published

1858
The first transatlantic
cable is laid between
Britain and the
United States

1860
Abraham Lincoln is
elected president

1854   1856   1858   1860

slowly gather Apache and Navajo onto the reservations. Although Carleton declares his intentions are to gently assimilate American Indians to U.S. culture, he kills many Indians while trying to force them onto reservations.

1861 The Central Pacific Railroad is chartered in California to build the western section of the transcontinental railroad.

1861–72 The Apache Wars begin in southern Arizona in 1861 when Apache chief Cochise escapes from an army post in Arizona with hostages. In 1871 Cochise opposes efforts to relocate his people to a reservation in New Mexico. In 1872 he finally agrees not to attack the U.S. Army in exchange for reservation land in eastern Arizona.

1862 The Homestead Act of 1862 is passed by the U.S. Congress. Nearly 470,000 homesteaders apply for homesteads in the next eighteen years.

1862–64 Little Crow's Uprising. The Santee Sioux, led by Little Crow, revolt against corrupt Indian agents in Minnesota who refuse to provide Indians with food they had been promised. The Sioux attack Minnesota settlements and the uprising quickly spreads to the eastern Dakotas. The uprising is defeated and 303 Sioux are sentenced to be hanged. President Abraham Lincoln overturns most of the execution orders, but 38 Indians are hanged, the largest mass execution in American history. Little Crow and his followers escape to Canada.

1863 John Bozeman blazes the Bozeman Trail after learning of a gold strike in present-day southwestern Montana.

1863 The Nez Percé of Oregon and Idaho are forced to sign the Thief Treaty. The treaty forces the Indians to va-

An emigrant party with their covered wagons.
(© Hulton Getty / Liaison Agency. Reproduced by permission.)

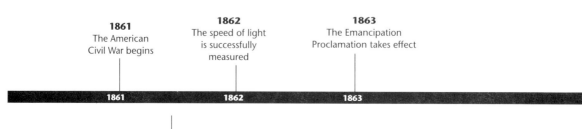

1861
The American
Civil War begins

1862
The speed of light
is successfully
measured

1863
The Emancipation
Proclamation takes effect

1861   1862   1863

cate lands wanted by whites, who had discovered gold on the land in 1860. The treaty reduces the Nez Percé land to one-tenth its former size.

November 29, 1864 Colonel John M. Chivington leads a force from Colorado in an unprovoked attack on a Southern Cheyenne and Arapaho camp at Sand Creek, killing an estimated five hundred men, women, and children. The Sand Creek Massacre is one of the first Indian battles to attract significant attention in the east.

1864 The "Long Walk" of the Navajo begins. Forces led by Kit Carson trap a huge number of Navajo in Canyon de Chelly in present-day Arizona, a steep-sided canyon in which the Navajo had traditionally taken refuge. The Navajo are marched southeast to Bosque Redondo, with many dying along the way.

1866 The first of the great cattle drives begins in Texas. Cowboys round up cattle and drive them northward to rail lines that reach into Kansas. In the years to come some eight million longhorn cattle travel the trails north to Kansas from ranches across Texas and throughout the Great Plains.

1867 Joseph McCoy, an Illinois livestock dealer, founds the town of Abilene, Kansas, as a gathering point for cattle drives from Texas. Rail lines stretching eastward from Abilene deliver cattle to eastern markets.

August 12, 1868 U.S. military authorities force Navajo chiefs to sign a treaty agreeing to live on reservations and cease opposition to whites. The treaty establishes a 3.5 million-acre reservation within the Navajo nation's old domains (a small portion of the original Navajo territory).

A cowboy on a cattle drive. *(Courtesy of the National Archives and Records Administration.)*

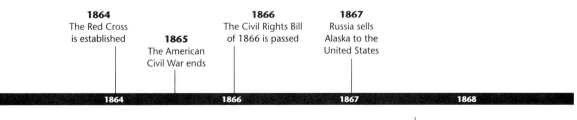

1864
The Red Cross is established

1865
The American Civil War ends

1866
The Civil Rights Bill of 1866 is passed

1867
Russia sells Alaska to the United States

1864   1866   1867   1868

May 10, 1869 The first transcontinental United States railroad is completed with the Golden Spike ceremony. The railroads joining the Atlantic and Pacific coasts are linked at Promontory Point, Utah, north of the Great Salt Lake.

1869 Brigadier General Ely S. Parker, a Seneca tribal leader and close friend of President Ulysses S. Grant, is appointed commissioner of Indian Affairs. It is the first time an Indian holds this post.

1870 Wodziwob, a Paiute Indian living on the California/Nevada border, is credited with beginning the Ghost Dance religion, which promises Indians that they will return to the life they had before European contact. The Ghost Dance movement lasts about two years in California, but it continues to exist in other areas for more than twenty years.

1870 The U.S. Supreme Court, in the case of *McKay v. Campbell,* decides that Indians are not U.S. citizens since their allegiance is to their tribe, not to the United States. Because of this ruling Indians are denied protections guaranteed by the U.S. Constitution.

1871 The famous cattle town of Dodge City, Kansas, is founded. Within a year the settlement boasts of a general store, three dance halls, and six saloons, and soon becomes a gathering place for cowboys fresh off the range.

1871 The U.S. Congress stops the practice of making treaties with Indians. Congress allows "agreements," which do not recognize tribes as independent nations. At the end of the treaty era, American Indian tribes still control one-tenth of the forty-eight states, or about one-fourth of the land between the Missis-

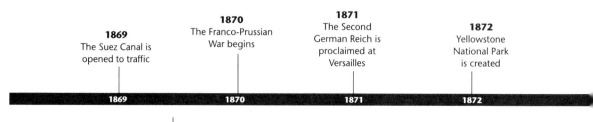

1869
The Suez Canal is opened to traffic

1870
The Franco-Prussian War begins

1871
The Second German Reich is proclaimed at Versailles

1872
Yellowstone National Park is created

1869   1870   1871   1872

sippi and the Rocky Mountains. By the early 1900s much of this land is owned by the U.S. government.

1874   An expedition led by Lieutenant Colonel George Armstrong Custer discovers gold in the Black Hills of South Dakota, sacred land for the Lakota Sioux, Cheyenne, and other tribes. In violation of the Fort Laramie Treaty, gold miners flood the Black Hills. Soon Indian and U.S. Army forces are fighting over this land.

1875   The results of the first river-borne exploration of the Colorado River are published by American geologist John Wesley Powell. After the American Civil War, the canyon of the Colorado River was the last unexplored region of the United States.

1875   U.S. president Ulysses Grant vetoes a bill that would protect the buffalo from extinction.

1875   In the winter of 1875, thousands of Indians from a number of tribes gather on the banks of the Little Bighorn River in southern Montana. There they plan their strategy for the defense of the Black Hills, ignoring or never learning of the U.S. Army's threat to hunt down and kill any Indians found off their reservations. For its part the army plans a major attack on the tribes for the spring of 1876.

June 25, 1876   At the Battle of Little Bighorn forces led by General George Armstrong Custer are defeated by combined Native American forces. The Indians' victory is their last major triumph against the whites.

1877   After the Battle of Little Bighorn, all of the Nez Percé Indians are ordered to report to reservations. Chief Joseph of the Nez Percé leads a band of his people on a long, torturous journey to elude army forces, but

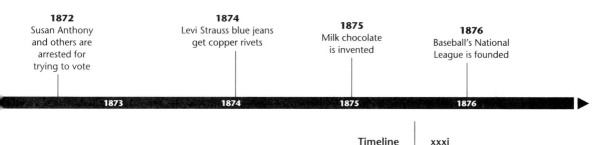

1872
Susan Anthony
and others are
arrested for
trying to vote

1874
Levi Strauss blue jeans
get copper rivets

1875
Milk chocolate
is invented

1876
Baseball's National
League is founded

1873   1874   1875   1876

they are eventually captured just 40 miles from the Canadian border.

1880 Cattle drives up the Chisholm Trail reach their peak.

July 18, 1883 Buffalo Bill's Wild West Show opens in Omaha, Nebraska. With riding, target shooting, and showmanship in an open-air spectacle, the show becomes an American favorite for the next twenty years.

1883–84 The Fence Cutter's War begins when a drought in Texas makes good grazing land scarce. Small ranchers and homesteaders pressure lawmakers to ban the fencing of public lands. When they receive no assistance, they band together in small groups with names like the Owls, Javelinas, or Blue Devils and, under the cover of night, tear down the offending fences.

1885 The cowboy era ends. Increased settlement of Kansas leads to the closing of the cattle towns, and expanding railroad lines mean that ranchers no longer have to drive cattle to railheads. Huge blizzards that strike the plains in 1886 and 1887 kill off cattle by the thousands, proving that cattle can't be left to fend for themselves. Finally, farmers claim increasing amounts of western land, and ranchers are forced to purchase and fence land for their cattle. Men who were once cowboys now become mere farmhands—but the legend of the cowboy lives on.

September 4, 1886 U.S. troops capture Apache chief Geronimo after four years of warfare with his band on the Mexican border.

April 22, 1889 In the Oklahoma Land Rush some fifty thousand settlers claim lands just opened to settlement, thus ending the Indian's claim to this territory.

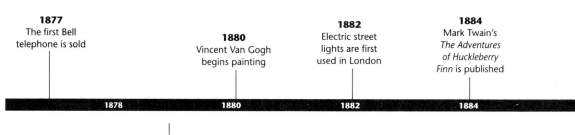

1877
The first Bell telephone is sold

1880
Vincent Van Gogh begins painting

1882
Electric street lights are first used in London

1884
Mark Twain's *The Adventures of Huckleberry Finn* is published

1878   1880   1882   1884

1889–90 The second Ghost Dance movement arises among Indians living on the Northern Plains, encouraging them to believe that they would return to the days before contact with whites had ruined their culture. The Ghost Dance religion spreads to many tribes throughout the West. The Bureau of Indian Affairs outlaws the Ghost Dance, and the army cracks down on participants.

February 10, 1890 Sioux chief Sitting Bull—hero of the 1876 Battle of the Little Bighorn—is shot dead by Indian police at Grand River as Sioux warriors of the Ghost Dance uprising try to rescue him.

December 29, 1890 The Battle of Wounded Knee ends the last major Indian resistance to white settlement in America. Nearly 500 well-armed troopers of the U.S. 7th Cavalry massacre an estimated 300 (out of 350) Sioux men, women, and children in a South Dakota encampment. The Army takes only 35 casualties.

1890 The Superintendent of the Census for 1890 declares that there is no longer a frontier in America. The census report's conclusion about the closing of the frontier encourages President Theodore Roosevelt to begin setting aside public lands as national parks.

1890–1900 At the end of the nineteenth century, most non-Indians believe that Native Americans as a group will not survive much longer. The term "Vanishing Americans" comes to be applied to Native Americans. This idea is used to justify continued taking of Native lands and moving the people to places far away. From an estimated population of 15,000,000 in the year 1500, the American Indian population declines to a low point of 237,196 in the 1900 U.S. Census.

Chiricahua Apache prisoners, including Geronimo (lower right corner).
(Courtesy of the National Archives and Records Administration.)

Hunkpapa Sioux leader Sitting Bull.
(Reproduced by permission of The Granger Collection, New York.)

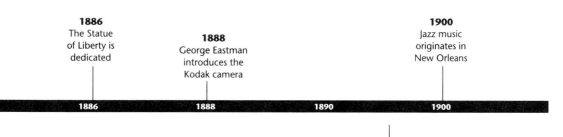

1886
The Statue of Liberty is dedicated

1888
George Eastman introduces the Kodak camera

1900
Jazz music originates in New Orleans

| 1886 | 1888 | 1890 | 1900 |

Words to Know

A

Annexation: The addition of territory to a country. Annexation became an issue in westward expansion when Southerners called for the United States to annex the Republic of Texas.

Argonauts: The name given to people who traveled to California via the water route from the east coast of the United States south along the Atlantic coast, across the Isthmus of Panama, and north on the Pacific Ocean.

C

Californios: Descendants of the original Spanish settlers in California.

Cattle Drive: Moving a herd of cattle from the open range to a railroad line. Cattle drives were led by bands of cowboys who tended the cattle.

Cholera: An acute intestinal infection. Cholera causes violent vomiting, fever, chills, and diarrhea. This infection killed hundreds of emigrants making their way west.

Colonies: Regions under the political control of a distant country.

Continental Divide: The line connecting the highest points of land in the Rocky Mountains. Waters on the west side of the divide flow into the Pacific Ocean, while those on the east side flow into the Gulf of Mexico.

E

Emigrants: People who leave one region to move to another. Those who moved from the East to settle in the West during westward expansion were known as emigrants.

F

49ers: People who traveled to the gold fields of California in 1849.

French and Indian War: A war between the British and combined French and Indian forces from 1755 to 1763 over control of the fur trading regions of the American interior.

Frontier: A term used by whites to refer to lands that lay beyond white settlements, including lands that were already occupied by Indians and Mexicans. In the United States the frontier existed until 1890 when Americans had settled the entire area between the Atlantic and Pacific Oceans.

G

Gadsden Purchase: In 1853 the United States purchased a strip of land on the southern borders of present-day New Mexico and Arizona from the Mexican government for $10 million. The land was used primarily to build a railway line connecting Texas to California.

Ghost Dance: A religious movement that was adopted by some Plains Indians in the 1880s and 1890s. The religion predicted that magical powers would allow the Indians to gain back all their land from the whites.

Great Migration: The mass movement of emigrants westward on the Oregon Trail that began in 1843 and eventually carried some 350,000 settlers to the West.

Great Plains: The vast area of rolling grasslands between the Mississippi River and the Rocky Mountains.

H

Harrison Land Act of 1800: This act allowed settlers to purchase land in parcels as small as 320 acres, a size more suited to family farming than early land legislation allowed. The act also allowed land to be purchased on credit, with one fourth of the cost as a down payment and the remainder due in four years.

Homestead Act of 1862: An act passed by Congress that gave settlers up to 160 acres of free land if they settled on it and made improvements over a five-year span. This act was responsible for bringing thousands of settlers into the west.

I

Indian Removal Act of 1830: An act passed by Congress calling for the removal—voluntary or forced—of all Indians to lands west of the Mississippi.

L

Louisiana Territory: Over 800,000 acres of land west of the Mississippi that was acquired from France for $15 million by President Thomas Jefferson in the Louisiana Purchase of 1803.

M

Manifest Destiny: The belief that by acquiring and populating the territories stretching from the Atlantic Ocean west to the Pacific Ocean, Americans were fulfilling a destiny ordained by God. This idea has been criticized as an excuse for the bold land grabs and the slaughter of Indians that characterized westward expansion, but those who believed in it thought they were demonstrating the virtues of a nation founded on political liberty, individual economic opportunity, and Christian civilization.

Mexican-American War: This war between the United States and Mexico, fought between 1846 and 1848, began as a battle over the southern border of Texas but soon expanded as the United States sought to acquire the territory that now includes Arizona, California, Colorado, Nevada, New Mexico, Utah, and Wyoming.

Missionaries: Proponents of a religion who travel into unexplored territories to try to convert the indigenous peoples to their religion. Spanish missionaries had an important influence in California; Protestant missionaries in Oregon and Washington; and Catholic missionaries throughout the French-influenced areas of the East.

N

Northwest Ordinance: Also known as the Ordinance of 1787, this ordinance passed by Congress paved the way for the orderly admission of new territories and states into the United States.

Northwest Passage: A mythical water route that linked the Atlantic Ocean to the Pacific Ocean; this passage was long sought by explorers of North America.

Northwest Territory: The unsettled area of land surrounding the Great Lakes and between the Ohio River and the Mississippi River that was given to the United States in the Treaty of Paris (1783). It included the present states of Ohio, Indiana, Illinois, Michigan, Wisconsin, and part of Minnesota.

O

Ohio River Valley: The area west of the Appalachian Mountains that includes part or all of the present-day states of West Virginia, Ohio, Kentucky, Indiana, and Illinois, as well as the far western parts of Pennsylvania and New York.

Ordinance of 1785: An ordinance passed by Congress that established a pattern for the surveying and division of all territories westward from the point where the Ohio River leaves the state of Pennsylvania.

Oregon Country: The name given to a vast expanse of land west of the Rocky Mountains and north of the Spanish territory containing the present-day states of Washington, Oregon, Idaho, and western Montana. This territory was jointly occupied by the British and the United States until 1846, when England ceded the territory to the United States.

Oregon Trail: A 2,000-mile trail that led from St. Joseph, Missouri, to the mouth of the Columbia River in Oregon. Thousands of settlers traveled on the trail from the 1830s to the 1890s. A major branch of the trail, the California Trail, led settlers to the gold fields of California.

P

Pantheism: A belief in and worship of all gods, or a god that resides in everything.

Proclamation of 1763: A British order that recalled all settlers from west of the Appalachian Mountains and forbid further emigration into the area west of the Appalachians.

R

Rendezvous: A gathering or meeting. The annual mountain man Rendezvous was a gathering of trappers and traders in the Rocky Mountain region. At the Rendezvous, fur trappers sold the furs and bought the goods that would allow them to survive through the next year. The mountain men entertained themselves during the Rendezvous with drinking, singing, dancing, and sporting contests.

S

South Pass: A low mountain pass over the Continental Divide located in present-day Wyoming; this pass was a major milestone on the Oregon Trail.

Speculator: Also known as a land speculator, an investor who bought land from the federal or state governments at a low price and sold it at a much higher price to settlers who wished to move to the frontier.

T

Telegraph Act of 1860: An act of Congress that granted to the lowest bidder public lands and a yearly contract for operation of a telegraph line connecting the East to San Francisco, California.

Territory: The name given to a region before it became a state. The Northwest Ordinance paved the way for the orderly admission of territories into the Union.

Trans-Appalachian West: The area of land that stretched west from the crest of the Appalachian Mountains to the Mississippi River.

Treaty of Ghent: Signed in 1814, this treaty ended the War of 1812 by granting the United States undisputed claim to the Northwest Territory and restoring American shipping rights to France.

Treaty of Guadalupe Hidalgo: This treaty with Mexico, signed on February 2, 1848, ended the Mexican-American War and granted to the United States territory including all or part of the present-day states of Arizona, California, Colorado, Nevada, New Mexico, Utah, and Wyoming.

Treaty of Paris (1763): In this treaty, which ended the French and Indian War, France relinquished its claim to Canada and the Ohio Valley and handed its holdings west of the Mississippi River to Spain. As a result, England and its colonies gained complete control over the settled regions of the present-day United States.

Treaty of Paris (1783): A treaty between England and the United States that granted the newly formed United States of America its independence and all the territory from the Great Lakes south to the Gulf of Mexico and from the Appalachians west to the Mississippi River.

V

Vaqueros: Hispanic men who worked on the ranches of Spaniards who settled in southern California and Mexico. Vaqueros were the first cowboys.

W

War of 1812: A war fought between England and the United States from 1812 to 1814 that was aimed at settling control of the trans-Appalachian west and shipping disputes between the two countries. Many Indian tribes sided with the English. The American victory established complete American control of the area.

Research and Activity Ideas

The following list of research and activity ideas is intended to offer suggestions for complementing social studies and history curricula, to trigger additional ideas for enhancing learning, and to suggest cross-disciplinary projects for library and classroom use.

Traveling West: You're living in the east in 1849, and hear rumors of gold in California. You decide to pack up your belongings and travel west in search of your fortune. What will you need to pack? How will you get there? Will you go alone or with a group of other goldseekers? Draw up a plan for your journey that includes a list of those things you will take and a description of the route on which you will travel. Your plan should address problems you may encounter and what preparations you've made to overcome these obstacles.

Indian Cultures Before and After Contact: There were hundreds of Indian tribes living throughout North America in the years before Americans claimed the continent for their own, and every one of these tribes changed when they came into contact with white people. Choose one Indian tribe and try to under-stand how their lives changed as the result of contact. Write a "before contact" description that describes Indian social practices, religious beliefs, and economic practices. Then, write an "after contact" description of how Indian culture changed as a result of contact with whites.

The Wild West: Many people have formed opinions of the American West by watching movies. But do movies tell an accurate story about life in the West? Watch one of the many classic film Westerns—*Shane, Stagecoach, She Wore a Yellow Ribbon, High Noon, The Searchers,* or a film suggested by your teacher—and compare and contrast the image of the West offered by the film with your more balanced understanding of the true nature of Western settlement.

Home on the Range: As settlers moved onto Western lands one of their first tasks was to build some form of shelter. In the east, log cabins were the first structure built; on the Plains, the first settlers built sod houses. Research one form of shelter that interests you, and discover what was needed to build it. Draw up a plan for constructing your first home on the range.

Judging Atrocities: When we look back at the way Americans treated Native Americans, we are often appalled at the cruelty and violence of Americans' attacks on Indian cultures. But Americans in the nineteenth century viewed things differently, believing that there were legitimate reasons for waging war on the Indians. Stage a class debate concerning American treatment of Indians in the nineteenth century. You might consider the following: Was the Indian Removal Act of 1830 a fair way to deal with conflicting claims to the lands? What role did Manifest Destiny play in American relations with Indians? Were Indians justified in their violence towards whites? Were army attacks on Indians at Sand Creek and Wounded Knee justified?

The Vastness of the West: Using a map of the United States, use pushpins to mark some of the major landmarks in the West. You might mark the site of the California Gold Rush; the Black Hills of South Dakota; Independence, Missouri, the staging point for trails west; Santa Fe, New Mexico; and other sites that interest you. Now figure out the distance between these points. Keeping in mind that travelers in the old West could usually cover ten to fifteen miles in a day, figure out how long it would take you to travel by wagon between different sites. How long would it take you to travel these same distances by car or by airplane?

Dinner is Served: Travelers on Western trails were said to live on a diet of coffee and hard biscuits. Using your library or the internet, locate and prepare some of the dishes that westerners ate every day on cattle drives or on wagon trains. What would it be like to eat these foods every day?

Your Town and the West: If you live west of the Appalachian mountains you live in an area that was once considered the frontier. Use your local library to learn about the role your town (or a town you are interested in) played in the expansion of the United States. Why was your town founded where it is? Is it near a river or a railway line? How did your town change as it moved from frontier village to an established town? Create a presentation to share what you've learned with your classmates.

Women and the West: Imagine you are a woman whose family has moved west to homestead on the Plains in the 1870s. What is a woman's role in establishing a homestead? Discover how women contributed to the settling of the West. Write a to-do list for one day or one week. Outline your tasks and describe how you will complete each task.

Negotiating a Treaty: You are an Indian leader and you must negotiate a treaty with a territorial governor who wants you and your people to move off the lands you've lived on for as long as you can remember. The governor offers you land in Indian Territory, and promises you that the "Great White Father" will always protect you—but he also suggests that his army will force you off the land if you don't leave peacefully. How would you argue for your right to stay? What arguments can you give that will make the governor agree to let you stay where you are? Either write a speech that this Indian leader will give, or stage a debate between the governor and the leader.

Westward Expansion Almanac

Claiming the Near West: Territorial Expansion to 1812

From the moment that Europeans set foot on the North American continent in the sixteenth century, they began to expand their influence westward. By the mid-eighteenth century that expansion had progressed to the point that there were thirteen British colonies poised on the eastern coast of North America. These colonies had established themselves over a period of years by fighting a series of skirmishes with the Native American inhabitants of the region. By the 1760s they had largely carved out their geographic boundaries, which generally stretched from the east coast of North America to the crest of the Appalachian Mountains. But the population of these colonies continued to grow, fed not only by internal population growth but also by a continued stream of immigrants from England and other European countries, including Germany, Holland, Ireland, and Scotland. This increased population as well as the deteriorating quality of the soil on eastern farms put pressure on the poorly defined western boundaries of these colonies. The colonies were poised to expand westward, but how would they do so?

Up until the end of the War of 1812 (1812–14), the westward expansion of the colonies into what is known as the trans-Appalachian frontier (the area of land stretching from the crest of the Appalachian Mountains to the Mississippi River) was conducted within a complex struggle among a variety of forces. The French, Spanish, British, colonial Americans, and Native Americans all sought to protect their interests in the area that stretched between the Appalachian Mountains and the Mississippi River. The story of how the colonies (which became an independent nation during this period) expanded westward in the years leading up to the War of 1812 is one of political maneuvering, fierce military confrontations, and a steady trickle of settlers carving their homes out of the wilderness. By the end of the War of 1812, the major political obstacles to U.S. control of the West had been removed, and a model was set for the continued expansion of the nation westward from the Mississippi River.

Disrupting the balance of power

During the first half of the eighteenth century, there was a three-way balance of power in North America. The British-backed colonies had extended their control up to the crest of the Appalachian Mountains, and the French boasted a lucrative fur-trading empire extending from the Appalachian Mountains westward into the Ohio River Valley (an expansive area west of the Appalachians that includes part or all of the present-day states of West Virginia, Ohio, Kentucky, Indiana, and Illinois, as well as the far western parts of Pennsylvania and New York). The British and French, both of whom longed to gain complete control over North America, had to contend with the presence of significant Indian populations in the region, and for many years avoided direct military confrontation with each other. These Indian tribes largely supported the French, who lavished them with gifts and treated them like partners, but traded with the English when necessary.

Beginning in the 1740s, however, English traders began to venture out into the Ohio Valley, establishing relations with tribes that had previously traded only with the French. In the late 1740s the Ohio Company, a land-speculation company (a company that buys land with the intention of selling it for a profit), founded a settlement at the point where

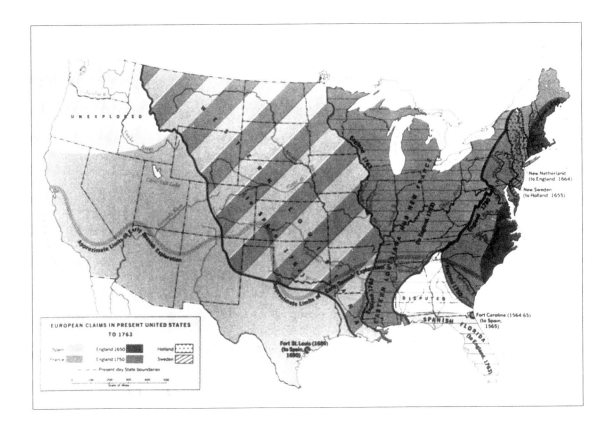

the Monongahela and Allegheny Rivers meet to form the Ohio River. (The site is now known as Pittsburgh, Pennsylvania.) French governors in Canada feared that this was the beginning of an English attempt to dominate the interior of the continent, and they began to build a series of forts to ward off English settlement. When they built Fort Duquesne (pronounced doo-KAYNE) near present-day Pittsburgh in 1754, the governor of Virginia (who claimed the land for the British colony) sent an armed force under the command of George Washington (1732–1799) to expel them from the area. The French defeated Washington and his men at the Battle of Fort Necessity on July 3 and 4, 1754, thus beginning the French and Indian War.

European claims in the United States in 1763.
(Courtesy of the National Park Service, Department of the Interior.)

The French and Indian War (1754–63)

The French and Indian War began badly for the British. British and colonial forces led by General Edward

Braddock (1695–1755) were soundly beaten by a combined French and Indian force when the British attempted to take Fort Duquesne in 1755, and they continued to suffer defeat after defeat between 1755 and 1757. American colonists resisted the burden of financing the war, which the British were forcing them to pay for. But the tide turned when the new leader of the British troops, William Pitt (1708–1778), committed his forces to a sustained campaign and began encouraging cooperation with American colonial forces. In a string of victories, the British and American forces captured the French fort at Louisbourg on the St. Lawrence River, Fort Frontenac on Lake Ontario, and Fort Duquesne. British general James Wolfe led the defeat of the main French army at Quebec in 1759, but the war did not officially come to an end until the Treaty of Paris was signed in 1763. Under the treaty, France relinquished its claim to Canada and the Ohio Valley and turned over its holdings west of the Mississippi River to Spain.

"In 1763," writes historian Elliott West in *The Oxford History of the American West*, "England suddenly found itself the master of eastern North America. Just as quickly, it began to learn how success bred difficulties." Indian tribes that had long sided with the French remained hostile to the English, and they launched a series of attacks on British positions throughout the Ohio Valley. This loosely organized coalition of Indians, created in part by an Ottawa chief named Pontiac (c. 1720–1769), captured several British forts and harassed frontier settlers throughout the region. Seeking to avoid further bloodshed, the British issued an order known as the Proclamation of 1763 that recalled all settlers from west of the Appalachian crest and forbade further emigration into the area. The proclamation enraged many colonists and proved largely ineffective. The colonists thought that their victory in the recent French and Indian War entitled them to push farther into the interior. By disobeying the proclamation, the colonists took yet another step toward breaking their ties with the British.

Opening the West

To the British, slowing westward expansion made good sense. Further westward emigration could only bring continuing costly wars with the Indians, and the opening of more land for settlers would attract emigrants from England and deplete the labor force there. Moreover, the British feared that if the colonies grew further, they would become ever more difficult to govern. The colonists, however, had other needs and ideas. The rapid growth of the colonial population in the 1700s placed real pressures on the land. As land was divided among growing families, and as the fertility of the soil declined after more than a century of use, it became increasingly difficult to support a family on an eastern farm. Accustomed to open land, American farmers and potential settlers felt that they needed at least a hundred acres to support a family. The possession of this amount of land helped make good citizens, they believed, and was thus essential to colonial life. It only made sense to them that they take possession of the fertile land in the Ohio Valley.

Settlers began moving into the areas around Fort Duquesne (now named Fort Pitt) after 1760. Scotch-Irish farmers from North Carolina moved into eastern Tennessee around 1771, seeking to avoid the corruption, high taxes, and inadequate representation they complained of back home. Settlers in both these areas had to look out for the American Indians whose territory they were invading. The early settlers of Kentucky did not have such worries, for there were no permanent Indian settlements in the fertile valleys they occupied. Judge Richard Henderson (1735–1785) spearheaded the development of Kentucky when he "purchased" millions of acres in central Kentucky from some Cherokee Indians and in 1775 sent a company led by frontiersman Daniel Boone (1734–1820) to live in the area. (Henderson's "purchase" of Indian land, like many such purchases, played on the Indian's misunderstanding of land ownership; it never occured to many Indians that land could even be sold.) Such settlers overlooked the Proclamation of 1763 and ignored any previous claims to the land they desired. And despite further attempts by the British to halt emigration, settlers continued to move west.

The Revolutionary War (1776–83)

The clash between colonial desires and British demands on the frontier was just one of many factors that led to the war for independence that the colonies waged against England beginning in 1776. Indian tribes saw that their interests lay with the British, and they cooperated with the British in numerous battles along the western frontier. South of Kentucky, Cherokee leaders attacked white settlements in the summer of 1776. In western New York and northwestern Pennsylvania, loyalists and Iroquois warriors conducted hundreds of raids against colonial settlements under the leadership of British colonel John Butler (1728–1796) and Mohawk warrior Joseph Brant (1742–1807). Counterattacks by colonial forces destroyed dozens of towns and left the area devastated. And in Kentucky, the Shawnee, the Delaware, and their allies terrorized white settlements, killing hundreds of settlers between 1777 and 1782. All such attacks were encouraged if not actually aided by the British.

Despite their setbacks in the West, colonial forces prevailed in their war for independence, and the British surrendered in 1783. The 1783 Treaty of Paris granted the newly formed United States of America its independence and all the territory from the Great Lakes south to the Gulf of Mexico and from the Appalachians west to the Mississippi River. (The Spanish, of course, still retained Florida and the area west of the Mississippi.) It was a vast and ungovernable territory, and the British hoped that, despite the treaty, they could continue to exert their influence in the trans-Appalachian area, profiting from the fur trade and disrupting American settlement. For their part, the Americans looked to the new territory as a land of opportunity, capable of providing the resources needed by the citizens of a growing nation—if only it could be claimed from the Native Americans.

The new nation had more than Indians to worry about as it surveyed its western territories. It also had to settle the conflicting claims of the different colonies (now states). When the colonies had first formed, they claimed vast stretches of unsurveyed land. As that land began to be settled, conflicting claims to territory brought many of the colonies into dispute. Following the Revolutionary War, however, Virginia, Connecticut, and Massachusetts handed over their interior holdings to the national government. The holdings included all claims north of the Ohio River and west of Pennsylvania. This region, known as the Northwest Territory or the Old Northwest, allowed the new nation the opportunity to expand in an organized fashion.

Excerpts from the Land Ordinance of 1785

May 20, 1785

An Ordinance for ascertaining the mode of disposing of Lands in the Western Territory.

BE it ordained by the United States in Congress assembled, that the territory ceded by individual States to the United States, which has been purchased of the Indian inhabitants, shall be disposed of in the following manner:

A surveyor from each state shall be appointed by Congress or a Committee of the States, who shall take an oath for the faithful discharge of his duty, before the Geographer of the United States....

...The Surveyors, as they are respectively qualified, shall proceed to divide the said territory into townships of six miles square, by lines running due north and south, and others crossing these at right angles, as near as may be, unless where the boundaries of the late Indian purchases may render the same impracticable....

The lines shall be measured with a chain; shall be plainly marked by chaps on the trees, and exactly described on a plat; whereon shall be noted by the surveyor, at their proper distances, all mines, salt-springs, salt-licks and mill-seats, that shall come to his knowledge, and all water-courses, mountains and other remarkable and permanent things, over and near which such lines shall pass, and also the quality of the lands.

There shall be reserved for the United States out of every township the four lots, being numbered 8, 11, 26, 29, and out of every fractional part of a township, so many lots of the same numbers as shall be found thereon, for future sale. There shall be reserved the lot No. 16, of every township, for the maintenance of public schools within the said township, also one-third part of all gold, silver, lead and copper mines, to be sold, or otherwise disposed of as Congress shall hereafter direct....

(Journals of the Continental Congress, ed. by J. C. Fitzpatrick, Vol. XXVIII, p. 375 ff.)

The Ordinance of 1785

The national legislature soon passed two laws that were crucial to the history of westward expansion: the Ordinance of 1785 and the Northwest Ordinance. The Ordinance of 1785 established a pattern for the surveying and division of all territories westward from the point where the Ohio River leaves the state of Pennsylvania. "That first square inch of the first surveyor's stake," writes West, "was a kind of polestar of national development, the anchored point of reckoning for more than a billion acres. Nowhere else in the world would an area of such size be laid out in a uniform land system." The entire Northwest Territory was to be surveyed into sections (measuring one square mile, or 640 acres). These sections were to be grouped into townships (six square miles, or 36 sections), and one section was to be set aside for public schools. The effects of this ordinance on the landscape were and are incalculable, for the ordinance placed a gridwork pattern atop the tumult of natural features, leading to the creation of roads, towns, and farms that obeyed the logic of the surveyor's stake rather than the lay of the land. And though the land was offered for sale at one dollar an acre, the minimum sale of 640 acres put land prices out of reach for some potential settlers and made farm sizes unmanageable. (This element of the ordinance would later be changed.)

The Northwest Ordinance

While the Ordinance of 1785 provided for the orderly arrangement of the land, the Northwest Ordinance, also known as the Ordinance of 1787, provided for the orderly establishment of future states. It declared that the Northwest Territory would be divided into three to five territories. Such territories would first be ruled by a governor, his secretary, and three judges, appointed by the national government. When five thousand free males lived in the territory, elections could be held to form a legislature. When sixty thousand free inhabitants were counted, the territory could petition for statehood. The new state would enjoy all the rights and privileges of existing states. The Northwest Ordinance also established a system of laws in the territories, forbade slavery, and guaranteed certain civil rights. Thirty-one of the thirty-five states west of the Appalachians became states through this process.

The Ordinance of 1785 and the Northwest Ordinance attempted to impose order on the growth of the United States, but the actual growth of the nation was far from orderly. There were two problems: the land was already occupied by Native Americans, many of whom had lived there for centuries, and the rush of settlers and land speculators into the newly opened territory defied organization. In order for settlement to progress, the land first had to be claimed from the Indians, who would fight for their right to live in the territory. Then it had to be divided equitably among players of unequal power.

Taking Indian land

The third article of the Northwest Ordinance made the Indians a promise: "The utmost good faith shall always be observed towards the Indians; their lands and property shall never be taken from them without their consent; and in their property, rights, and liberty, they shall never be invaded and disturbed, unless in just and lawful wars authorized by Congress; but laws founded in justice and humanity, shall from time to time be made for preventing wrongs being done to them, and for preserving peace and friendship with them." The authors of the ordinance may have meant what they wrote, but in the years to come every element of their promise to the Indians was broken or severely distorted. Indian lands were systematically invaded; Indian property was ruthlessly destroyed; and the only laws made were intended to strip Indians of any claim to the land on which they had hunted and lived for years.

Though relations between whites and Native Americans had quieted just after the end of the Revolutionary War, after 1786 hostilities between Americans and Indians on the frontier began to heat up. Acting in concert, Indians led by Miami chief Little Turtle (c. 1752–1812) began to attack farmsteads in Kentucky, killing as many as one settler per week. State militias retaliated, heightening the tensions between the two sides. In 1790, concerned about the Indians' coordinated efforts and aware that they were receiving encouragement from British troops who had still not left the territory, President George Washington sent forces to strike against what he called "certain banditti [bandits] of Indians from the northwest side of the Ohio." The Indians had a score of triumphs, including a 1791 rout of forces led by territorial Governor Arthur St. Clair. In that battle, Little Turtle's forces killed 630 out of 1,400 men and captured hundreds of weapons. When treaty negotiations between the two sides failed, Washington sent General Anthony Wayne (1745–1796) on a more sustained campaign against the Indian forces. Wayne's troops scored a major victory over a combined force of eight hundred Indians at the battle of Fallen Timbers in 1794. The defeat was particularly dispiriting for the Indians, for they learned during the battle that they could not depend on support from the British forces stationed in nearby Fort Miamis. The battle of Fallen Timbers was not conclusive, but it indicated to the Indians that the Americans were willing to commit substantial resources to settling the Old Northwest.

Land sales

Despite their promises that Indians would retain claim to their land, the national and state governments were quick to sell off vast tracts of land on which Native Americans were still living. Such land sales brought immediate revenue to governments still struggling to pay off debts accumulated during the Revolutionary War (1776–83), but they didn't bode well for the lone settler hoping to buy a small chunk of land on which to start a farm. Land speculators proved to be the biggest purchasers of land. The Ohio Company of Associates bought five million acres of land in southern Ohio at a cost of about nine cents an acre; New York sold more than five million acres at an average price of twenty cents an acre. The worst case of land speculators getting land cheaply occurred when the Georgia legislature was bribed into selling thirty-five million acres at just over a penny an acre. Wealthy land speculators held on to the land until the prices rose and then sold it for a large profit.

Unable to purchase land, some settlers, called squatters, simply claimed a patch of land that they liked. Others paid the prices demanded by the land speculators but complained loudly to their representatives. Popular uproar over the excesses of the land speculators soon persuaded legislators to change land-sale policies. The Harrison Land Act of 1800 allowed settlers to purchase land in parcels as small as 320 acres (down from 640 acres), a size more suited to family farming. The act also allowed land to be purchased on credit, with a fourth of the cost as a down payment and the remainder due in four years. This act helped encourage an ever-increasing number of emigrants to commit to the difficult life of the pioneer settler.

Carving farms from the forests

The stream of emigrants (people who leave an area to settle in a new area) began to work its way west during the last years of the eighteenth century. Settlers tended to move due

westward from their present locations. Thus the upper Ohio Valley was settled primarily by the former residents of New England, New York, and Pennsylvania, while the southern Ohio Valley and the Gulf frontier were settled by Virginians, Carolinians, and Georgians. The majority of the settlers intended to farm, but first they had to carve their farms out of the dense forest that carpeted most of the land. Most such families were self-supporting: They grew beans, squash, and corn; hunted for the game that abounded in the woods; and fished in the lakes and streams. Farming families usually kept some domestic animals, the most common being pigs. Pigs require no pastures, rooting for their food wherever they find it, and settlers found uses for every last bit of the animal, from snout to hooves.

The first settlers in the northern areas were subsistence farmers (farmers who produce just enough to support themselves), scratching a living from the land for a few years and then moving on when the soil began to wear out. Later

Emigrants moving from Connecticut to eastern Ohio.
(Reproduced by permission of Archive Photos, Inc.)

farmers practiced more sustainable agriculture, plowing the land, rotating crops, and fertilizing with manure. On cleared lands many farmers began to harvest wheat, which by the early 1800s had become a major cash crop. On the southern frontier, cotton quickly became the dominant crop. After the invention of the cotton gin in 1793, it became very profitable to grow cotton. As in the north, the first settlers cleared the land and moved on. But in the south, wealthy planters bought up property and combined it into large plantations. Rich in capital and slaves, these plantation owners produced goods for a global economy (to be sold around the world). Their example encouraged others to believe that the frontier was not just a place for "backwoods farmers" but could provide real economic opportunity. Cattle ranches also proved profitable enterprises on the southern frontier; prior to the War of 1812, more land was dedicated to cattle raising than to any other economic activity.

Though the American frontier is often depicted in terms of farms and plantations, in truth towns and cities were important centers of frontier life. Most towns formed along major rivers, which provided easy transportation of goods to market. Pittsburgh, Pennsylvania; Lexington, Kentucky; and Cincinnati, Ohio, all became important centers of trade and even manufacturing. New Orleans, Louisiana, at the mouth of the Mississippi, was of course a major shipping and trading center. These cities were lively and even dangerous places. They served the needs of many different people—farmers, fur trappers, Indians, and merchants—many of whom sought in the city amusements they could not find elsewhere. Gambling houses, brothels, and saloons thrived in these wide-open towns. Not all was wild, of course. A variety of Protestant churches thrived on the frontier, with the Methodists making particular efforts to reach people and establish congregations, especially in the northern territories.

Obstacles to expansion

In the years following the Revolutionary War (1776–83), much changed in the trans-Appalachian West. Kentucky became a state in 1792, and Tennessee followed in 1796. Many thousands of settlers moved out into territory

The early settlers of the Ohio Valley had to carve their farms out of the dense forest. Most settler families were self-supporting: They grew beans, squash, and corn; hunted for the game that abounded in the woods; and fished in the lakes and streams. *(Reproduced by permission of Archive Photos, Inc.)*

that only a few years earlier had been largely possessed by Indians. The white people in the trans-Appalachian West soon outnumbered the Indians, and they had behind them the force of the national government and the solid weight of public opinion in favor of moving ever westward. Yet the growing nation still faced major obstacles. British forces remained in place throughout the Northwest Territory, and they encouraged Indians who wished to battle the intrusive Americans. Equally important, the nation was becoming increasingly dependent on the Mississippi River and its principal port of New Orleans, but both the city and the Louisiana Territory (the area between the Mississippi River and the Rocky Mountains) were controlled by the Spanish. Should the Spaniards turn against the United States, all of the western settlements would be threatened. As the century turned, the fate of westward expansion was still in doubt.

The Louisiana Purchase

The problem of Spanish control of the Louisiana Territory and New Orleans was removed in a strange twist of diplomatic fate. The United States had long feared that the Spanish would restrict trade along the Mississippi, and their fears were confirmed in 1802 when Spanish authorities barred American traders from using the port of New Orleans. When American authorities protested the closure of the port, they learned that the Louisiana Territory had actually been given to France in the secret Treaty of San Ildefonso two years earlier. President Thomas Jefferson (1743–1826) instructed diplomat Robert Livingston (1746–1813) to negotiate with France for the reopening of the port. In the process of these negotiations, Livingston and James Monroe (1758–1831) soon learned that France was interested in doing far more than opening the port—it was willing to sell the entire territory. The two negotiators, surprised by the offer from French ruler Napoleon Bonaparte (1769–1821) and acting without authorization from President Jefferson, negotiated the purchase of the Louisiana Territory for about fifteen million dollars. In April 1803 the French government accepted the offer.

The acquisition of the Louisiana Territory put Jefferson in a difficult position. There was no public support for the ac-

LOUISIANA PURCHASE

Pacific Ocean

Fort Clatsop

Oregon (Columbia) R.

Oregon Country

ROCKY

MOUNTAINS

British Possession

Yellowstone R.

Hidatsa and Mandan Villages

Fort Mandan

Lake Superior

Lake Michigan

Mississippi R.

Louisiana Purchase

Missouri River

St. Louis

Spanish Possession

Mississippi R.

Gulf of Mexico

0 — 300 miles
0 — 300 kilometers

quisition of this territory, and the U.S. Constitution made no provision for the purchase of territory from a foreign country. Jefferson feared that purchasing the land was not even legal. Yet Jefferson and Congress could not pass up the opportunity to nearly double the size of the country with a single, inexpensive purchase (the land cost about four cents an acre). Though no one knew exactly how far the borders of the Louisiana Territory extended, the Congress approved the Louisiana Purchase on December 20, 1803. With that one acquisition, the United States gained 800,000 square miles of territory.

With the Louisiana Purchase the United States gained territory stretching from the Mississippi River to the Rocky Mountains and from the Gulf of Mexico to Canada. *(Reproduced by permission of The Gale Group.)*

The coming of the War of 1812

All of the territory in the world would do Americans no good if they could not control it, and in the years leading up to the War of 1812 the United States came to realize that it must once again fight England to defend its rights as a sovereign nation (a country that is free to determine its own destiny). The War of 1812 is often called the Second War for Independence, for despite granting the United States its independence in 1783, the British continued to station British forces in the Northwest Territory and encourage Indian attacks on U.S. settlements. And, after 1805, as part of their war effort against the French, the British repeatedly disrupted U.S. shipping to France. Though the shipping and trade issues became the subject of diplomatic negotiations, many historians agree that the real cause of the war between the United States and Britain was the United States' desire to secure control of its western territories and prevent further British meddling on the continent. The so-called "War Hawks," members of Congress from the western states, even hoped that they could wrest control of Canada from the British, thus further expanding American control. Those in the West also saw war as a legitimate way to drive troublesome Indians off the land Americans wanted.

Tecumseh and Indian resistance

The greatest threat to American lives in the years leading up to and including the War of 1812 came from Indians determined to stop westward expansion. Surveying the steady encroachment of white men onto Indian lands in the present-day states of Ohio and Indiana, a Shawnee chief named Tecumseh (1768–1813) spearheaded the formation of a confederation of Indian tribes that hoped to stop the white advance. He was aided by his brother, Tenskwatawa (c. 1768–1834), a one-eyed prophet who had stirred excitement among Indian tribes with his visions of a unified and triumphant Indian nation. Tecumseh's influence spread far to the south as well, where he had secured the cooperation of the Creeks, Cherokee, and Choctaw. In a speech to these tribes quoted in Ray Allen Billington's *Westward to the Pacific,* Tecumseh called for "War now. War forever. War upon the living. War upon the dead; dig up their very corpses from the graves; our country must give no rest to a white man's bones."

By 1808 Tecumseh's confederation was organizing to oppose the land grabs of territorial Governor William Henry Harrison (1773–1841) and had formed a village called Prophetstown in north-central Indiana. Harrison had negotiated a treaty with a fragment of a tribe, and he believed this treaty gave him the right to take over three million acres of prime Indiana land. The stage was set for a confrontation. Harrison's forces met a group led by Tenskwatawa on November 7, 1811, at Prophetstown and routed the Indian forces. When the actual war with England began in 1812, Tecumseh allied himself with the unreliable British forces and participated in some 150 battles with American forces. Tecumseh himself was killed, and his followers demoralized, when Indian forces protecting the retreating British were thoroughly beaten at the Battle of the Thames (October 5, 1813).

Tecumseh's southern allies, who called themselves Red Sticks, fared no better. In an early battle, they succeeded at slaughtering five hundred people who had taken refuge in Fort Mims on the Alabama River. American retaliation was swift. Led by Andrew Jackson (1767–1845), a military force cornered and killed more than eight hundred Indian warriors, effectively ending Indian resistance on the southern frontier. As a result of these and other confrontations during the War of 1812, organized Indian resistance to westward expansion ended. Leaderless and with their best warriors killed, the Indians signed treaties that granted white men access to vast tracts of land.

Though the war against the Indians was conducted on the western frontier, American forces met the British in the east, on the sea, and on the Great Lakes. The British navy

 The Battle of New Orleans

Ironically, the most important battle of the War of 1812 (1812–14) was fought after the Treaty of Ghent was signed (though neither side knew it). British commander Sir Edward Pakenham led a force of seventy-five hundred British troops in an effort to capture the city of New Orleans and thus cripple American trade. After easily defeating a tiny American naval fleet, Pakenham ordered his men to march on the city on January 8, 1815. Awaiting him was a band of western frontiersmen, six thousand strong, led by the famous Indian fighter General Andrew Jackson. The strategically placed U.S. forces rained bullets on the British, killing two thousand soldiers in less than an hour and losing only a few American lives. The battle secured the Mississippi Valley, made a hero of Jackson (who would later become president), and sparked a wave of pride among American citizens.

Shawnee chief Tecumseh convinced Native American peoples to form a confederation to better defend themselves against European Americans' encroachment. *(Reproduced by permission of the Granger Collection, New York.)*

defeated the Americans on the seas and burned Washington, D.C. American forces triumphed on the Great Lakes, thanks to the heroic efforts of Captain Oliver Perry (1785–1819), and drove the British from the interior of the United States. In the end the war was something of a stalemate, but as with the Revolutionary War, the British simply didn't have the will to conduct a long war across the sea. The Treaty of Ghent, signed late in 1814, gave the United States undisputed claim to the inland Northwest and restored American shipping rights.

Conclusion

With its triumph in the War of 1812, the United States surveyed the vast western landscape without having to worry about European meddling or organized Indian resistance. Finally able to take advantage of the Louisiana Purchase, the nation expanded westward quickly, establishing states throughout what became known as the Midwest and the South, and sending settlers out on a network of trails that would take them all the way to the Pacific coast. There would certainly be obstacles in the years ahead—battles with Indians, war with the Mexicans over Texas, and a long-simmering conflict over the expansion of slavery into new territories—but after 1812 the United States was far more confident and aggressive in staking its claim to a land that stretched from sea to shining sea.

For More Information

Books

Billington, Ray Allen, with James Blaine Hedges. *Westward Expansion: A History of the American Frontier.* New York: Macmillan, 1949.

Edwards, Cheryl, ed. *Westward Expansion: Exploration and Settlement.* Lowell, MA: Discovery Enterprises, 1995.

Erdosh, George. *Food and Recipes of the Westward Expansion.* New York: PowerKids Press, 1997.

Mancall, Peter C., ed. *Westward Expansion, 1800–1860.* Detroit: Gale, 1999.

Wexler, Alan, ed. *Atlas of Westward Expansion.* New York: Facts On File, 1995.

Web sites

The American West. [Online] http://www.americanwest.com (accessed April 4, 2000).

National Archives and Records Administration. "The Louisiana Purchase." *American Originals.* [Online] http://www.nara.gov/exhall/originals/loupurch.html (accessed April 4, 2000).

The West. [Online] http://www.pbs.org/weta/thewest/ (accessed April 4, 2000).

Sources

Billington, Ray Allen. *Westward to the Pacific: An Overview of America's Westward Expansion.* St. Louis: Jefferson National Expansion Historical Association, 1979.

Faber, Harold. *From Sea to Sea: The Growth of the United States.* New York: Charles Scribner's Sons, 1992.

Milner, Clyde A., II, Carol A. O'Connor, and Martha A. Sandweiss, eds. *The Oxford History of the American West.* New York and Oxford: Oxford University Press, 1994.

Smith, Carter, ed. *The Conquest of the West: A Sourcebook on the American West.* Brookfield, CT: Millbrook Press, 1992.

White, Richard. *"It's Your Misfortune and None of My Own": A New History of the American West.* Norman: University of Oklahoma Press, 1991.

Opening the West

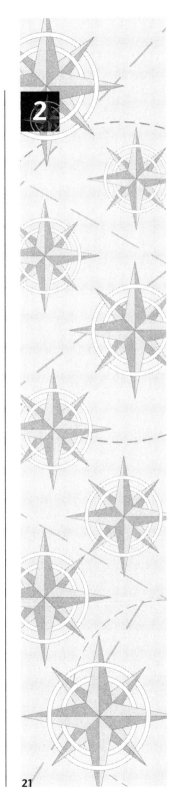

2

As the British colonies on the eastern seaboard grew ever more crowded in the mid-1700s, colonists began to look westward, beyond the Appalachian Mountains, and imagine the incredible riches the continent had to offer. At first, only the hardiest souls wandered far from civilization into the unknown. The stories these early adventurers told—first of the thick forests of the Ohio Valley, and later of the mineral-rich mountains in California, Colorado, and Nevada; the grassy plains of Texas and the Oklahoma and Kansas territories; and the fertile Willamette Valley of the Oregon territory—thrilled and shocked the incredulous but curious easterners.

Early wars and land purchases legalized Americans' claim to the continent (see Chapter 1). But these wars did not open the West—individuals did. Acting alone or in small groups, brave individualists ventured into virgin territory to claim what seemed to be "free" land or to profit from the abundant wild game. Without governmental protections, these frontiersmen stood alone in the wilderness. To keep their claims in the trans-Appalachian area (the area of land that stretched west from the crest of the Appalachian Mountains to the Mississippi River), early settlers fought almost constantly with Indians. "For the frontiersman who found his cabin in flames and his family mutilated, horror quickly hardened into a desire for vengeance. Backwoods morality teamed God and right against the 'redman,'" according to frontier historian Paul O'Neil in *The Frontiersmen.*

While these individuals' farms helped stake America's claim to the area between the crest of the Appalachian Mountains and the Mississippi River, the trappers who traipsed even farther west, through the wilderness beyond the Mississippi River did not. More permanent settlements were needed there to establish America's claim to the rest of the continent.

The fur trade

Fur trappers of the Far West accommodated the cultural differences between whites and Indians for the benefit of trade. Many allied themselves with Native Americans to learn more about the wilderness they roamed. Combing thousands of miles to collect animal pelts for trade, these independent trappers also gathered stories of the marvelous frontier. Their pelts and stories poured into the trading center of St. Louis and into the eastern states; the pelts became fashionable hats, and the traders' stories thrilled the easterners, helping to create a national desire to see the West.

As profitable as the fur trade became, however, trappers did not provide America with a stable presence in the Far West; only settlements could secure that. Families needed to be persuaded to cross the Mississippi River in search of homes. Towns needed to be built. So ultimately, Americans needed to discover what every square mile of their country had to offer and promote the best places for settlement. First, explorers blazed trails across the continent, and then the U.S. Army sent engineers to explore the boundaries of the country. After the Civil War (1861–65), the "Great Surveys" detailed the mysteries of the interior. These excursions provided maps of the continent and prompted many to flock westward and settle all worthy territory. Pulled by stories and guided by maps, America fulfilled what many called its manifest destiny: to settle the continent from coast to coast.

Claiming the land

The rapid population growth in the American colonies during the 1700s motivated colonists to move west. American farmers felt that they needed at least one hundred acres to support a family. As lands were divided and dispersed among growing families, and as the fertility of the soil declined after more than a century of use, it became increasingly difficult to support a family on an eastern farm. It only made sense to the colonists that they take possession of the fertile land in the Ohio Valley (an expansive area west of the Appalachians that includes part or all of the present-day states of West Virginia, Ohio, Kentucky, Indiana, and Illinois, as well as the far western parts of Pennsylvania and New York).

The settling of the trans-Appalachian area began slowly. Limited numbers of settlers moved into the areas around Fort Duquesne (pronounced doo-KAYNE; now named Fort Pitt) after 1760 and Scotch-Irish farmers from North Carolina moved into eastern Tennessee around 1771. The settlers of the trans-Appalachian area were hardy backwoodsmen who braved the wilderness to carve out settlements and claim new land for the young country. Without maps or support from their government, these men cleared the land for their family farms and stood alone against Indians defending their claims to the land. The American settlers had only their own strength and skill with a flintlock rifle or an ax for protection.

Men like Daniel Boone and James Harrod ventured into the uncharted forests across the Appalachian Mountains to ready the area for settlement in the 1760s and 1770s. Although these men were interested in settling the frontier, they did not want to replicate life in the East. Boone scorned the settled towns of the east and preferred not to live "within 100 miles of a d——d Yankee," noted Paul O'Neil in *The Frontiersmen*. After years of hunting in and exploring the rich forests of Kentucky, Boone cut the first road over the Cumberland Gap (a natural passage through the region west of the Appalachians) to found Boonesborough in Kentucky in 1775. Judge Richard Henderson had employed Boone to lead a group to settle the millions of acres in central Kentucky that Henderson had purchased from some Cherokee Indians.

Little by little, others followed, using the same tools and steely determination to settle the fertile valleys between the Appalachian Mountains and the Mississippi River. Many of those who settled the area during this time were the first whites to do so, for while British and French fur traders had roamed the woods for years, they had not established permanent settlements. And all these settlers ignored the Proclamation of 1763, which had declared the Appalachian Mountains the western boundary of the colonies due to ongoing conflicts with the Native American population in the region beyond the Appalachians.

Life on this new frontier was hard. After carving their farms out of the thickly forested valleys, settlers had to defend their new homes against attack. Early on, Indians opposed Americans encroaching on their land and allied themselves with French or British trappers. Indians would burn the crops and cabins and attack the settlers. Until the War of 1812 (1812–14) established the Mississippi River as the new western border of the United States, Indian raids were, in the words of O'Neil, "as much a part of border life as hunting or planting corn."

Discovering the land's riches: Lewis and Clark

With the Louisiana Purchase of 1803, the United States acquired from France more than 800,000 acres of land, stretching from west of the Mississippi to the Rocky Mountains (see Chapter 1), doubling the size of the United States. Americans had been busily settling the Near West and began to wonder about the land across the Mississippi. Intrigued by the notes of British fur trader and explorer Alexander Mackenzie (c. 1755–1820), the first white man to cross the Rocky Mountains, President Thomas Jefferson engaged Captains Meriwether Lewis (1774–1809) and William Clark (1770–1838) to seek out the Northwest Passage, a direct water route to the Pacific Ocean, which many hoped would facilitate profitable trading with other countries. Lewis and Clark welcomed the president's request, even though they would be on land claimed by the British once they crossed the Rockies. Not only were they enthusiastic, but the two good friends were also up to the task. The twenty-nine-year-old Lewis and the thirty-three-year-old Clark were both well-trained military men and well versed in woods-manship and Indian matters.

Lewis and Clark assembled a group of explorers called the "Corps of Discovery," which included fourteen soldiers, nine Kentuckians, two French river men, a slave named York, and Lewis's pet Newfoundland dog, Sea-man. On May 14, 1804, twenty-two oarsmen rowed a square-sailed keel-boat (a shallow riverboat used for hauling freight) up the Missouri River near St. Louis, along with two groups of six and seven men in two pirogues, or canoes. Two hunters with horses patrolled the banks of the river for game. Along the way the Corps also added a number of interpreters who spoke various Indian languages.

Meeting different cultures

Clark recorded every twist and turn of the river and commented on significant geological features along their route. Lewis tried to befriend the more than fifty Indian tribes they encountered, bestowing gifts upon the chiefs and relating stories of the powerful United States and the "Great Father" Jefferson (President Thomas Jefferson) in Washington, D.C., who would welcome visits from chiefs and send gifts to tribes who remained peaceful. At these meetings, the Corps would put on a show to entertain the tribes: the soldiers would march in full uniform, and Lewis would fire a gun. As entertaining as the Corps' show was, Seaman the dog and the black slave, York, proved tremendously interesting to the Indians as well. Indians were fascinated with the "unpainted man-with-the-black-skin," calling him "Big Medicine."

Just as the Indians were fascinated with the Corps, the Corps too found the Native Americans interesting. Never before had the Corps seen people who strapped planks to babies' heads to flatten their foreheads; nor had they seen people whose noses were pierced with shells. Lewis recorded

William Clark. *(© Bettmann/ Corbis. Reproduced by permission.)*

Meriwether Lewis. *(© Bettmann/Corbis. Reproduced by permission.)*

every detail of each meeting, describing how each tribe reacted to his speech about the United States and detailing various Indian ceremonies, daily routines, and tribal organization. The Corps' initial discoveries were sent back to St. Louis on a keelboat on April 7, 1805. This trove of information included Clark's chart of the fifty different tribes they had encountered; a dictionary of the Mandan tribe's language; a map of the Missouri River; live animals, including magpies, a prairie dog, and a sharp-tailed grouse; the skins and skeletons of other animals unknown in the East; a variety of plant specimens; and a container of mice and insects. In addition, forty-five Native Americans accepted voyage on the boat bound for the Great Father. As the boat left, Lewis and Clark continued westward with their Corps, which now numbered thirty-one and included Indian interpreter Sacajawea and her two-month-old son (see box on p. 28-29).

The expedition made its way to the head of the Missouri River in Montana and, with Sacajawea acting as an interpreter to the Shoshone (pronounced shuh-SHOW-nee) tribe, was pointed in the direction of the "great or stinking lake," which Lewis recorded as the Shoshones' term for the ocean, according to the *Original Journals of the Lewis and Clark Expedition*. Late in 1805, the group saw Indians wearing sailors' clothes and knew they couldn't be far from the ocean. In fact, they were on the Colombia River in present-day Oregon. In mid-November they reached the Pacific coast in what is now northwestern Oregon. Though they had reached their destination, the party was unenthusiastic about spending the winter at Fort Clatsop, which consisted of two rows of hastily constructed log cabins. The Corps suffered pesky fleas, spoiled fish for food, rain every day but twelve, mildewed clothing, and neighboring Indians stealing their supplies. Unwilling to wait longer for the ship Jefferson had promised would take them home around Cape Horn, on the southernmost tip of South America, the expedition started for home on March 23, 1806.

Dividing the party

When the Corps reached Travelers' Rest Creek, near present-day Lolo, Montana, Lewis and Clark split their party in two so they could explore even more of the West on their way home. Lewis's party of nine braved swarms of mosquitoes to explore the Marias River. Clark divided his group of twenty-two, sending one group down the Missouri River and the other, including himself, overland to the Yellowstone River, where they would then paddle downriver to the Missouri.

Lewis's party met with Blackfeet Indians, who did not respond well to Lewis's speech. The Blackfeet were not interested in ruining their business connections with the Canadians to trade with the Americans. But more detrimental to the meeting was Lewis's acknowledgment of his friendship with the Nez Percé and Shoshone tribes, which were enemies of the Blackfeet. At night, Blackfeet warriors turned the explorers' guns on them, and in the struggle the Lewis party killed two Blackfeet warriors—the only time members of the expedition killed Indians. To avoid reprisal, Lewis and his party rode their horses more than 120 miles in twenty-four hours to escape Blackfeet territory. Luckily, when they arrived at the Missouri River, the Corps boats were waiting for them. Three days later, Lewis's party caught up with Clark, who had led the others downriver to hunt and to escape the mosquitoes.

Returning to civilization

By September 23, 1806, the Corps had finished its journey. All the explorers except Sergeant Charles Floyd, who had become ill and died near present-day Sioux City, Iowa, arrived in St. Louis two years, four months, and ten days after leaving. The journey had taken so long that the

Sacajawea (also Sacagawea, Sakakawea)

For years, historians scoured American history looking for instances of genuine Indian and American cooperation. Sacajawea's aid to the Lewis and Clark expedition had, for many years, seemed one of the best examples. Though she played a relatively minor role in the expedition, she was among the first Indian women, if not the first, to play any part in helping white expansion.

Born around 1788 in the Shoshone tribe, Sacajawea was captured by the Hidatsa tribe of North Dakota when she was twelve. Mountain man and fur trader Toussaint Charbonneau, who had lived with the Hidatsa for several years, bought Sacajawea from the Hidatsa in about 1804 to be his wife. Lewis and Clark met Charbonneau in the Mandan villages at the bend of the Missouri River in Dakota country in 1805 and hired him as an interpreter. Before the Corps of Discovery left the Mandan, Sacajawea gave birth to a son, Jean Baptiste, who was nicknamed "Pomp." The seventeen-year-old Sacajawea carried her son on her back in a cradle board all the way to the Pacific Ocean.

Not long after leaving the Mandan village, Lewis and Clark discovered Charbonneau was a fine cook but a terrible guide. While steering a pirogue along the Missouri River, Charbonneau, who could not swim and was, according to Lewis, "perhaps the most timid waterman in the world," nearly lost "almost every article indispensably necessary to ... insure the success of the enterprise in which, we are now

well-wishers who had sent them off were astonished to see them return, having heard rumors that the Corps had been slaughtered by Indians or enslaved by the Spanish. Nevertheless the explorers had returned with news of a "practical route" across the country that would afford "immense advantages to the fur trade" because "the Missouri and all its branches ... abound more in beaver and common otter than any streams on earth," according to Lewis's letter to the president upon his return.

Lewis and Clark had established the commercial value of the new territory rather than the suitability of the land for settlement as the earlier backwoodsmen had done. Their report made it clear that abundant game could enrich the young country, and Americans jumped at the chance. Trappers swarmed into the West.

launched," according to *Along the Trail with Lewis and Clark*. A gust of wind caught the sail and tipped the boat until it filled to within an inch of the top. Charbonneau lost his wits and proved unable to manage the situation. Luckily, Private Pierre Cruzatte and Sacajawea remained calm. Lewis remarked that their "resolution and fortitude" saved the cargo.

Sacajawea also proved better able to guide and interpret for the Corps than her husband did. She gathered healthful vegetation from the forests to improve the expedition's menu and could speak with the Shoshone tribes they would soon encounter. The first band of Indians the expedition met was led by a chief named Cameahwait, who turned out to be Sacajawea's brother. Their joyous reunion made it possible for the Corps to trade for horses and other supplies needed to cross the Rocky Mountains.

When the expedition returned to the Mandan villages on the way back to St. Louis, Sacajawea and Charbonneau left the Corps. In 1809, Sacajawea and Charbonneau visited Clark in St. Louis and left their son behind to be educated. There are conflicting accounts as to what happened to Sacajawea after her visit with Clark. One version states that she died of fever in 1812. Another suggests that she remained in St. Louis for a time, went to live with the Comanche tribe, and eventually rejoined her relatives on the Wind River Reservation of Wyoming, where she died of natural causes in April 1884.

The inhabited West

The explorers who ventured across the Mississippi did not find the land unsettled or unclaimed, as many of the backwoodsmen had found the trans-Appalachian region. (Though native peoples lived on much of this land, Americans didn't consider the Indian lands settled.) Unlike the area between the Appalachians and the Mississippi, the Far West and the Southwest (parts of present-day California, Arizona, New Mexico, and Texas) had been claimed and settled by the Spanish. Spain had claimed all of present-day New Mexico in 1598, and in 1769 Spanish missionaries arrived on the California coast and set out to convert the more than three hundred thousand indigenous peoples, whom they called Diggers, to Christianity. In an attempt to extend their empire farther north into California, the Spanish began

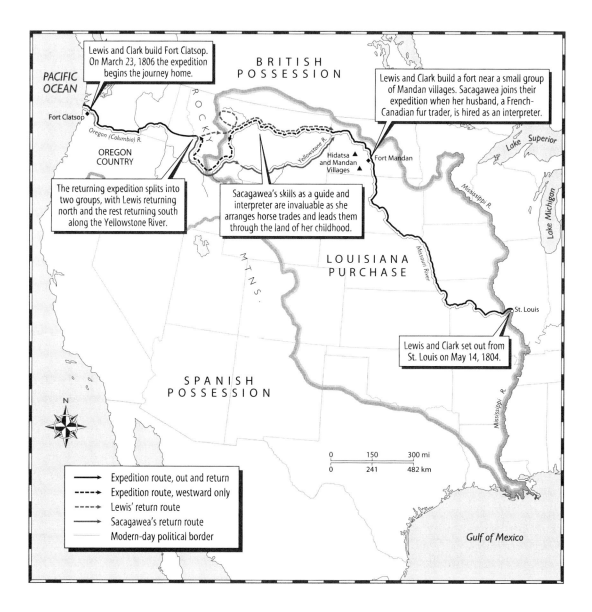

Map showing the routes taken by Lewis, Clark, and Sacajawea during their exploration of the American West. *(Map by XNR Productions. Reproduced by permission of the Gale Group.)*

building missions (religious settlements), pueblos (villages), and presidios (forts), beginning in San Diego and extending northward all the way to San Francisco Bay. By the turn of the century, they had gathered nearly the entire population of California Indians south of San Francisco Bay into their missions. But life in the missions destroyed the Indians' lives and culture. Forced to labor in the missions, the baptized Indians were essentially slaves, and to make matters worse, they were not immune to many of the Spaniards' diseases. By 1817, 90 percent of the mission Indians had died from disease and abuse.

Some of the first U.S. expeditions across the Mississippi River were intended to establish trade with the Spanish. In 1806, Army Lieutenant Zebulon Montgomery Pike (1779–1813) led fifteen men from St. Louis to explore the southern border of the Louisiana Territory. Instead of finding the headwaters of the Arkansas or Red River, as he had hoped to, Pike encountered many Indian villages and Spanish settlements in New Mexico. He was quite impressed by a mountain peak looming high above the flat plains of present-day Colorado, which would later bear his name, but ultimately he was unable to ascend its peak and declared that no human could. (Fourteen years later, three men did attain the summit of Pikes Peak.)

Zebulon Montgomery Pike led fifteen men to explore the southern border of the Louisiana Territory. (© CORBIS. Reproduced by permission.)

When Pike returned with news of the affluent Spanish settlements, many American traders flocked into the Southwest. Although the Spaniards forbade foreigners from trading in Spanish territories and threw early traders into jail, the Mexicans, who took control of the area in 1821, proved better trading partners. And by 1824, the United States sent a federal survey team to map out and clear what would become the Santa Fe Trail, which would open the Southwest to thousands of wagons carrying settlers as well as traders.

Mexican independence also benefited American traders in California. When Mexico declared its independence from Spain in 1821, it gained the California territory. And in 1834, when the Mexican government ended the dominance of the Spanish missions, it granted large tracts of land to the Californios, descendants of the original Spanish settlers. These ranchos were tended by the first cowboys, called vaqueros. Wealthy Californio Mariano Vallejo remembered the days when he and his peers dominated California society

Pikes Peak is named after Zebulon Montgomery Pike who declared the peak too high for any human to reach. (© David Muench/ CORBIS. Reproduced by permission.)

(quoted by Gradalupe Vallejo in *Century Magazine*): "We were the pioneers of the Pacific coast, building towns and Missions while General [George] Washington was carrying on the War of the Revolution. We often talk together of the days when a few hundred large Spanish ranches and Mission tracts occupied the whole country from the Pacific to the San Joaquin." The Californios organized great ranching empires and became rich selling cowhides to Russian, English, French, and

American traders who stopped at California ports. The Californios traded the hides for manufactured goods, bright cloth, jewelry, tobacco, furniture, and a wealth of other goods that they could not produce themselves. The influence of the Californios declined, however, when the United States claimed California and the other southwestern territories following the Mexican-American War in 1848.

Founding Astoria

After 1807, the promise of abundant furs in the West was the main reason Euro-Americans ventured across the Mississippi. Merchants were also lured west in search of a convenient trade route to China and India. Four years after Lewis and Clark returned and detailed their trip to the Pacific, John Jacob Astor (1763–1848), one of the wealthiest Americans of his time, formed the Pacific Fur Company with the encouragement of Thomas Jefferson. He hoped to open a line of trading posts between Missouri and the Oregon Country. The main outpost, to be called Fort Astoria, was on the Oregon coast, at the mouth of the Columbia River. This outpost would funnel goods from the inland areas across the Pacific and provide a center for international maritime trade. In addition, Astor hoped his post would "carry the American population across the Rocky Mountains and spread it along the shores of the Pacific," according to W. Irving in *Astoria*. In 1810 Astor sent thirty-three men by sea from New York to the mouth of the Columbia and sixty-four trappers and guides overland, to found Fort Astoria.

In March 1811, the *Tonquin*, captained by former naval officer Jonathan Thorn, landed in Oregon. Thorn proved to be a reckless leader, losing seven men while attempting a landing in rough seas and leaving fewer than half his men to build the new fort while he and the other half ventured north to trade with the Indians. After Thorn lost his temper and struck a Salish Indian chief while trying to make a deal, the tribe killed him in retaliation the next day, along with many of his crew. One of his wounded men lit the ship's cache of gunpowder and accidentally blew the *Tonquin* to pieces. The remainder of the party forged ahead with plans for the fort.

Seven months passed before the first of the overland party made it to the fort. Unaccustomed to the trials of the

wilderness, many of the party had died en route. Only forty-five of the original sixty-four made it to Fort Astoria. In 1813, a supply ship brought reinforcements to the fort, and it seemed as if the venture would succeed. But the Americans and the British were in the midst of the War of 1812 (1812–14) and hostilities between them had reached a high point. Captain William Black landed and purchased the fort for the British, renaming it Fort George in October 1813. The Treaty of Ghent, signed twelve months later at the end of the War of 1812, reinstated the fort as an American outpost. Although the fort was a disaster in business terms and brought death to sixty-five of the men who tried to found it, Fort Astoria helped legitimize America's claim to the Pacific coast, setting the stage for future American settlement of the area.

John Jacob Astor. (Reproduced by permission of the National Portrait Gallery.)

Trappers map the West

Although it had existed in the trans-Mississippi West for almost two decades, the American fur trade truly began to flourish in the 1820s. Trappers who combed the area related the geography of the West, and slowly a map of the region emerged via word of mouth. The trappers told of mountain vistas, geysers, and lakes of salt. They described buffalo skulls scattered across the plains and fights with grizzly bears. But many would lament, as Jim Bridger (1804–1881) did, that "They said I was the d——dest liar ever lived. That's what a man gets for telling the truth," according to Bil Gilbert in *The Trailblazers*. Though the trappers' stories often fell upon disbelieving ears, their tales circulated through the civilized East and fueled a wave of interest in settling the West.

Trade in Santa Fe, in present-day New Mexico, opened to Americans in 1821, when Mexico won its independence from Spain. In 1823 Edwin James and Stephen Long published the details of their expeditions in the Rocky Mountains, which increased American interest in the area. Trappers gathered at the annual Rendezvous near the common borders of present-day Idaho, Wyoming, and Utah (see box on p. 36) to sell their pelts and obtain supplies for the coming year. Pelts were shipped overseas on trading vessels or carried overland or on rivers to eastern markets. By the 1830s, however, overtrapping of beaver and changes in fashion put the fur trade in jeopardy. Heavy competition over the next twenty years made the American fur trade unprofitable by the 1840s. Unable to find many beavers to trap, trappers established farms or general trading posts in the Rocky Mountains they had come to know so well. One of the most famous trappers was Jim Bridger, who established a ranch in southwest Wyoming that catered to settlers making their way west.

Though the era of mountain men had come to an end, their work would usher in the next great era of emigration. The keen sense of the continent the mountain men had gained while combing the country for fur proved invaluable to later explorers, who hired the mountain men as guides in their search for viable travel routes for settlers.

By the 1840s, Americans, feeling the impact of increased European immigration, began to look on the trans-Mississippi region not as a vast wealth-building resource for those willing to risk their lives but as a potential home in which to raise American families. As early as the 1830s, artists and scientists had portrayed and detailed the natural wonders of the continent, and by the 1840s political movements began to use these pictures and scientific discoveries to further expansionist goals of claiming the entire continent for the United States. Notions of manifest destiny, the idea that Americans were preordained to inhabit the continent from coast to coast, fueled what amounted to a holy war or crusade toward the Pacific Ocean.

Topographical engineers

While the mountain men trapped and explored the unknown regions of the continent for profit, the United States Army formed the Corps of Topographical Engineers in 1838 to look at the land with an eye toward settlement. The thirty-six officers who made up this group were the best the

The Mountain Man Rendezvous

The annual Rendezvous was the most significant social and business event of the American fur trade during the 1820s and 1830s. Each summer in late June or early July, Rocky Mountain fur trappers and their Indian allies met with the trading companies in order to purchase supplies and exchange a year's worth of pelts. The fur-trading companies, including the two largest, the American Fur Company and the Rocky Mountain Fur Company, would send a supply train from St. Louis loaded with clothing, ammunition, traps, sugar, coffee, flour, and anything else a trapper might need. Trappers would be lucky to bring in eight hundred dollars' worth of pelts to trade for essential supplies. The annual Rendezvous was usually held near the common borders of present-day Idaho, Wyoming, and Utah.

The Rendezvous was the only time trappers could be found in a group—most of their time was spent combing the rivers and mountains alone or in small bands. By the time a mountain man reached the Rendezvous, he might have traveled more than three thousand miles in search of pelts. Tired of their year-long isolation, trappers made the Rendezvous a raucous celebration of surviving the year's hardships and danger. The mountain men challenged each other to wrestling and shooting matches, horse racing, and even eating contests. They drank, gambled, fought, exchanged tall tales, and bartered for wives.

When the fur-trading industry declined in the 1840s, the Rendezvous ended. Having befriended the Indians and adopted many of their customs, many fur trappers continued to live in the mountains rather than returning to civilization. Some of the most famous, including Jim Bridger, Kit Carson, Tom Fitzpatrick, and Jedediah Smith, acted as guides to the explorers and settlers of the West.

military had to offer, having graduated at the top of their classes at the West Point military academy. The Corps of Engineers made maps and surveys of the frontier from the 1840s to the 1860s. The Corps marked the 49th parallel as the boundary between Canada and Oregon and in 1849, after the Mexican-American War, established the boundary between Mexico and the United States, which ran fifteen hundred miles from the Gulf of Mexico to the Pacific Ocean.

The Army Corps of Topographical Engineers was instrumental in opening the West for settlement. Leading expeditions into the frontier, the corps helped determine which

parts of the frontier were best for settlement. Of all the engineers, John Charles Frémont (1813–1890) became by far the most famous. Known as "the Pathfinder," Frémont led five expeditions into the West between 1842 and 1854. Though Frémont was not a skilled explorer—he often needed help staying on others' paths and found few new routes himself—he was a masterful promoter of the West. A charismatic speaker and glamorous figure, Frémont influenced many Americans' decision to go west.

During the1820s and 1830s, the annual mountain man Rendezvous occurred each summer in late June or early July. Rocky Mountain fur trappers and their Indian allies met with the trading companies in order to purchase supplies and exchange a year's worth of pelts. *(Courtesy of the Library of Congress.)*

John Frémont, promoter of the West

Unlike the other engineers, Frémont did not attend West Point; instead, he was appointed to the corps as a civilian by a powerful friend named Joel Poinsett (1779–1851), the secretary of war under President Martin Van Buren (1782–1862) who helped set up the corps. Given the title of second lieutenant, Frémont worked under the extremely gifted surveyor Joseph Nicollet. A few years later, Frémont married Jessie Benton (1824–1902), the daughter of expansionist Senator Thomas Hart Benton (1782–1858) of Missouri. Benton pushed through an appropriation of thirty thousand dollars for a survey of the Oregon Trail; Frémont would lead the survey, but he was guided by the famous mountain man Kit Carson (1809–1868).

In addition to the routine drawing of maps and descriptions of the land, Frémont, as instructed by Benton, set out to romanticize the West and make western travel appealing to those east of the Mississippi. Benton and others who promoted the idea of manifest destiny reasoned that the mountain men, who were often regarded as outcasts, were not enough to support American claims to the continent. Their concerns about ownership of the continent were understandable: Mexico owned the Southwest outright, and the United States and Britain jointly owned the Oregon Country. Supporters of manifest destiny pushed for the more "civilized" settlement of the Far West and tried to appeal to farmers, ranchers, storekeepers, preachers, and miners, people who would give the American government a reason to spend money on roads and forts in the West and to support the United States's claim to the area. Frémont's accounts of his adventures—such as climbing high mountains and navigating white-water rapids—enticed many to venture into the Far West.

One of Frémont's most memorable stories was of a mountain summit, recalled in his *Report of the Exploring Expedition to trhe Rocky Mountains:*

> Here, on the summit, where the stillness was absolute, unbroken by any sound, and thus the solitude complete, we thought ourselves beyond the region of animated life; but while we were sitting on the rock, a solitary bee (*bromus, the bumble bee*) came winging his flight from the eastern valley, and lit on the knee of one of the men. It was a strange place, the icy rock and the highest peak of the Rocky Mountains, for a lover of warm sunshine and flowers; and we pleased ourselves with the idea that he was the first of his species to cross the mountain barrier, a solitary pioneer to foretell the advance of civilization.

Frémont combined his romanticized adventures with practical advice on food and shelter and supply lists for the emigrants wishing to make the journey. His report of his ex-

pedition would usher in an era of unprecedented interest in settling the
trans-Mississippi region.

Despite Frémont's enthusiasm,
his was not the only account of the expedition. His topographer, Charles
Preuss, wrote an account of the same
mountain ascent that was less glamorous: "The hike was disagreeable all
around. No supper, no breakfast, little
or no sleep—who can enjoy climbing a
mountain under these circumstances?
Moreover, all the men, with perhaps
two exceptions, would have much preferred to stay in camp. What possible
interest do these fellows have in such
an undertaking?" according to Bil
Gilbert in *The Trailblazers*. Indeed,
twenty years before Frémont's expedition, Major Stephen H. Long had
dubbed the Great Plains the "Great
Desert," and Long and most of the
other travelers to the region declared it
"wholly unfit for cultivation, and of
course, uninhabitable by a people depending upon agriculture
for their subsistence," as quoted in *The Trailblazers*. Long went
on to assert that the Plains would "serve as a barrier to prevent
too great an extension of our population westward." But Frémont's account of the Plains could not have been more different. Frémont noted that the region "reminds us of cultivated
gardens and civilization." In the end, Frémont proved quite
able to persuade others to his view, and legislators were so
taken with his report in 1843 that Congress ordered the distri-
bution of ten thousand copies. And in the early 1840s, thousands of wagon trains assembled to journey west.

Hearing of profitable trade with the Mexicans, John
Bidwell started out for California with the first of the Oregon
Trail wagon trains. Religious leader Brigham Young (1801–
1877) and the twelve thousand Mormons who followed him
read Frémont's and others' reports of the West to locate the
perfect spot for their religious refuge (present-day Salt Lake
City). Missionaries (proponents of a religion who travel into

John Charles Frémont was
not a skillful explorer, but
his romanticized accounts
of his adventures in the
West enticed Americans to
venture into the Far West.
*(Courtesy of the Library of
Congress.)*

The Colorado Valley as photographed during the Topographical and Geological Survey carried out by the American geologist John Wesley Powell. *(Photograph by Beaman. © Hulton Getty/ Liaison Agency. Reproduced by permission.)*

unexplored territories to try to convert indigenous peoples to the missionaries' religion) organized to save the souls of the numerous native peoples on the frontier, a trend that ended quickly after the brutal massacre of Marcus and Narcissa Whitman at their Oregon mission (see Chapter 10).

Mapping the inland territories

By the end of the Civil War (1861–65) the army had defined the boundaries of the continent and detailed its natural assets. The army had consolidated its survey findings on one map drawn to scale 1:3,000,000 by Lieutenant Gouverneur Kemble Warren (1830–1882), but much of the inland territory had yet to be mapped. People were naturally curious about these unmapped portions of the country, and the Homestead Act of 1862, which offered 160 acres of land to anyone able to settle and work it, created a need for these areas to be explored to find good places for settlement.

The fifteen years following the Civil War became known as the period of the "Great Surveys." Ferdinand Vandiveer Hayden, Clarence King, John Wesley Powell, and the army's Lieutenant George Montague Wheeler led most of the surveys. Exploring what would become Nebraska, Colorado, Wyoming, Utah, Nevada, California, Arizona, and New Mexico and some of Montana, Idaho, and Oregon, these men and their crews detailed the region's geologic structure and assessed its mineral deposits, navigated its rivers, and described wildlife and vegetation, providing instruction for the best use of the land. Written without the grand exaggerations and misleading romantic tales used by Frémont, these surveys scientifically recorded the abundance and vastness of the nation and were enhanced by the new technology of photography (photographers often accompanied the surveyors on their treks). By 1879 these surveys would complete the work started by Lewis and Clark in 1804. Surveyor Hayden noted that the goal was to "lay before the public such full, accurate and reliable information as will bring from the older states the capital, skill, and enterprise necessary to develop the great natural resources," according to Gilbert's *The Trailblazers*. Leaving nothing to the imagination, the Great Surveys would create the foundation for the settlement of the West.

For More Information

Books
Wishart, David J. *The Fur Trade of the American West: 1807–1840*. Lincoln: University of Nebraska Press, 1979.

Web sites
"The Adventures of Daniel Boone, Formerly a Hunter; Containing a Narrative of the Wars of Kentucky." *Archiving Early America: Historic Documents from Eighteenth Century America*. [Online] http://www.early america.com/lives/boone/index.html (accessed April 5, 2000).

"The Journals of Lewis and Clark." *American Studies @ The University of Virginia: Hypertexts*. [Online] http://xroads.virginia.edu/~HYPER/ JOURNALS/toc.htm (accessed April 5, 2000).

Mountain Men and the Fur Trade: Sources of the History of the Fur Trade in the Rocky Mountain West. [Online] http://www.xmission.com/~drudy/ amm.html (accessed April 5, 2000).

Rabbit, Mary C. *The United States Geological Survey: 1879–1989, USGS Circular 1050*. [Online] http://www.usgs.gov/reports/circular/c1050/index.htm (accessed April 5, 2000).

Sources

Berry, Don. *Mountain Men: The Trappers of the Great Fur-Trading Era, 1822–1843*. New York: Macmillan, 1966.

Blumberg, Rhoda. *The Incredible Journey of Lewis and Clark*. New York: William Morrow, 1987.

Clark, Ella E. *Sacagawea of the Lewis and Clark Expedition*. Berkeley: University of California Press, 1979.

Fifer, Barbara, and Vicky Soderberg. *Along the Trail with Lewis and Clark*. Great Falls: Montana Magazine, 1998.

Frémont, John C. *Report of the Exploring Expedition to the Rocky Mountains*. United States Government, Washington, D.C., 1845.

Gilbert, Bil. *The Trailblazers*. New York: Time-Life Books, 1973.

Irving, W. *Astoria*. New York: The Century Co., 1909.

Jackson, Donald, ed. *Letters of the Lewis and Clark Expedition with Related Documents: 1783–1854*. Urbana: University of Illinois Press, 1962.

O'Neil, Paul. *The Frontiersmen*. Alexandria, VA: Time-Life Books, 1977.

Thwaites, Reuben Gold, ed. *Original Journals of the Lewis and Clark Expedition*. 8 vols. New York: Dodd, Mead & Co., 1904–1905.

Vallejo, Guadalupe. "Ranch and Mission Days in Alta California." *Century Magazine* (December 1890).

Driving the Indians Westward: Indian Removal to 1840

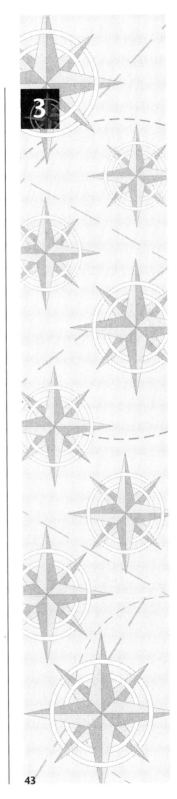

For more than three hundred years, white men battled Native Americans for control of the North American continent. From the early seventeenth century, when European settlers landed on the shores of the present-day United States, to nearly the dawn of the twentieth century, white settlers and soldiers waged an unrelenting war to claim the lands that Native Americans, or Indians, had long known as their own. The three-and-a-half-century war between whites and Indians consisted of battles large and small; of organized campaigns by the U.S. Army and daring daylight raids by Indian warriors; of extreme brutality and rare kindness. Though the underlying cause of the wars was the hunger of white settlers and governments for land, the tensions were heightened by the huge cultural differences that separated the two peoples. Whites and Indians thought very differently about land, family, promises, and warfare—differences that only added to the tragedy of what is known as Indian removal.

First encounters

The very first encounters between whites and Indians in what would become the United States were peaceful and mutually beneficial. In fact, Indians probably ensured the survival of the colony that was established at Jamestown, Virginia, in 1607. Ill prepared for the harsh winters, the British colonists died in massive numbers until a local Algonquian Indian leader known as Powhatan (c. 1550–1618) provided them with food. Later the Indians helped the colonists plant native foods and harvest a weed known as tobacco (which would later become a major source of colonial income). Of course, the most famous instance of Indian friendship with settlers occurred at Plymouth, Massachusetts, where Indians helped the Pilgrim colonists grow food and learn how to use the land. Such Indian-white cooperation is now celebrated with the Thanksgiving holiday. White colonists also proved helpful to Indians, largely by providing them with guns, which made the Indians' hunting much easier than it had been with the bow and arrow.

Following God's plan

The many Native American peoples living in North America when white settlers began to arrive in the 1600s and 1700s had fully developed traditions and established ways of life. They built dwellings, hunted and farmed for their food, raised families, and worshiped in their own way. Yet the white colonists failed to appreciate the unique cultures of the native peoples. All they saw were uncivilized, primitive people who failed to use the land wisely and worshiped strange gods. Inspired by the belief that they needed to convert the Indians to Christianity, and eager to remake the landscape into the productive farms they had left behind in Europe, the colonists who would become Americans set about to claim both Indian land and Indian souls.

It is impossible to overemphasize the strength of the colonists' preconceptions. They firmly believed that God rewarded the people who made productive use of the land. The Indians that they saw wandered freely over the land, hunting where they wished and never building fences. What could be better, what would be more in line with God's plan, they thought, than to subject this land to orderly and productive

use? The white settlers firmly believed that by doing this, they were acting according to the plan of their Christian God. Indians, on the other hand, worshiped nature gods in ways that to the settlers seemed "primitive" and "childish." According to author Don Nardo in *The Indian Wars,* one white minister described the Indians as living in a "miserable, Godless state of sin." The Bible gave the colonists guidance in dealing with the Indians; according to the Book of Psalms, "God will give him [the Christian] the heathen [non-Christians to convert and watch over], and the uttermost parts of the earth for his possession." Such beliefs made it seem to the settlers not just natural but necessary to lay claim to the land before them.

In early encounters between Native Americans and British settlers, the Native Americans believed that the European Americans were a group with whom they might learn to coexist. Here, Ottawa chief Pontiac holds out a peace pipe to British major Robert Rogers.
(Courtesy of the Library of Congress.)

The white tide

While white colonists were unified by a common vision of their role in the new land, the various Indian tribes held a variety of religious and cultural beliefs. For years the Indians had been living lightly on the land, sometimes clashing with other tribes but never facing a unified and powerful foe. When white groups began settling on the land, the Native Americans saw them as yet another small tribe with whom they might trade, battle, and eventually learn to coexist. They had no notion that they faced a large and powerful enemy that would not be scared off by a few midnight raids or the loss of a few scalps.

Early hostilities

Given their vastly different expectations, it is unsurprising that conflict soon erupted between white colonists and the tribes they encountered. The first full-scale Indian war occurred in 1622, when chief Powhatan's younger brother, Opechancanough, led an attack on Jamestown, Virginia, to protest white use of Indian land, killing 350 colonists. The colonists struck back violently, burning Indian villages and killing all the Indians they found, including women and children. For twenty years the colonists harassed the Indians in this manner, until they agreed to sign a treaty granting the colonists control of all the land along the Atlantic coast.

A similar conflict shook New England in 1675 and 1676. The Wampanoag leader Metacomet (c. 1639–1676), known to the settlers as King Philip, organized several of the local tribes and attacked white settlements throughout New England. This clash between white and Indian forces, known as King Philip's War, ended in the destruction of nearly every major Indian village in the area and in the near-elimination of the Narraganset tribe. These early clashes set a pattern for future conflicts. Indians would attack whites who had encroached on them in some way. Offended that their will was being resisted, whites would organize massive counterattacks and drive the Indians from their land. Thus every Indian attack was met with an overwhelming display of force and determination until the white settlers had conquered every last bit of Indian land.

Dividing the land

By the middle of the eighteenth century, the growing British colonies had claimed most of the land stretching from the Atlantic Ocean to the crest of the Appalachian Mountains, several hundred miles to the west. Yet they faced organized resistance in their attempts to move west of the Appalachians. The French government had a significant trading empire in the region west of the Appalachians. French forces protected the region and provided aid and support to the Indians. Determined to drive the French out of North America, the British sent troops to assist the colonists during the French and Indian War (1754–63; see Chapter 1). The British won the war; they now faced only Indian resistance to further westward expansion.

Native American resistance was fierce. Indian tribes that had long sided with the French remained hostile to the British and launched a series of attacks on British positions throughout the Ohio Valley. This loosely organized coalition of Native Americans, created in part by an Ottawa chief named Pontiac (c. 1720–1769), captured several British forts and harassed frontier settlers. Seeking to avoid further bloodshed, the British issued an order known as the Proclamation of 1763, which recalled all settlers from west of the Appalachian crest and forbade further emigration into the area. Though the proclamation temporarily halted white expansion onto Indian lands, it enraged many colonists, who felt that their victory in the French and Indian War entitled them to push farther into the interior. This attempt to limit colonial expansion eventually backfired, for the colonists ultimately revolted against British rule in part so that they could claim the interior of the continent for their own.

In the years following the French and Indian War, the colonists were more concerned with the difficulty of enduring British rule than with their conflicts with the Indian tribes to the west. In 1776 they declared independence from England, starting the Revolutionary War, and by the time the war ended in 1783, they had claimed control of the original thirteen colonies and of a large portion of land that became know as the Northwest Territory or the Old Northwest. The Northwest Territory stretched between the Appalachian Mountains and the Mississippi River to the west (including the present states of Ohio, Indiana, Illinois, Michigan, Wisconsin, and part of Minnesota). The Americans—as they were now rightly known—saw the new territory as a land of opportunity, capable of providing the space needed by the citizens of a growing nation—if only it could be claimed from the hostile Indians. The Northwest Territory became the site of furious battles with the Indians in the years to come.

Fighting for the Old Northwest

The Old Northwest was home to many Native American tribes, notably the Ottawa, Chippewa, Shawnee, and Potawatomi. Its dense forests, wide rivers, and fertile valleys provided these groups with all that they needed to survive. But the Americans were not content to let the Indians use this land in a traditional, Native American way; they saw in the rich Ohio River Valley a place where gentlemen farmers could establish family farms, using the land to provide for their families while they developed the virtues that would make good citizens in a growing democracy. This vision of the American future was offered most eloquently by Thomas Jefferson (1743–1826), framer of the Declaration of Independence and soon to be the third president of the United States. In 1787 Jefferson authored the Northwest Ordinance, which provided for the orderly establishment of future states in the Old Northwest. (See Chapter 1 for more information about the Northwest Ordinance.) Jefferson was a vocal supporter of the virtues of yeoman farmers (owners of small farms) developing western lands. "Those that labor in the earth," he once wrote in *Notes on Virginia*, "are the chosen people of God, if ever He had a chosen people." The earlier Ordinance of 1785, which provided for the orderly surveying and sale of western lands, had only encouraged the movement of settlers into the Old Northwest. (See Chapter 1 for more information about the Ordinance of 1785). At the end of the eighteenth century, large numbers of Americans began to cross the Appalachians and settle in territory that was claimed by Indians.

The Indians who lived in the Old Northwest had seen enough to know that when white settlers came into an area, they eventually drove Indians out. So when settlers began taking advantage of these new ordinances, the Indians in the Old Northwest resisted their advance. They attacked settlers' camps and burned their farms. But still the whites moved in. One Indian chief, a Shawnee named Tecumseh (1768–1813), believed that the only way to stop the white advance was for all the tribes to unite and fight them. Though he was based in present-day Indiana, Tecumseh roamed far across the frontier, traveling as far south as Georgia and north into present-day Michigan. Tecumseh was a powerful speaker, and he gave voice to the frustrations and anger of many Indian warriors. In a speech to Indian tribes quoted in Ray Allen Billington's *Westward to the Pacific,* Tecumseh called for "War now. War forever. War upon the living. War upon the dead; dig up their very corpses from the graves; our country must give no rest to a white man's bones." Tecumseh even forged alliances with the British, who hoped to maintain their presence in the Old Northwest even though they had been defeated in the Revolutionary War (1776–83).

Little Turtle's War

The first major confrontation in the Old Northwest was known as Little Turtle's War. Alarmed at the number of Indian attacks on American settlers, President George Washington (1732–1799) sent a force of fourteen hundred soldiers under General Josiah Harmar into the Ohio Valley in 1790. Believing he had intimidated the combined Shawnee, Potawatomi, and Chippewa forces into retreat, Harmar gave chase and suddenly found his troops in a deadly ambush. The Indians won the battle. Washington next sent a larger force under General Arthur St. Clair, but they were badly defeated in a battle along the banks of the Wabash River. Finally, Washington sent a force of three thousand soldiers under General Anthony Wayne (1745–1796) to drive the Indians from the country. Wayne built several strong forts and pledged himself to protecting the region's white inhabitants. Alarmed at the growing American strength, two thousand warriors led by Turkey Foot and Blue Jacket faced Wayne's force of thirty-five hundred in a stand of storm-damaged trees known as Fallen Timbers. In a fierce battle, Wayne's troops defeated the combined Indian forces and forced them to sign a treaty granting all of Ohio and much of Indiana to the United States. Though they had made a strong stand, the Indians had lost this stage of the war.

Defeating Tecumseh

Tecumseh refused to sign the treaty following the battle of Fallen Timbers and instead recommitted himself to or-

General William Henry Harrison. *(Reproduced by permission of Archive Photos, Inc.)*

ganizing the tribes. "The whites," said Tecumseh, "are already nearly a match for us all united, and too strong for any one tribe to resist.... Unless every tribe unanimously combines to give check to the ambition and avarice of the whites, they will soon conquer us apart and disunited, and we will be driven away from our native country and scattered as autumnal leaves before the wind," according to Nardo. General William Henry Harrison (1773-1841), acting on the orders of President James Madison (1751–1836), negotiated treaties with the Miami and Delaware Indians, but Tecumseh vowed that he would never honor such treaties, for he believed that land could not be sold. Thus the battle lines were drawn.

In early November 1811, Harrison led a force of soldiers to attack Tecumseh's headquarters at Prophetstown on the banks of the Tippecanoe River (in present-day northwestern Indiana). Tecumseh was away, and the Indian forces were led by his brother, Tenskwatawa (c.1768–1834), who was also known as the Prophet. Tenskwatawa told his followers that he had cast a spell over the nearby troops and that they would easily defeat the heavily armed soldiers. Early in the morning of November 7, the Indian forces attacked Harrison's men, only to be mowed down by a torrent of musket fire. Harrison's troops counterattacked and burned Prophetstown to the ground. Enraged by the defeat, Indians across the Old Northwest raided white settlements. It was not long, however, before such minor skirmishes were swallowed up in the tumult of the War of 1812 (1812–14).

Essentially a war between the British and the Americans over control of the Old Northwest, the War of 1812 gave the Indians an opportunity to ally themselves with the British in hopes of driving out the Americans. Tecumseh led a band of warriors to several successes, though he grew increasingly frustrated with what he saw as the cowardice of British lead-

ers. Tecumseh hungered for a final showdown that would once and for all drive the Americans from Indian lands. On October 5, 1813, Tecumseh decided to make his stand along the banks of the Thames River north of Lake Erie (in present-day Ontario). The British troops who fought alongside Tecumseh retreated after a powerful charge by mounted U.S. soldiers. Surrounded and outmanned, Tecumseh and his men fought on in bloody, hand-to-hand combat. Tecumseh was soon killed, and his followers retreated. White soldiers skinned one Indian they believed to be Tecumseh, hoping to make tobacco pouches of his skin and sell them for souvenirs. But several Shawnees rescued their leader's body and buried it in an unknown location. With Tecumseh's body were buried his dreams of stopping the white advance. The Americans won the War of 1812 and laid a secure claim to the lands of the Old Northwest. Emboldened by the purchase of the Louisiana Territory in 1803 (see Chapter 1), they looked westward to new lands.

Native American forces led by Tecumseh's brother, Tenskwatawa, were soundly defeated by American troops led by William Henry Harrison at the Battle of Tippecanoe. *(Reproduced by permission of CORBIS/ Bettmann.)*

Driving Native Americans westward

Whites had always justified evicting Indians from their lands by explaining that there was plenty of land to the west where the displaced tribes could settle. Such arguments ignored the fact that tribes preferred not to live alongside their traditional enemies or to change their entire lifestyle simply because white settlers wanted to "improve" their land. But increasingly, it was to the lands west of the Mississippi that the Indians were banished.

Andrew Jackson, Indian fighter

Though the War of 1812 eliminated the threat of "hostile" Indians in the Old Northwest, a number of large, established tribes continued to stand in the way of white settlement in the southern half of the growing nation. The man most closely associated with the removal of the southern tribes is Andrew Jackson (1767–1845). Jackson, "a tough, profane, brawling ramrod of a man," in the words of historians Robert M. Utley and Wilcomb E. Washburn, was given the task of suppressing the Creek Indians during the War of 1812. At the start of the war, the Creek had mounted a series of ferocious attacks on white settlements in the Alabama and Louisiana territories. Jackson was determined to strike back, and he did this so effectively that he nearly exterminated every Creek warrior. Shortly after their final defeat, Creek chief Bill Weatherford, who was only part Indian, came alone to Jackson's camp. "I am in your power," he told General Jackson, according to Utley and Washburn. "I have done the white people all the harm I could; I have fought them, and fought them bravely; if I had an army, I would yet fight, and contend to the last: but I have none; my people are all gone. I can now do no more than weep over the misfortunes of my nation." Jackson released Weatherford and then went on to negotiate treaties that stripped the Creek nation of nearly twenty-three million acres of land. It was the first of many victories for Jackson.

The Seminole wars

Another fierce tribe, the Seminole, hectored American settlements from their bases in Spanish-controlled Florida.

When a band of Seminole attacked a boatload of U.S. soldiers' families in southern Georgia, the U.S. War Department tapped Andrew Jackson to defeat them. On the pretext of chasing Indian killers, Jackson marched on Florida, attacking both Indian and Spanish towns. Though he scored no major victories over the Seminole, his efforts did persuade the Spanish to sell Florida to the United States in 1819 for five million dollars. Jackson became governor of the territory, and as white settlement in the territory increased, he kept up the pressure on the Seminole. It was not until the late 1830s, however, that the fierce tribe was finally defeated and forced to retreat to lands beyond the Mississippi or into the Florida swamps, well out of reach of white settlements.

Andrew Jackson (left) meets with a Seminole man. Before becoming president of the United States, Andrew Jackson led forces to defeat the Creek and Seminole nations. *(Courtesy of the Library of Congress.)*

Indian removal

Andrew Jackson became president of the United States in 1829 and oversaw a concerted effort to remove Native Americans from all lands east of the Mississippi. In his first address to Congress as president, Jackson asked: "What good man would prefer a country covered with forests and ranged by a few thousand savages to our extensive Republic, studded with cities, towns, and prosperous farms, embellished with all the improvements which art can devise or industry execute, occupied by more than twelve million happy people, and filled with all the blessings of liberty, civilization, and religion?" Pressured by the governments of frontier states that complained of the difficulties they faced in dealing with conflicts between Indian tribes and white settlers, Congress passed and Jackson signed the Indian Removal Act of 1830. The Indian Removal Act called for the removal—voluntary or forced—of all Indians to an area west of the Mississippi. The actual Indian Territory that was defined by Congress in 1834 was far smaller than the "all lands west of the Mississippi" that whites had once promised. In fact, the Indian Territory covered only parts of the present-day states of Oklahoma, Nebraska, and Kansas.

Indian removal progressed throughout the 1830s. The Cherokee tribes of Georgia, realizing that warfare against the whites was futile, took their case against Georgia's discriminatory laws to the U.S. Supreme Court. The Court actually ruled in favor of the Cherokee, stating that Indian tribes were "domestic dependent nations" that could conduct their own political processes and were afforded the protection of the federal government. But Jackson ignored the ruling and supported Georgia's efforts to drive the Indians from the state. Some Indians left voluntarily, carrying their belongings to a new and unfamiliar land. Others resisted. The Creek in Alabama were dragged away in chains, and soldiers drove the Choctaw from Mississippi in the dead of winter, killing many along the way. All in all, thousands of Indians died as they were driven from their native lands.

The Trail of Tears

By the late 1830s the Georgia Cherokee, an educated and prosperous tribe, had done all they could to stay on their ancestral lands, including starting the first Native American newspaper, the *Georgia Phoenix,* to promote their cause. But in

1838 Jackson's successor as president, Martin Van Buren (1782–1862), ordered U.S. troops and the Georgia state militia to remove the remaining seventeen thousand Cherokee by whatever means necessary. According to Utley and Washburn, commanding General Winfield Scott (1786–1866) ordered that "every possible kindness ... must ... be shown by the troops." But kindness is hardly the word to describe the horrors that were inflicted upon the Cherokee. Write Utley and Washburn: "Yet, on the sunny May morning when the soldiers set about their task, some of them raped, robbed, and murdered the Indians.... The army kept the Cherokee penned up in concentration camps throughout the stifling summer; many died, and many more fell ill. In the fall and early winter contingents started west, some in flatboats, some in wagons, some on foot."

The Cherokee thus began a forced march of some twelve hundred miles. Dozens died every day on the journey, falling prey to disease, starvation, or exposure. Those who survived were robbed by marauding parties of white men along the way, claiming Cherokee goods in exchange for ills done to them by other tribes. In all, four thousand Cherokee died before they reached their destination in present-day Oklahoma in March 1839. The trek is remembered by the Cherokee as the "Trail of Tears."

Whites believed that Indian removal had solved the territorial disputes to everyone's satisfaction. Settlers would no longer be bothered by Indian attacks, and the Indians could pursue their lifestyle on lands of their own in the west. But in reality, Indian removal would stop neither westward expansion nor the Indian wars.

Manifest destiny and the plight of Native Americans

Prior to the 1830s, many politicians, military leaders, and American citizens believed that the policy of removing Indians to western lands, separate from the white settlers, was best for everyone. Though there were some who thought that the only good Indian was a dead Indian, others regretted the difficulties that western expansion had caused for Native Americans and honestly hoped that the Indians would find a stable life in the Indian Territory. Yet the changing nature of American expansion in the years to come made it clear that settlers would not stop at the Mississippi and that the Indian wars were far from over.

At the turn of the eighteenth century, few Americans could imagine that their country would ever need to expand beyond the Mississippi River. The land east of that mighty river seemed capable of providing for the growing population for generations to come. Moreover, early explorers had indicated that much of the land west of the Mississippi was undesirable, either too arid or too mountainous to serve a nation of farmers. In fact, many maps depicted the area west of the Mississippi as the Great American Desert. But wars, gold, and a hunger for expansion soon changed these attitudes. Settlers who had ventured into Texas soon found themselves at odds with the Mexican governors of the territory. The Texans wanted to secede from Mexico and become part of the United States. Eventually Americans joined the dispute between the Texans and the Mexicans, fighting a war with Mexico. The Mexican-American War (1846–48) earned the United States a vast territory that included present-day Texas, New Mexico, Arizona, Nevada, and California, which virtually doubled the size of the country. (See Chapter 4 for more information about the Mexican-American War.)

The western lands acquired from Mexico might well have remained relatively uninhabited and unvisited were it not for the California gold rush of 1849, which drew many thousands of gold seekers across the country to settle in California. Within a few years the United States had added vast tracts of western land and a new state on the shores of the Pacific Ocean. Finally, an 1846 treaty with the British gave the Americans unimpeded control of the present-day states of Idaho, Oregon, and Washington. There was now no reason for Americans not to spread across the entire continent. Throughout the 1830s and 1840s there developed a national fervor for building the nation until it reached from coast to coast. This fervor was known as manifest destiny—the belief that it was God's intended plan for the Americans to control a vast empire stretching from the Atlantic to the Pacific. It was an old ideology, expanded to fit new circumstances. And it meant the doom of all those Indian tribes that had as yet escaped the white man's wrath.

For More Information

Books

Drinnon, Richard. *Facing West: The Metaphysics of Indian-Hating and Empire Building.* Minneapolis: University of Minnesota Press, 1980.

Hook, Jason. *American Indian Warrior Chiefs: Tecumseh, Crazy Horse, Chief Joseph, Geronimo.* New York: Firebird Books, 1990.

Lawson, Don. *The United States in the Indian Wars.* New York: Abelard-Schuman, 1975.

Prucha, Francis Paul. *The Sword of the Republic: The United States Army on the Frontier, 1783–1846.* New York: Macmillan, 1969.

Rogin, Michael Paul. *Fathers & Children: Andrew Jackson and the Subjugation of the American Indian.* New York: Vintage Books, 1976.

Utley, Robert M. *Frontier Regulars: The United States Army and the Indian, 1866–1890.* New York: Macmillan, 1973.

Utley, Robert M. *Frontiersmen in Blue: The United States Army and the Indian, 1848–1865.* New York: Macmillan, 1967.

Waldman, Carl. *Atlas of the North American Indian.* New York: Facts on File, 1985.

Web sites

"Battle of Fallen Timbers." *Ohio History Central.* [Online] http://www.ohio kids.org/kids/ohc/history/h_indian/events/bfallen.html (accessed April 6, 2000).

Georgia College and State University. *Ina Dillard Russel Library Special Collections: Native American Resources.* [Online] http://library.gcsu.edu/~sc/resna.html (accessed April 6, 2000).

National Historic Trail: The Cherokee Trail of Tears, 1838–1839. [Online] http://rosecity.net/tears/trail/tearsnht.html (accessed April 6, 2000).

State Library of North Carolina. "Andrew Jackson." *North Carolina Encyclopedia.* [Online] http://statelibrary.dcr.state.nc.us/nc/bio/public/jackson.htm (accessed April 6, 2000).

Tecumseh. [Online] http://www.geocities.com/SouthBeach/Cove/8286/warrior.html (accessed April 6, 2000).

"William Henry Harrison Biography" *Grolier Online: The American Presidency.* [Online] http://gi.grolier.com/presidents/ea/bios/09pharr.html (accessed April 6, 2000).

Sources

Axelrod, Alan. *Chronicle of the Indian Wars: From Colonial Times to Wounded Knee.* New York: Prentice Hall, 1993.

Billington, Ray Allen. *Westward to the Pacific: An Overview of America's Westward Expansion.* St. Louis, MO: Jefferson National Expansion Historical Association, 1979.

Brown, Dee. *Bury My Heart at Wounded Knee*. New York: Holt, Rinehart & Winston, 1970.

Morris, Richard B. *The Indian Wars*. Minneapolis, MN: Lerner Publications, 1985.

Nardo, Don. *The Indian Wars*. San Diego, CA: Lucent Books, 1991.

Utley, Robert M., and Wilcomb E. Washburn. *Indian Wars*. Boston: Houghton Mifflin, 1987.

Claiming the Far West: Territorial Expansion after 1812

T hough America had won its independence from England in the Revolutionary War (1776–83), the years following that war were hardly peaceful. Conflict with Indian tribes throughout the trans-Appalachian west (the area between the Appalachian Mountains and the Mississippi River) kept settlers there from feeling comfortable in their new land. Fears that the Spanish would block American access to the port of New Orleans at the mouth of the Mississippi River alarmed both farmers and politicians. Most important, the British remained a force in the trans-Appalachian region, maintaining forts and supporting Indian hostilities. By the end of the War of 1812 (1812–14), however, these problems had largely been solved. The Indians had been defeated in the east, and the British no longer tried to exert an influence in the American territories. Moreover, the purchase of the Louisiana Territory (the area between the Mississippi River and the Rocky Mountains) in 1803 meant that Americans controlled the important trading route along the Mississippi River. (See Chapter 1 for full details on all these events.)

The Louisiana Purchase opened vast expanses of land to American control, doubling the size of the young nation. A country that had once thought it would stretch only to the Mississippi River now saw its horizon expand all the way to the Rocky Mountains, and perhaps beyond to the Pacific. The possibilities of western expansion sparked dreams of exploration, of conquest, of empire, of a nation stretching from sea to shining sea. But the realization of those dreams would take another century and would involve luck, warfare, and diplomacy. As ever in America, pioneers and fortune seekers led the way, moving into new lands and bringing with them the support of an expanding nation.

The dreams of a president

One of the first Americans to embrace the dream of a coast-to-coast empire was President Thomas Jefferson (1743– 1826). Jefferson had read with interest Canadian fur trader Alexander Mackenzie's (c. 1755–1820) account of his 1793 explorations across the Canadian Rocky Mountains and to the shores of the Pacific. In his book, *Voyages from Montreal,* Mackenzie outlined his vision of a continental fur trade controlled by the British. As it became clear that the United States could expand that far west, Jefferson began to dream of an expedition that would explore the far western lands and establish a claim for American control of the fur-rich regions there. Gathering together two experienced young military officers, Meriwether Lewis (1774–1809) and William Clark (1770–1838), Jefferson gave them these instructions in a letter dated January 20, 1803, quoted in Donald Jackson's *Letters of the Lewis and Clark Expedition with Related Documents: 1783–1854:* "The object of your mission is to explore the Missouri River, & such principal streams of it, by its course & communication with the waters of the Pacific Ocean, may offer the most direct and practicable water communications across this continent, for the purposes of trade."

Lewis and Clark set out from St. Louis in May 1804 at the head of a party of thirty that included soldiers, volunteer backwoodsmen, hunters, interpreters, two French voyageurs (fur traders), and a black slave named York. Tak-

ing detailed notes as they traveled, the party ascended the Missouri River, dodged trouble with Indians in present-day South Dakota, and holed up for the winter with a band of Mandan Indians in present-day North Dakota. Over the winter they hired a French interpreter, Toussaint Charbonneau, who brought along with him his Indian wife, Sacajawea (c. 1788–c. 1812 or 1884). Sacajawea's knowledge of Indian culture helped the party befriend a band of Shoshone Indians, who provided the travelers with horses and pointed them toward a passage across the difficult Rocky Mountains. Lewis

Sacajawea's knowledge of Native American cultures and languages and of the geography of the West contributed to the success of the Lewis and Clark expedition. *(Drawing by Alfred Russel. Reproduced by permission of Corbis-Bettmann.)*

and Clark led their party across the mountains and eventually down the Columbia River. On December 3, 1805, they reached the Pacific, thus staking the United States's claim to the vast lands that would become known as the Oregon Country. (However, it would be 1848 before those claims were secure.)

The drive for expansion

As news of Lewis and Clark's voyage reached the American people, it excited an impulse for westward expansion that was already strong. Ever since the Revolutionary War (1776–83), Americans had seen their future in the West. The western lands, they believed, could be cleared and farmed, made subject to the settler's seemingly irresistible impulse to tame the land. Every man could own his own farm, provide for his family, and become a citizen in the expanding republic. Not only would the land be tamed and farmed, asserted religious leaders; it would also be Christianized. They believed that the Native Americans living on the land were uncivilized but would become civilized through their experience of Christian religions—or would die resisting. The Louisiana Purchase and the success of Lewis and Clark's expedition only encouraged Americans' desire for western land.

This enthusiasm combined with a variety of other factors to create a national mood that fueled expansion. Among the most pressing of the expansionist forces was population growth. Thanks to a high birthrate and continued immigration, the American population grew from about five million in 1800 to nearly twenty-three million by the middle of the nineteenth century. Of these, some four million moved into the western territories between 1820 and 1850. Economic depressions in the late 1810s and 1830s also encouraged expansion as people turned to the cheap western lands for sustenance. Finally, a number of popular writers encouraged Americans to think of themselves as a "superior people" whose job it was to civilize peoples they considered inferior—namely, the Indians.

By the 1840s, very few Americans questioned whether the United States should be expanding into the lands west of

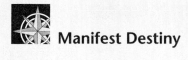

Manifest Destiny

Though the drive to expand the United States across the continent was expressed in many ways by many influential people, the person most associated with the phrase "manifest destiny" was newspaperman John O'Sullivan. In 1845 he wrote an article in the *United States Magazine and Democratic Review* that suppored the annexation of Texas and spelled out the justification for America's westward march. O'Sullivan maintained that since countries such as Britain, France, Spain, and Mexico had never shown any hesitation in taking lands that would benefit their country, America should forthrightly claim those lands, including Texas, that were rightly hers. Though O'Sullivan's language is outdated, his final point rings clear to this day:

> Why, were other reasoning wanting, in favor of now elevating this question of the reception of Texas into the Union, out of the lower region of our past party dissensions, up to its proper level of a high and broad nationality, it surely is to be found, found abundantly, in the manner in which other nations have undertaken to intrude themselves into it, between us and the proper parties to the case, in a spirit of hostile interference against us, for the avowed object of thwarting our policy and hampering our power, limiting our greatness and checking the fulfillment of our manifest destiny to overspread the continent allotted by Providence for the free development of our yearly multiplying millions.

the Mississippi River; they only asked how that expansion would occur. As Mexico and the United States argued over the borders of the Republic of Texas, formerly part of the nation of Mexico, indignant Americans proclaimed their nation's natural right to control the breadth of the continent. Most Americans assumed without question that their nation would eventually extend from the Atlantic to the Pacific Ocean, while some even imagined control of all of North and South America. In 1845, as war with Mexico loomed, John L. O'Sullivan, editor of the *United States Magazine and Democratic Review,* defined this faith in American expansion as the nation's "manifest destiny." The idea of manifest destiny implied that Americans had the God-given right to acquire and populate the territories stretching west to the Pacific. This idea has been criticized as an excuse for the bold land grabs and the slaughter of Indians that characterized expansion, but those who believed in it thought they were demonstrating the virtues of a nation founded on political liberty, individual economic opportunity, and Christian civilization.

Texas

On February 14, 1819, American diplomat John Quincy Adams (1767–1848) and Spanish ambassador Luis de Onís signed a treaty that granted the United States the Spanish territory of Florida and established a border between the United States and Mexico in present-day Texas. The first part of the treaty was executed without dispute, but the border would soon become the bone of contention that would ultimately bring Texas into the union. Angry that the United States had largely ceded the Texas territory to the Spanish, American settlers began to move into East Texas in 1821. By that time, however, the land was no longer controlled by Spain but by Mexico, which had won independence from Spain that same year. As more and more settlers moved in, Mexico felt it needed to solidify its control of the region. Threatened by the settlers' democratic ideas and their Protestant religion, Mexico sent troops into Texas and banned further settlement in the 1830s.

Texas's American settlers decided to form their own provisional government in 1835 and hoped that either Mexico would recognize their independence or the United States would come to their defense and claim Texas as a state. But the path to self-government would not be easy. Bands of Texans achieved early successes against Mexican troops, but in 1836 a large army led by Mexican dictator General Antonio López de Santa Anna (1794–1876)—who referred to himself as the "Napoleon of the West"—moved on the Texans. Though Texas military leader Sam Houston (1793–1863) counseled retreat, a force of some 187 men under Lieutenant Colonel William B. Travis prepared to face the Mexicans from the stronghold of the Alamo Mission in San Antonio. With Travis were both American settlers and Mexican residents who resented the harsh rule of Santa Anna.

Remember the Alamo!

For ten days, Santa Anna and his men laid siege to the thick-walled Alamo. Both sides were equally dedicated: Santa Anna to the extermination of every last defender, and Travis and his men to "Victory or Death," as Travis wrote in a letter quoted by Harold Faber in *From Sea to Sea*. Death it would be, as the Mexicans finally overwhelmed the Texans on March 6, 1836, killing every male, including Travis and famous frontiersmen Jim Bowie and Davy Crockett. The Mexicans spared the lives of a number of women, children, and slaves (though the exact number is not known it is reported variously between three and thirty). But the Mexicans paid a high price for their victory: they lost about fifteen hundred men.

When word reached Houston of the massacre at the Alamo and of another at a town called Goliad, he helped form an army to defeat Santa Anna. In late April 1836, Houston prepared to lead a ragtag band of nine hundred men against Santa Anna's thirteen hundred. "Victory is certain!" Houston told his men. "Trust in God and fear not! The victims of the Alamo and the names of those who were murdered at Goliad cry out for cool, deliberate vengeance. Remember the Alamo! Remember Goliad!" Roused for battle behind their inspirational leader, the Texans surprised the Mexicans on the plains of San Jacinto, won a decisive victory, and captured Santa Anna. In exchange for his life, Santa Anna granted the Texans independence.

The annexation of Texas

Sam Houston became the president of the Republic of Texas on October 22, 1836. In the same election, the citizens of Texas voted six to one in favor of the immediate annexation (acquisition) of Texas by the United States, with statehood assumed to follow soon after. But the United States, under President Andrew Jackson (1767–1845), was not ready to move so quickly. There was no doubt that they wanted the territory, which included most of present-day Texas and parts of New Mexico, Colorado, Wyoming, Kansas, and Oklahoma. The question was, would Texas be a free or a slave state (that is, a state in which slavery was illegal or legal)? Southerners who wanted to extend the institution of slavery into new territories argued that Texas should be admitted as a slave state; northerners feared giving the slave-holding states more power and argued that all new territories admitted into the union should be free. The solution to this dilemma was nearly ten years in the making.

With slave and free states equally balanced and with relative peace on the American borders and the border with

Texas, there were few compelling reasons to speed annexation. But in the 1840s things began to change. Mexico sent troops into Texas after vowing that it would reclaim the Republic, and Indian raids on frontier settlements had settlers calling for military support. Texas sent envoys to England and France to ask for assistance.

Southerners who feared that Texas would enter the nation as a free state wanted to take advantage of the large number of slave owners already in the state and pushed for immediate annexation. U.S. diplomats hated the idea that England or France might regain influence on the continent through aiding Texas. The stalemate ended when expansion-minded American President John Tyler (1790–1862) reopened talks of annexation in 1843. In 1845 Tyler's successor, James K. Polk (1795–1849), outmaneuvered opponents of adding Texas to the Union and sent a resolution to Congress calling for the admission of Texas as a state. On February 16, 1846, Texans raised the United States flag in their capital, and the matter was resolved with Texas joining the United States as a slave state. There remained the minor problem of negotiating the western boundary of the state with Mexico; that problem would take a war to solve.

Acquiring the Oregon Territory

Ever since 1818 the United States and Britain had jointly occupied the Oregon Country, the northwestern corner of the United States that included the present-day states of Washington, Oregon, Idaho, and western Montana. British fur traders were most familiar with the region, for they had long operated there and had hopes of securing a fur empire in the Northwest. But because neither country had a significant presence in the region, there seemed no reason to push for absolute control. In fact, the joint occupation treaty was renewed in 1827. In the 1830s, however, the balance of power began to shift.

In the 1830s American settlers began to trickle westward on what would become the Oregon Trail (a route to the West that ran from Missouri to present-day Washington). In 1835, the first of the Protestant missionaries, Samuel Parker, came west to found missions to convert the Indians; he was

followed in 1836 by Marcus Whitman and his wife, Narcissa, who founded a mission in Walla Walla. The trickle of settlers turned into a steady stream by the 1840s. Parties of settlers arrived one hundred or more at a time, boosting the American population of the Oregon Country to 5000 by 1845, while the British could claim only 750 inhabitants. The settlers were backed by a solid wall of public opinion—the enthusiasm for America's manifest destiny was at its peak in the mid-1840s. What had once seemed a distant land not worthy of conflict now was viewed as an indispensable piece of the American empire.

President Polk, the same man who had pushed through the acquisition of Texas, was eager to obtain Oregon for the United States, and he used his political skills to that end as soon as he was elected. In his inaugural address on March 4, 1845, he declared: "Nor will it become in a less degree my duty to assert and maintain by all constitutional means the right of the United States to that portion of our

Wagons on the Oregon Trail. *(Reproduced by permission of the Nebraska Division of Travel and Tourism.)*

territory which lies beyond the Rocky Mountains. Our title to the country of Oregon is clear and unquestionable, and already our people are preparing to perfect that title by occupying it with their wives and children." After lengthy though peaceful negotiations with the British, the United States obtained on June 10, 1846, all the territory south of the 49th parallel (the line of latitude that now defines the United States's northern border with Canada). As with the Louisiana Purchase, the United States had enlarged its territory dramatically with the stroke of a pen.

War with Mexico

Nowhere was the power of manifest destiny felt more strongly than in the brewing conflict with Mexico. According to historian Harold Faber:

> "The vision of golden California as part of the United States was the real cause of the Mexican War. There were tensions on the Mexican border, there were problems concerning the annexation of Texas, there were insults and misunderstandings on both sides—all this was true enough. But behind the hostile attitudes and moves was the fact that the United States was determined to expand to the Pacific. Neither Indians nor the elements nor the legality of Mexican claims was going to stand in the way. Manifest destiny was in the air Americans breathed, and President Polk was determined to do all in his power to stretch the geographical limits of the United States to the Pacific Ocean. Polk did not want war, he merely wanted the fruits of war, the land and territory of a neighboring country."

At the center of the dispute that would lead the United States and Mexico into war in 1846 was the question of the border between the newly established state of Texas and its former ruler, Mexico. The United States claimed as the border the river known as the Rio Grande, but the Mexicans insisted that the border should be the Nueces River, well east of the Rio Grande. The territory about which they were arguing was not vast, but it was important to both countries. Of lesser importance were financial claims and ill feelings resulting from the recent acquisition of Texas. It should have been an easy matter to negotiate—but negotiation did not come easily for either side.

President Polk sent diplomat John Slidell (1793–1871) to Mexico City to negotiate with the new Mexican president, José Joaquín Herrera. But at the same time he charged General

Zachary Taylor (1784–1850), Colonel Stephen W. Kearny (1794–1848), and Commander John D. Sloat to prepare for war from their separate outposts near the border with Mexico. Herrera wanted peace, but he was hounded by critics who charged that he would meekly give away Mexican territory to a country that most Mexicans perceived as aggressive and greedy. Faced with this political pressure, Herrera refused to talk with Slidell. Both sides held their breath to see what the other would do. On April 24, 1846, the Mexicans gave the Americans an excuse to fight by launching an attack on Taylor's forces on the Rio Grande. Telling Congress that the Mexicans had "at last invaded our territory and shed the blood of our fellow-citizens on our own soil," Polk declared war on Mexico in May 1846.

As wars go, the Mexican-American War (1846–48) was neither particularly bloody nor hard fought. Kearny led his troops and a mass of volunteers southwest on the Santa Fe Trail in the blistering heat of summer; more men died from the heat than in battle. In fact, Kearny took the New Mexican capital of Santa Fe without firing a shot and in August 1846 claimed New Mexico as U.S. territory. California had been claimed by American settlers in July 1846 in what was known as the Bear Flag Revolt. The Californians gladly raised the American flag over the territory when Commander Sloat arrived in Monterey, having met little resistance. With the seizure of New Mexico and California, the United States had met its objectives. But it seemed that Polk still had a score to settle with an old adversary: General Santa Anna, who had retaken control of Mexico shortly after the war began.

Storming Mexico City

Though they had already achieved their goals, American forces entered Mexico in early 1847. Future President Zachary Taylor led his outnumbered forces to a stunning victory in Monterrey, Mexico, and signed a peace treaty (though it was later invalidated by his political enemy, President Polk). General Winfield Scott (1786–1866), defying logic, landed his troops in Vera Cruz, on the eastern coast of Mexico, and then marched them across the Mexican continent and straight to the Mexican capital, Mexico City. Facing a force three times the size of his own, Scott defeated the Mexican troops under

The Gadsden Purchase

No sooner had Americans taken more than half a million acres of Mexican land in the Mexican-American War (1846–48) than they set their sights on a slice of land that lay just south of the borders of present-day New Mexico and Arizona. Railroad builders and their backers in Congress searched eagerly for a southern route that would link California to the settled areas in the East, and they found it—in Mexico. Luckily for the Americans, Mexico was in desperate need of cash. Thus, in 1853 James B. Gadsden (1788–1858), president of the South Carolina Railroad Company, negotiated with Mexican President López de Santa Anna to sell the 29,000 square miles of territory for $10 million. Stymied by political haggling, southern railroad builders lost the race to build the first transcontinental railroad, but their Southern Pacific line became an important connector between east and west.

Santa Anna in the Battle of Chapultepec and raised the American flag over the capital in September 1847.

Had they desired, the soldiers might have taken all of Mexico as an American possession. But racist American politicians did not want to rule over a land of nonwhites. Instead, diplomat Nicholas Trist offered the Mexican government eighteen million dollars in exchange for the cession of more than half a million acres of land. The Treaty of Guadalupe Hidalgo, signed on February 2, 1848, granted to the United States all or part of the present-day states of Arizona, California, Colorado, New Mexico, Utah, and Wyoming. It was a territorial addition second only to the Louisiana Purchase.

Populating the West

In the early 1800s, the idea that American territories would stretch all the way to the Pacific was merely a dream, and those who thought it possible assumed that such expansion could only occur in the distant future. But by 1854, Americans had claimed the territory that makes up the biggest part of the contiguous United States. Much of it remained wild, unclaimed by any settlers and inhabited by Indians if it was inhabited at all. But it was no longer foreign land, and it now seemed inevitable that Americans would spread out and populate the vast expanses that had once seemed so distant. Territorial expansion had largely ended; now it was time to populate the West.

Land and gold

Though fur trappers and mountain men had made forays into the Far West in the early nineteenth century, it wasn't until the opening of the various trails west in the

1820s and 1830s that significant numbers of American settlers moved beyond the Mississippi River. The Santa Fe Trail began to be a major commercial route in 1821, but it was the Oregon Trail that allowed first hundreds and then thousands of emigrants to leave their homes in the settled east and venture out in search of a new life. Between 1843, the year of the first Great Migration west, and 1869, when the transcontinental railway was finished, the Oregon Trail and its spur to California carried an estimated 350,000 pioneers across 2,000 miles of tortuous terrain. Drawing them west were the fertile land of Oregon and the goldfields of California.

In 1849, James Marshall discovered gold on the American River in the Sacramento Valley of California. The news of gold in California spread through the United States like wildfire. The *New York Herald* reported on January 11, 1849 that "The spirit of emigration which is carrying off thousands to California so far from dying away increases and expands every day. All classes of our citizens seem to be under the in-

An emigrant party with their covered wagons on the road to California through the Sierra Nevada mountain range. *(© Hulton Getty / Liaison Agency. Reproduced by permission.)*

fluence of this extraordinary mania." Emigration to the state had been a trickle, but now it turned into a steady flow. An estimated thirty-two thousand people took the overland routes to California in 1849, and another forty-four thousand came in 1850. The territory of California now had enough inhabitants to petition for statehood, which was granted in 1850. The United States now had an official outpost on the West Coast, and the Pony Express (an early postal service), telegraph lines, and eventually the transcontinental railroad all connected east to west (see Chapter 11). Construction projects like the railroad helped create settlements along the way and further sped the populating of the West.

The California gold rush was not the only mining boom to bring settlers to the West. In 1859 miners flocked to Nevada to exploit the so-called Comstock Lode of gold and silver. In that same year gold was discovered near Pikes Peak in Colorado, and gold, silver, and lead mining flourished there between 1859 and 1880. According to Roger Barr in *The American Frontier,* "The last great mining frontier opened in 1877, when gold was discovered in the Black Hills of the Dakota Territory." Mining brought droves of prospectors into the region, and they were soon followed by families and by merchants eager to profit by providing goods and services to the miners. In this way whole communities were founded. It is not a coincidence that the first western territories to attain statehood were mining states: California, which joined the union in 1850; Nevada, in 1864; and Colorado, in 1876.

Farmers and ranchers

Miners were not the only settlers in the American West. Writes Barr, "As in earlier American frontiers, it was farmers, the last in the line of frontiersmen, who truly conquered the West. Dissatisfied by the conditions at home, lured by the promise of free land, and aided by new technology, they came by the thousands to the Great Plains beginning in the 1850s." Farmers moving out onto the Plains had to learn new methods of farming, and they were aided by technological advances, such as John Deere's invention of the steel plow (1837), which made their work easier. Another invention, barbed wire (1874), allowed farmers to fence off

their land to keep the growing numbers of livestock from trampling their crops.

Farming in the West was greatly encouraged by the Homestead Act of 1862, which gave settlers up to 160 acres of free land if they settled on it and made improvements over a five-year span. The Timber Culture Act of 1873 granted an additional 160 acres to farmers who agreed to plant a portion of

Gold rush miners in California. The prospect of striking it rich attracted thousands of Americans to California between 1849 and 1850. *(Reproduced by permission of The Granger Collection, New York.)*

their land with trees. Though both acts were abused by land speculators (people who buy and hold on to land with the intention of later selling it for a profit), they did serve to draw many thousands of settlers from the crowded East and even from Europe into the wide-open spaces of the American West. Farming on the Plains was difficult, but by 1890 farmers had claimed more than 430 million acres of land—more land, writes Barr, "than all of their ancestors had claimed throughout American history." The biggest single land claim, known as the Oklahoma land rush, occurred on April 22, 1889, when in a single day some fifty thousand settlers claimed lands that had just been opened to settlement.

Cattle ranching vied with farming as the dominant industry in the Plains, for ranchers found that they could graze vast herds of cattle on the open grasslands that had only years before been roamed by buffalo and Indians. The construction of railroads meant that ranchers could get their cattle to slaughterhouses in the East. As soon as Joseph M. McCoy established a railhead (a point on a railroad where traffic stops) in Abilene, Kansas, in 1867, writes Barr, "the cattle industry was born. Between 1868 and 1871, nearly 1,500,000 cattle were driven from the Texas range north to Abilene and shipped east." The cattle boom did not last long, for increased competition among ranchers and between ranchers and farmers soon made cattle ranching less profitable. Though it enjoyed only a short life, cattle culture gave America one of its most enduring heroes: the cowboy.

The end of the frontier

By 1890 fourteen states and four territories had been carved out of the lands west of the Mississippi. Census figures for that year revealed that 8,525,000 people lived in these states and territories, 13.5 percent of the country's total population. A few years later, historian Frederick Jackson Turner noted in *The Frontier in American History*, "Up to and including 1880 the country had a frontier of settlement, but at present the unsettled area has been so broken into by isolated bodies of settlement that there can hardly be said to be a frontier line. In discussion of its extent, its westward movement, etc., [the frontier] can not, therefore, any longer have a place in census reports." The great American drive to expand across the breadth of the continent had ended.

Ever since the Revolutionary War, Americans had looked westward to the lands they had yet to conquer. For more than a century—in dramatic battles, vast land grabs, vicious wars against Indians, and the slow movement of settlers onto unclaimed land—Americans had pushed west. Spurred by their belief that the continent was destined to fall under their dominion, Americans established farms, founded communities, petitioned for statehood, and slowly but surely settled the West. In so doing they forged a unique nation, one in which individualism and democracy flourished alongside the darker traits of greed and racism.

For More Information

Books

Billington, Ray Allen, with James Blaine Hedges. *Westward Expansion: A History of the American Frontier.* New York: Macmillan, 1949.

Edwards, Cheryl, ed. *Westward Expansion: Exploration and Settlement.* Lowell, MA: Discovery Enterprises, 1995.

Erdosh, George. *Food and Recipes of the Westward Expansion.* New York: PowerKids Press, 1997.

Mancall, Peter C., ed. *Westward Expansion, 1800–1860.* Detroit: Gale, 1999.

Milner, Clyde A.,II, Carol A. O'Connor, and Martha A. Sandweiss, eds. *The Oxford History of the American West.* New York and Oxford: Oxford University Press, 1994.

Wexler, Alan, ed. *Atlas of Westward Expansion.* New York: Facts On File, 1995.

White, Richard. *"It's Your Misfortune and None of My Own": A New History of the American West.* Norman: University of Oklahoma Press, 1991.

Web sites

"All about the Gold Rush." *PBS: Online.* [Online] http://www.isu.edu/~trinmich/allabout.html (accessed April 12, 2000).

Brazoria County Historical Museum. "Award-Winning Austin Colony Exhibit." *Where Texas Began.* [Online] http://www.bchm.org/ (accessed April 12, 2000).

Daughters of the Republic of Texas. *The Alamo in 1836: Brief Chronology of Events Concerning the Alamo.* [Online] http://www.thealamo.org/alamo1836.html (accessed April 12, 2000).

"The Journals of Lewis and Clark." *American Studies @ The University of Virginia: Hypertexts.* [Online] http://xroads.virginia.edu/~HYPER/JOURNALS/toc.htm (accessed April 5, 2000).

Muzzey, David Saville. "The Mexican War." *Museum of the City of San Francisco.* [Online] http://www.sfmuseum.org/hist6/muzzey.html (accessed April 12, 2000).

Sources

Barr, Roger. *The American Frontier.* San Diego, CA: Lucent Books, 1996.

Billington, Ray Allen. *Westward to the Pacific: An Overview of America's Westward Expansion.* St. Louis MO: Jefferson National Expansion Historical Association, 1979.

Faber, Harold. *From Sea to Sea: The Growth of the United States.* New York: Charles Scribner's Sons, 1992.

Jackson, Donald, ed. *Letters of the Lewis and Clark Expedition with Related Documents: 1783–1854.* Urbana: University of Illinois Press, 1978.

Smith, Carter, ed. *The Conquest of the West: A Sourcebook on the American West.* Brookfield, CT: Millbrook Press, 1992.

Turner, Frederick Jackson. *The Frontier in American History.* New York: Henry Holt and Co., 1950.

Trails West

5

Between 1800 and 1870, nearly half a million Americans set out across the frontier on the many trails that led west from settled America. Whether they took the Santa Fe Trail, the Oregon-California Trail, the Mormon Trail, or one of many others, these trappers, traders, farmers, and families set out on a journey of discovery. Lured by promises—of gold, of lucrative trade, or of fertile farmland—these pioneers endured weeks and even months of arduous travel across vast plains and arid deserts and over high mountain passes to reach their destination and build the communities that defined the American West. The trails they blazed helped pave the way for the civilizing of the West.

The first expeditions

Until the Louisiana Purchase of 1803 (see Chapter 1), the western boundary of the United States was the Mississippi River. Mere political boundaries had never stopped trappers and traders from traveling beyond the Mississippi, but before 1803 there were no organized settlements west of the great river. With the Louisiana Purchase, however, the vast lands to the west of the Mississippi were suddenly opened to organized exploration and settlement. The first of several expeditions to explore the newly acquired Louisiana Territory was led by Captains Meriwether Lewis (1774–1809) and William Clark (1770–1838). Leading a group known as the Corps of Discovery, Lewis and Clark traveled northwest along the Missouri River, journeying nearly as far north as the present-day Canadian border before heading due west across the present-day states of Montana, Idaho, Washington, and Oregon, finally reaching the mouth of the Columbia River on the Pacific coast (see Chapter 2). Though the expedition (1804–1806) failed to locate the coveted Northwest Passage (a mythical water route linking the Atlantic to the Pacific), they were the first party of whites to cross the continental United States, they brought back a wealth of information about western geography, and they established claims to the Pacific Northwest that would aid the young country as it negotiated with British, Russian, and Spanish interests. Most important, the expedition enabled Americans to see the commercial advantages of moving west—especially for fur trapping—and stimulated the idea of western expansion.

First Lieutenant Zebulon Pike (1779–1813) started out on his own journey in 1806, the same year Lewis and Clark returned. His smaller expedition intended to survey the southwest corner of the Louisiana Territory, which butted up against Spanish territory. The Spaniards kept tight control over their border, for they wanted to dominate trade within their colonies and feared that the spirit that had sparked the American Revolution (1776–1783) might well creep into their distant Mexican colonies. When Pike's expedition accidentally strayed across the border, they were captured and imprisoned. While detained in Santa Fe (in what is now New Mexico), Pike observed that the Spanish kept the residents of the colony under tight control and that the prices of goods were unusually high because they had to be obtained from far-off Spanish outposts. After their release in 1807, Pike and his men returned home with stories of potential trade that stirred the hearts of Yankee merchants.

Trade with the colonies of New Spain would not come easily. In 1812 an expedition led by James Baird and Robert McKnight set out to open trade with Santa Fe. But Spanish officials captured the traders, auctioned their goods, and threw the ten men in jail, where they languished until 1820. Other traders met with similar though less dramatic fates. In the end it was no mere party of merchants that opened trade with the Southwest. Rather, in 1821 Mexico broke away from Spain and became an independent nation. In September of that year Mexico opened its borders with the United States. It would not be long before enterprising traders worked their way southwest—legally.

The father of the Santa Fe Trail

Like the traders who preceded him, William Becknell (c. 1796–1865) headed for Santa Fe in the summer of 1821 hoping to make a small fortune selling goods there. With a few companions and a string of pack mules, Becknell set out from Franklin, Missouri, which was at that point a major jumping-off point for the West. But Becknell's timing was better than that of his predecessors, for by the time he reached Santa Fe, the new governor, Facundo Melgares, welcomed the traders with open arms. Mexican men and women crowded into Santa Fe's central plaza to bid for Becknell's goods. The canny merchant realized that he could sell all that he could carry and soon laid plans to start regular expeditions from Missouri to Santa Fe. In this way the first of the trails west was formed as a commercial route.

Becknell's first journey led him out of Missouri and across the territory that would eventually become the state of Kansas. The trees of Missouri soon gave way to waving grass and then, as the travelers reached the Arkansas River in southwest Kansas, to an area that had become known as the Great American Desert. These rolling short-grass prairies, with their scarcity of water, intimidated many early travelers and encouraged Becknell to follow the Arkansas River into present-day Colorado and on toward the Rocky Mountains. Prodding his mules over the tortuous Raton Pass, Becknell then led them down through the high sandy plains of northern New Mexico and into Santa Fe. It was a fine route for mules, but Becknell wanted to bring wagons loaded with trade goods on his next journey. He would have to try another route.

Susan Shelby Magoffin: A Woman on the Santa Fe Trail

Historians have long asserted that the frontier shaped the American character, making Americans tougher, more practical, and more independent than Europeans, who lived in relative luxury. The diary kept by Susan Shelby Magoffin, *Down the Santa Fe Trail and into Mexico: The Diary of Susan Shelby Magoffin, 1846–1847,* certainly reinforces this assertion. Magoffin left Missouri a distinguished southern belle, delicate and refined, and traveled over the Santa Fe Trail with her husband in 1846. One thousand miles and several months later, she was a trail-hardened pioneer woman, afraid of nothing.

Eighteen years old and pregnant, Susan joined her new husband, forty-five-year-old trader Samuel Magoffin, on their honeymoon journey in a party that included sixteen wagons, two hundred oxen, her dog Ring, and her personal attendant, Jane. Early in the trip she wrote of the pleasure of picking wildflowers and berries and listening to birdsong. "Oh, this is a life I would not exchange for a great deal!" she wrote. "There is such independence, so much free uncontaminated air, which impregnates the mind, the feelings, nay every thought with purity."

The party soon faced difficulties. The Magoffins' carriage tipped over, smashing it and injuring the couple. They were forced to ration water and saw ominous signs of Indian parties in the area. When they reached Bent's Fort in present-day Colorado, Susan had a miscarriage and then observed sadly how well an Indian woman had fared in her own childbirth. "No doubt many ladies are ruined by too careful treatments during childbirth," she mused, wondering if the less pampered "custom of the [Indians]" was not better for woman and child. The Magoffins arrived in Santa Fe shortly after American troops took the city in the war with Mexico. Susan was by now a hardened veteran of the trail, capable of joining in the defense of the wagon train when they feared attack from Mexican troops.

Susan Magoffin was not the first woman to travel on the Santa Fe Trail, as was long believed, but she is representative of many of the women who left the East as refined and protected ladies and became over the course of their travel tough-minded survivors who were more than capable of carrying their load. Though the frontier was dominated by men, women proved themselves again and again on the trails leading west.

Near death on the Cimarron Cutoff

Traveling west in 1822 with a party of thirty men and three wagons, Becknell was determined to find a route that avoided the high mountains and headed directly to

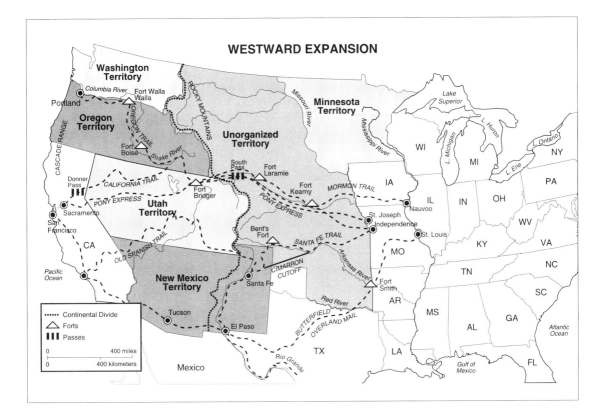

WESTWARD EXPANSION

Santa Fe. Shortly after reaching the Arkansas River, Becknell led his band southwest toward the Cimarron River and then across the sandy desert to meet the original trail due east of Santa Fe. The route nearly cost the entire party their lives. Once they had filled their water barrels at the Cimarron, the travelers had to venture fifty miles without another source of water. If they had been lucky, they would have made it in four days. But on this journey Becknell was not lucky, and soon he and his men faced the real danger of death by dehydration (the loss of water in the body). Ravaged by thirst, Becknell's men were reduced to killing their dogs and cutting off the ears of their mules to drink their blood. Finally, they managed to kill a buffalo that had recently drunk water and survived by drinking its stomach fluids. Was cutting off 100 miles and a difficult mountain pass worth this ordeal? Evidently many travelers thought so, for the Cimarron Cutoff, as it was known, became a much used part of the Santa Fe Trail.

The Santa Fe Trail and the Cimarron Cutoff were mainly used as commercial routes for traders heading to new markets in Mexico. *(Reproduced by permission of the Gale Group.)*

A bustling trade

"By 1824," writes historian Arthur King Peters in *Seven Trails West*, "Becknell had prospered enough to mount a full-scale caravan of twenty-four vehicles carrying a heavy and diversified cargo worth about $30,000, and armed with a small cannon to impress the Indians." Becknell's company returned that fall with "$180,000 in gold and silver and $10,000 worth of furs—a gross profit of 600 percent on their wagonloads of basic hardware, cutlery, and dry goods." Clearly there was money to be made on the Santa Fe Trail, and by the mid-1820s many were joining Becknell and the other early travelers in bringing their wares to Santa Fe. By the 1830s many traders had ventured even farther, taking the trail known as the Camino Real south through present-day New Mexico and on to the Mexican city of Chihuahua (pronounced chi-WA-wa). It is estimated that by 1846 the trade using the Santa Fe Trail had reached $1 million from a traffic flow of 363 wagons and 750 men; by 1860 trade topped $3.5 million. Such trade was conducted not only by American merchants but also by enterprising Mexican adventurers.

Travelers on the Santa Fe Trail faced several dangers. The most pressing, if they took the Cimarron Cutoff, was thirst. Many travelers told harrowing tales of the horrors they encountered as they faced death in a land without water. Equally daunting were the prairie fires. Whether started by lightning or a carelessly tended campfire, a prairie fire could sweep across the land with devastating speed, consuming all in its path. "The [perils of] these prairie conflagrations ... when the grass is tall and dry ... [can be] sufficient to daunt the stoutest heart," Santa Fe Trail traveler Josiah Gregg said (as quoted in *Trails West*).

Danger on the trail

The danger most associated with wagon travel, of course, was Indian attacks. Though the risk has been exaggerated by movies and television shows, it was very real, especially as greater numbers of whites ventured across the Native American lands that the Santa Fe Trail traversed. The tribes that lived in the lands crossed by the eastern half of the trail—the Osage and the Kansas, or Kaw—generally left the travelers alone or negotiated treaties. But the Comanche, Kiowa,

Pawnee, Cheyenne, Arapaho, and Apache warriors who patrolled the western reaches of the trail were widely feared for their fierce attacks. A soldier named Henry Inman, quoted in *Trails West,* remembered that a landmark known as Pawnee Rock provided cover for Native Americans who would "dash down upon the Santa Fe traders like hawks, to carry off their plunder and their scalps." The ground around Pawnee Rock, he recalled, was littered with the graves of victims of the Indians' attacks. Travelers were well armed and often towed a cannon behind their wagons to announce their readiness to fight, but the small bands were often at the mercy of the Indians.

Late in the 1830s military patrols began accompanying the travelers to offer them protection. Moreover, traders began to establish outposts and forts along the trail to offer shelter. Bent's Fort, on the northern section of the trail, became an important post after its founding in 1833. Later the military constructed a number of forts along the trail, including Fort Mann (1847), Fort Atkinson (1850), Fort Union (1851), Fort Larned (1859), and Fort Lyon (1860). Tensions between the Mexicans and the Americans heightened after Texas's 1836 revolution and its annexation by the United States in 1845 (see Chapter 4). In 1846, during the Mexican-American War (1846–48), General Stephen Watts Kearny led his army down the trail and into battle with the Mexicans. The increased military presence on the trail helped ward off Indian attacks.

After the United States claimed the present-day states of New Mexico, Arizona, Colorado, Nevada, and California from Mexico in 1848, trade along the Santa Fe Trail changed. The trail became, according to *Trails West* contributor Marc Simmons, "one of the principal highways binding America's East to the infant West. The volume of trade steadily increased. By the early 1850s, new mail and stagecoach service contributed to the growing traffic." The trail continued to be an important link between east and west through the 1850s and 1860s. In 1862 one of the pivotal western battles of the Civil War (1861–65) was fought at Glorieta Pass, New Mexico. Confederate troops, having conquered Albuquerque and Santa Fe, moved northward along the Santa Fe Trail, intent on capturing Fort Union and securing the Colorado goldfields for the Southern forces. But Union forces met the Confederate soldiers at the pass, burned their supply train, and drove them southward, securing a decisive victory for the North.

The Santa Fe Trail, like all the trails that led west, fell victim to the rise of the railroad. By 1872 the Atchison, Topeka and Santa Fe Railroad had reached Dodge City, Kansas, and by 1878 it reached the foot of Raton Pass. Finally, in 1880, the railroad stretched all the way to Santa Fe. The local paper carried the headline "The Old Santa Fe Trail Passes into Oblivion." More than a hundred years later, however, one can still find traces of the trail and of the forts along the way in parks scattered across Missouri, Kansas, Oklahoma, New Mexico, and Colorado.

The Oregon Trail

The Oregon Trail was the most famous, the most traveled, and the longest of the trails that stretched across the American West. Between 1843, the year of the first Great Migration (the mass movement of settlers west), and 1869, when the transcontinental railway was finished, the Oregon Trail and its spur to California carried an estimated 350,000 pioneers across 2000 miles of difficult terrain. The pioneers who traveled west on this trail dreamed that they would find a better life, richer farmland, and more independence in the West. Many reached their goals; sadly, others died along the way. Even after trains made transcontinental travel easier and cheaper, some pioneers continued to use the trails to cross the country as late as 1895. During its peak years, the Oregon-California Trail was an essential link connecting east to west.

Blazing the trail

The most famous of the western trails had humble beginnings. The first white man to follow the route that became the Oregon Trail actually began on the West Coast. In 1811, fur magnate John Jacob Astor (1763–1848) had sent men to establish a settlement at the mouth of the Columbia River in Oregon Country (as it was known), where he hoped he could compete with the British for control of the region's fur trade. But no sooner had the men built a small trading post than they came under attack by local Indians. A tragic mistake ignited the store of gunpowder aboard their ship, sinking the ship and killing those who remained aboard. (See Chapter 2 for more about the trading post, Fort Astoria.) The inhabitants of Astoria, as the post was called, were stranded. They

OREGON TRAIL

Oregon Territory

PORTLAND

CASCADES

ROCKY MOUNTAINS

Minnesota Territory

Unorganized Territory

CALIFORNIA TRAIL

Great Salt Lake

OREGON TRAIL

SACRAMENTO

Utah Territory

INDEPENDENCE

California

Pacific Ocean

New Mexico Territory

Texas

| 0 | 400 miles |
| 0 | 400 kilometers |

The Oregon-California Trail was one of the longest and most traveled trails leading west. *(Reproduced by permission of the Gale Group.)*

had no choice but to send a party of men east to find help and supplies. The man they chose to lead the way was Robert Stuart, a twenty-seven-year-old Scotsman.

Stuart and a group of seven men departed on the arduous journey on June 29, 1812. The party first followed rivers eastward, but with the help of some friendly Shoshone Indians they decided to take a more direct land route. Their progress was nearly stopped shortly thereafter, when a band of Crow Indians stole the men's horses. From that point on, Stuart's party would travel on foot. In late October 1812, Stuart located a broad pass through the mountains. From South Pass, the men moved steadily downhill for a thousand miles, following the Sweetwater and North Platte Rivers until they reached the broad Missouri River. On March 30, 1813—ten months after they began—the party reached the small town of St. Louis. Luckily, Stuart kept a detailed journal documenting his route; his *The Return from the Mouth of the Columbia to*

Missouri helped guide the many travelers who would eventually travel the same region.

Early travelers

Stuart's journey did not spark a rush of pioneers moving westward. Indeed, for the next thirty years the only white men to venture out into the Louisiana Territory and Oregon Country were fur trappers, who rarely followed set routes but instead ranged widely across the land. In 1830 a group of these fur traders led a train of ten wagons on the Oregon Trail to their annual Rendezvous (a regular social gathering for trappers and traders; see Chapter 2). These were the first wagons on the Oregon Trail, and the men—Jedediah Smith, David E. Jackson, and William Sublette—believed that wagons could make it all the way to the coast.

A party of missionaries undertook a similar venture in 1836. Hoping that they could convert Indians to Christianity, Presbyterian ministers Marcus Whitman and Henry Spalding joined a group of fur traders heading west. In September of the same year they arrived at a fur-trading outpost near present-day Walla Walla, Washington. Their journey was notable because the two missionaries brought along their wives; Eliza Spalding and Narcissa Whitman became the first white women to cross the Oregon Trail, proving that families could make the journey. The couples established separate missions. The Whitmans' mission ended in tragedy in 1847 when Indians attacked and killed most of the inhabitants (see Chapter 10). But until that time the mission stood as a welcoming point on a trail that grew increasingly crowded in the 1840s.

The Great Migration

For years, cautious observers in the East had warned against selling one's belongings, packing a wagon, and heading west. Newspaper editor Horace Greeley (1811–1872) called westward travel "palpable suicide," and statesman Daniel Webster (1782–1852) warned that the Far West was a "region of savages and wild beasts," according to Arthur King Peters in *Seven Trails West.* But that mood began to change in the 1840s, thanks to a number of factors. A long economic downturn that lasted from 1837 to 1842 encouraged many to seek their

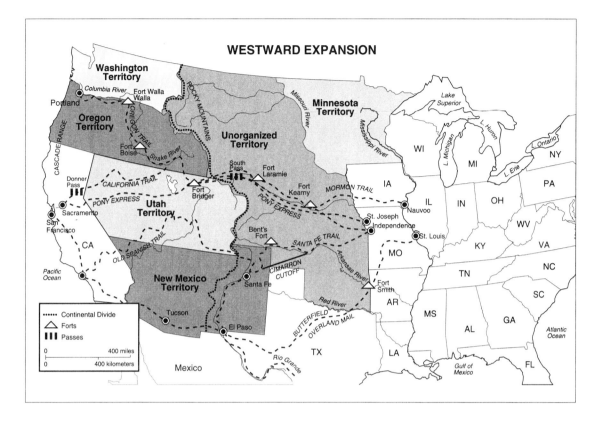

WESTWARD EXPANSION

Map of the routes west including the Oregon-California Trail, which headed west out of Independence, Missouri. *(Reproduced by permission of the Gale Group.)*

fortune in the West; Congress hinted that it would give land to Oregon settlers; Britain ceded the present-day states of Oregon and Washington to the United States in 1846; and the California gold rush of 1849 to 1850 beckoned many who were hungry for instant riches (see Chapter 6). The Great Migration, the name given to the first major exodus of emigrants westward, drew one thousand settlers onto the Oregon Trail in 1843, and more came every year after that. The small trail soon became a highway stretching to the promised land. Many Americans felt that it was their "manifest destiny" to secure these western lands (see Chapter 4). Manifest destiny was the belief that Americans had the God-given right to acquire and populate the territories stretching west to the Pacific.

For the first several years after 1843, the vast majority of western settlers ended up in Oregon Country, but by 1846 the trend began to change. Once word of gold in California reached the East, the number of travelers going south to California was four times that of those venturing north into Oregon. Those going to Oregon had promises of vast acres of fertile farmland, but California had gold—and a warmer climate.

The routes west

For most, the Oregon-California Trail began in Independence, Missouri, the western outpost of a young nation sprawling across the continent. Others left from St. Joseph or Westport, Missouri, and others still from Council Bluffs in present-day Iowa. These towns were booming with the business of outfitting wagon trains. Merchants sold wagons, guns, tools, livestock, food, and other supplies. Saloons, gambling halls, and brothels entertained the men during the evening. Emigration societies organized their members months in advance, and they met in the early spring to prepare for their departure. As soon as the ground thawed and the spring rains ceased, usually in April or early May, the parties would venture westward together, in groups small and large.

The pioneers' first stopping point was at Fort Kearny along the south bank of the Platte River in present-day Nebraska. Wide and shallow, the Platte was also their first major obstacle. Described by an observer quoted in *Seven Trails West* as "two to three miles wide and fully knee deep," the river mired the wagons in mud, and pits of quicksand threatened to swallow livestock alive. Past the Platte the land began to dry out, its colors changing from greens to dusty browns. Bison, prairie dogs, and antelope dotted the horizon; they were sometimes joined by bands of Indians who watched the travelers from a distance, rarely bothering to attack. Studying their trail guides, the pioneers looked for milestones like Courthouse Rock, Chimney Rock, and Scotts Bluff at the far end of present-day Nebraska.

Fort Laramie, in present-day Wyoming (see map on p. 87), provided the travelers with a "civilized" rest stop on their journey. Originally opened by the American Fur Company, the fort was purchased by the U.S. Army in 1849. There the travelers could fix their wagons, rest their stock, and trade news. Until Fort Laramie, the trail was ill defined and allowed the wagons to drive four abreast or more. After Laramie the wagons progressed in single file for hundreds of miles. Over the years the wagons wore deep ruts in the soft sandstone over which they traveled. In some places those ruts can still be seen today.

Eagle Rock at Scotts Bluff in Nebraska. Scotts Bluff was a milestone for pioneers on the Oregon Trail. *(© Dave G. Houser/CORBIS. Reproduced by permission.)*

Slowly gaining elevation, the travelers hoped to reach Independence Rock by Independence Day, July 4. This meant they had a good chance of getting to their destination before winter set in. On Independence Rock the pioneers carved their names in the soft rock, a tradition begun years before by mountain men. The carvings were a form of communication with those who followed, and they still speak to those who see them today. Reaching South Pass (see map on p. 87), from which point all waters flowed westward to the Pacific Ocean, might have seemed a letdown, for the pass was no high mountain outlook but rather a high, flat plain toward which the travelers had been ascending gradually for hundreds of miles. Just west of South Pass the travelers had to make a decision: would they continue north and west to Oregon or journey southward to the Great Salt Lake and onward to California? Some had decided ahead of time, but many travelers made the decision that would shape their destiny on the spot.

On to Oregon

Those choosing Oregon took Sublette's Cutoff, headed toward Soda Springs—where they bathed in the rejuvenating waters—and stopped for a rest at Fort Hall. They had come two-thirds of the way. Soon the wagon trains located the Snake River, named for its twisting course, and followed it for 250 miles. Crossing the Snake was one of the most perilous parts of the journey. Travelers often chained their wagons together in order to cross 600 feet of rapidly moving river or sent their belongings on separate rafts. More mountains remained—100 miles of the Blue Mountains—but once those were crossed the pioneers journeyed downward to the Columbia River, where they passed the Whitman Mission before reaching Fort Walla Walla. A short trip down the Columbia took them to their final destination—the broad, fertile Willamette Valley (pronounced wil-LAM-it).

The California branch

Beyond South Pass, many travelers chose to leave the Oregon Trail and venture southward on the California Trail. It was a more difficult journey, with higher mountains and more arid deserts, but the lure of gold proved sufficiently

strong. Many took the Mormon Trail toward Salt Lake City to restock before moving on. From Salt Lake City, some took the Old Spanish Trail that led toward Los Angeles, a route that promised refuge from snow. But most kept on the Oregon Trail to the north of the Great Salt Lake, looking for the California Trail that would take them down through present-day Nevada and across the Sierra Nevada Mountains into California.

By late summer or early fall, the emigrants found themselves following Nevada's Humboldt River, a sluggish stream that ends in a barren valley known as the Humboldt Basin. The travelers next had to traverse the dreaded Forty-Mile Desert. With scorching heat, no food or water to be found, and sand so deep that it threatened to swallow up oxen and wagons, the Forty-Mile Desert was an excruciating ordeal. Venturing through a bone-dry desert littered with the carcasses of dead livestock, traveler Margaret Frink is quoted in *Gold Fever!*: "The dead animals ... lay so thick on the ground that the carcasses, if placed together, would have reached across many miles of that desert. The stench arising was continuous and terrible." Upon reaching the end of the desert, traveler J. H. Beadle wrote: "At last we got into the hind end o' creation—seventy miles 'thout [without] a drop o' water or a spear o' grass." And still the journey was not over, for the high and rocky Sierra Nevada Mountains lay ahead. The weary travelers had to cross them before the snow started to fall.

The mountains were hot and dry by day and freezing cold by night. On some mornings the gold seekers woke to find ice skirting the streams they followed into the mountains. And in the Sierra Nevadas the Indians were a real threat. Emigrant William Swain, quoted in *The World Rushed In,* wrote to his wife that the Diggers, as the Indians were called, "are thieves, nothing conciliates them and no amount short of *all* will satisfy them.... Passed several wagons that had lost their stock by the Indians and were unable to pursue their journey." Swain's fellow travelers were so worn down from the journey that some of them looked like "living caricatures of the human species, some of them mounted on poor, dusty looking mules, others on miserable looking worn down horses, all dressed in dusty, ragged clothes, as most of us are." Finally, however, the travelers crossed the last mountain pass and began to travel down into the Sacramento Valley. Some found gold and became rich. Some, like the Donner Party, were not so lucky (see box).

Stocking a wagon

A successful trip west took strength, endurance, luck—and a well-stocked wagon. Outfitters developed special wag-

Several factors, including the loss of many of their livestock, left the Donner Party in a desperate situation. *(By Charles Nahl. Reproduced by permission of Corbis-Bettmann.)*

ons strong enough to endure the beating given by 2000 miles of rough trails, light enough to be pulled by a team of oxen or mules, and big enough to carry all of a family's belongings. These wagons, (known as prairie schooners because their billowing canvas covers looked like a ship's sails from a distance) were about ten feet long, four feet wide, and two feet deep. Their sides were bowed out so that the contents got shifted toward the center, and the cracks between the wood were sealed to keep water out during river crossings. The wagons were usually pulled by a team of four oxen or six mules. Extra livestock were often brought along to let the animals work in shifts. In the end, most pioneers preferred the cheaper, stronger, hardier oxen to the mules.

The wagons could carry from 1,600 to 2,500 pounds of household goods, and families filled them to the brim. Food, of course, was essential. The early guidebooks recommended that each emigrant bring 200 pounds of flour, 150

The Donner Party

In the spring of 1846 a party of eighty-one men, women, and children set off from Independence, Missouri, on the Oregon Trail, bound for California. Leading the party was James Frazier Reed; he was joined by his family, by the families of Jacob and George Donner, and by several other families. They are known to history as the Donner Party, and their story is one of the most gruesome and tragic tales to emerge from the decades-long exodus of pioneers westward.

Their journey was ill-fated from the start. Heavy rains delayed their crossing of the Platte River, and a bad decision about which route to take beyond South Pass meant that they had to spend precious days carving a trail through thick underbrush.

Then, according to Arthur King Peters in *Seven Trails West,* as they crossed the salt desert of present-day Utah, "oxen gave out and wagons had to be abandoned; Indians made off with much of the stock; thirst, hunger, and cold exacted their toll." By the time they had crossed the desert, the members of the party were deeply divided, arguing among themselves. Matters worsened when Reed stabbed one of the ox drivers to death, supposedly in self-defense. The party still had to cross the mountain pass, but it was getting quite late in the season.

As they approached the pass, snow began to fall. Unable to progress, the party camped at Truckee Lake (now called Donner Lake). Some of the party had fallen behind and camped a few miles away at Alder

pounds of bacon, 10 pounds of coffee, 20 pounds of sugar, and 10 pounds of salt. (In addition to the food they carried, pioneers supplemented their diet with wild game, berries, and—if they had brought along a cow—fresh milk.) Cooking supplies allowed pioneer wives or the party cook to prepare meals, but the cook had to be flexible and learn to cook over a campfire. Many families brought along furniture, mirrors, and heirlooms, though they often regretted the extra weight when the trail got rough. Barrels of water, rope, and wagon-wheel grease also added weight. Spare parts—including spokes, axles, and canvas roofs—could be carried under the wagon bed.

A typical day on the trail began at six in the morning, when the pilots (as the party guides were known) rousted the pioneers from their sleep to get started before the day got hot. A midday break, called "nooning," gave the oxen a rest and

Creek. The parties took shelter in an abandoned trapper's cabin and built two more cabins and rough lean-tos. The snow continued to fall, piling up around their campsites and frustrating their attempts to leave. Finally, in December, a party of seventeen (including two Native American guides) set out to get help. Running out of food, they resorted to eating the flesh of several party members who had died. The Indian guides were killed and eaten as well. The survivors of the rescue party secured help for some members of the original Donner Party, but others remained stranded.

The last rescue party, which arrived at Truckee Lake in April 1847, made a gruesome discovery. All of those who had remained were dead but one. Lewis Keseberg, an educated German, was found nearly starving, sitting amid the remains of human corpses, brewing a pot of stew made from human organs. According to Peters, one member of the rescue party recalled seeing, "bodies terribly mutilated, legs, arms, and skulls scattered in every direction." Facing starvation, the members of the Donner Party had again resorted to cannibalism.

It is not known exactly how many members of the Donner Party ate human flesh in order to survive. But the cannibalism helped make the Donner Party notorious. Thirty-nine members of the Donner Party died on their terrible journey, either on the trail, at Truckee Lake, or in trying to reach the California settlements. Theirs was the most tragic and horrific of all westward journeys.

allowed them time to graze. As soon as this break was over, the parties were back on the trail until about five in the afternoon. On an average day a party of pioneers could expect to travel about 15 miles; on some days they traveled more and on others much less. Sometimes entire days would be spent just crossing a river. At the end of the day the wagons were pulled into a circle to provide a corral for the animals and to act as a defense against Indian attacks (which were rare). The evening campfire provided the members of the wagon train with the rare opportunity to relax; the adults talked as the sky darkened, and the children played nearby. Campfires were made from whatever wood could be found or from buffalo chips (the polite name for dried buffalo dung). As the fires died, the emigrants drifted off to their makeshift sleeping arrangements. Some slept inside the wagon, but most stretched out with a blanket on the ground. After a long day

A family of four poses in front of the wagon that will also be their home for the several months it takes to cross the continent.
(Courtesy of the National Archives and Records Administration.)

of travel, even the hard earth must have been a comfort. A few sentries stayed awake to ward off wild animals and look out for Indian thieves.

Indians on the trail

Though legend has it that wagon trains crossing the prairie were under constant attack from marauding bands of Indians, in truth Native Americans posed little danger to the emigrants. Much of the contact between whites and Indians was peaceful, as Indians provided directions to emigrants passing through their lands, or as the emigrants traded their guns for Indian horses. Some of the tribes demanded that travelers pay a toll to cross their land. But not all relations between Indian and whites were peaceful. Indians sometimes slipped into camps at night and stole horses and other goods. The Pawnee tribe gained a reputation for thievery. Other tribes,

such as the Crow and the Blackfoot, disliked the emigrants crossing their tribal lands and raided the camps or caught and killed stragglers. In the end, though, few whites were killed by Indians on the Oregon-California Trail. Of the 250,000 settlers who traveled the trails in the 1840s and 1850s, it is estimated that only 362 died at the hands of Indians.

Much of the contact between whites and Native Americans was peaceful, as Indians provided directions to emigrants passing through their lands, or as the emigrants traded their guns for Indian horses. (© CORBIS. Reproduced by permission.)

Death on the trail

While Indians did not pose a grave danger to emigrants, life on the trail was certainly dangerous. Long days of traveling under a burning sun were difficult in themselves, and these difficulties were compounded by the sometimes backbreaking labor of fording streams and climbing steep mountain trails. Accidents cost many lives, especially for children. It was not uncommon for a child to fall off a wagon and be crushed beneath the heavy wheels. Pregnant women also suffered under the strain of the journey. Many a grave marker along the trail lamented the passing of a wife or child.

The most pressing danger was disease. Pneumonia, whooping cough, measles, smallpox, and other sicknesses took many lives, but the biggest killer was cholera. An acute intestinal infection, cholera causes violent vomiting, fever, chills, and diarrhea. As the sickness swept through the camps, it killed quickly, sometimes in a matter of hours. Those who survived were severely weakened. The disease raged on the trail, especially in the 1840s. One emigrant described the road from Independence to Fort Laramie as a graveyard. Though accurate death rates are not available, it is estimated that at least 20,000 of the 350,000 people who ventured forth on the Oregon-California Trail died on the way. That means that one in seventeen of the emigrants did not reach his or her destination and that there were an average of ten graves per mile of the trail. On the Oregon-California Trail, dreams came at a cost.

Other dreams, other trails

Though the Santa Fe and the Oregon-California Trails were the most famous and the most-traveled, they were certainly not the only trails that settlers, traders, and soldiers used as they worked their way west across the continent. Indeed, countless trails, named and unnamed, reached out from civilization into the rapidly receding frontier. Many of these trails have been commemorated by the stories told by travelers or by the parks built years after; others have simply been forgotten. (For information on the Mormon Trail, see Chapter 10.)

The Gila Trail

The Gila (HEE-lah) Trail was one of the most desolate and difficult of all the trails to cross the American West. Linking Santa Fe, New Mexico, and El Paso, Texas, with California, the trail stretched across the deserts of present-day southern New Mexico, Arizona, and California before branching to reach the coastal cities of San Diego and Los Angeles. Archaeologists have discovered evidence that the trail was used by Indians as long as twenty thousand years ago, and some of the first Spanish explorers, including Francisco Vásquez de Coronado (c. 1510–1554), used the trail in the 1540s as they

searched for the mythical Seven Golden Cities of Cíbola. Once this area came under Spanish control, missionaries regularly traveled along the banks of the Gila River. It wasn't until 1825, however, that a white man, James Ohio Pattie, left Santa Fe and traveled into present-day Arizona on what would become the Gila Trail. His trail blazing set the stage for the more intense use of the trail that began in the 1840s.

Early travelers on the Gila Trail were astounded by its difficulty. According to *Trails West* contributor Don Dedera, early traveler Dr. John S. Griffin called the land "utterly worthless ... the cactus is the only thing that grows.... Every bush in this country is full of thorns ... every rock you turn over has a tarantula or centipede...." Further, according to Dedera, a "U.S. senator dismissed the region as 'just like hell. All it lacks is water and good society.'" Not only was the desert a formidable obstacle, but Indian attacks were a greater danger on this trail than on nearly any other. Yavapai, Apache, and Navajo

There were many difficulties to be faced on the trails. The pioneers endured, hoping for a better life in the West. *(Reproduced by permission of Archive Photos, Inc.)*

Indians all resented white intrusions onto their native lands. Apache warrior Cochise (c. 1812–1874) was widely feared along the trail in the 1860s for his daring raids on travelers and on early settlers in present-day Arizona.

Despite the difficulties, more and more white travelers used the Gila Trail beginning in the 1840s. The annexation of Texas in 1845 and the U.S. victory in the Mexican-American War in 1848 removed a major obstacle to American travel across the Southwest. The California gold rush of 1849 drew hundreds and then thousands of gold prospectors across the desert. Soon cattle drivers began herding cattle from Texas to California, where their livestock drew a high price in the inflated markets. By the mid-1850s perhaps one hundred thousand travelers had used the Gila Trail. One of the more prominent users of the Gila Trail was John Butterfield's Overland Mail service. Using more than 250 coaches; several hundred wagons; and employees, horses, and mules numbering in the thousands, the Overland Mail began to make twice-weekly trips between St. Louis, Missouri, and California in the late 1850s, carrying news of goldfield riches and the coming Civil War.

The Gila Trail, like all the others, eventually succumbed to the railroad. But it brought many thousands of travelers across the southern reaches of the present-day United States, including the settlers who would establish the first towns in present-day Arizona.

The Bozeman Trail

Mile for mile, the Bozeman Trail may have been the bloodiest of the western trails. Like many western trails, the Bozeman Trail was blazed to lead travelers first to gold and second to promises of fertile land. The father of the Bozeman Trail was John Bozeman (1835–1867), who pioneered the trail in 1863 after learning of a gold strike in present-day southwestern Montana. Crow Indian raiders took everything but Bozeman's life on his first trip, but he was undaunted. By July 1863 he had recruited a party to leave the Oregon Trail near the northernmost reaches of the North Platte River and travel northwest into the High Plains country, an area that was home to many Native Americans. The trail this party followed carried travelers for only a few years, until 1868, but it made a crucial contribution to the settling of Montana and to the eventual defeat of the many Native American tribes that claimed the vast and empty lands of present-day Wyoming and Montana as their own.

Though whites viewed northeastern Wyoming and eastern Montana as a wasteland, the Crow and other Native Americans who lived there loved their land deeply. Driven westward by the relentless pressure of the expanding United States, other Indian tribes—notably the Sioux and the Cheyenne—joined the Crow on this land beginning in the 1850s. By the early 1860s these tribes had recognized that the only way to defend their territory was to halt any white attempts to settle on their land, for once whites built homes and farms, the army was never far behind. As determined as Bozeman was to settle southwestern Montana, the Indians were determined to keep white men out.

According to *Trails West* contributor Louis de la Haba, after 1864 "emigrant and freight trains used the trail with increasing regularity. Just as regularly, Indians attacked the travelers, running off livestock, stealing horses, ambushing stragglers, and scalping their victims." Travelers who left records noted an extraordinary number of sites where Indian warriors had attacked and killed previous travelers. By 1866, after hearing frequent complaints about Indian harassment, the federal government began to establish a military presence along the Bozeman Trail. Colonel Henry B. Carrington tried to negotiate a treaty with the Indians but was famously rebuffed by the Sioux chief Red Cloud. "You are the white eagle who has come to steal the road," Red Cloud told Carrington. "The Great Father [the president] sends us presents and wants us to sell him the road, but the white chief comes with soldiers to steal it before the Indian says yes or no. I will talk with you no more." Red Cloud recognized that the claims to this land would have to be settled in battle.

The Sioux scored one of the great Indian victories over white forces late in 1866. One of Carrington's officers, Captain William J. Fetterman, ventured out to scare off the Indians who had been attacking wood-gathering parties. Warned not to venture beyond the nearby Lodge Trail Ridge, the arrogant Fetterman led a group of seventy-eight soldiers over the ridge and into the waiting arms of some three thousand Sioux. All of the soldiers were killed, and many were horribly mutilated. Fetterman and his second in command, Captain Frederick H. Brown, seem to have done each other the favor of a bullet shot to the head, thus avoiding torture at the hands of the Indian warriors. It was a tremendous victory for the Indians, but it only heightened the desire of white forces to rid the land of the Indian menace.

The Bozeman Trail was largely abandoned after 1868. The railroad had made the trail obsolete, and few white travelers cared to brave the perils of crossing a land that remained in the control of hostile Indian forces. The Indians quickly destroyed the forts built along the trail and reclaimed control of much of the territory. It would be more than a decade before white forces would again attempt to drive the Indians from this land.

Trails' end

The many trails that led traders, gold seekers, farmers, and other emigrants west in the middle decades of the nineteenth century left their mark on the landscape and on the American memory. Physical traces of the trails remain to this day: deep wagon-wheel ruts are still visible in deserted stretches of the mountainous West, and many forts attract tourists eager to understand this romantic part of the near past. The impression on the American memory is even deeper, for the pioneers seemed to embody the very spirit of America. Brave, persistent, and tough, the pioneers who crossed the country on these trails endured many hardships while pushing onward toward their goal: a new life in the West.

For More Information

Books

Billington, Ray Allen. *Westward to the Pacific: An Overview of America's Westward Expansion.* St. Louis, MO: Jefferson National Expansion Historical Association, 1979.

Catrow, David. *The Story of the Oregon Trail.* Chicago: Children's Press, 1984.

Faragher, John Mack. *Women and Men on the Overland Trail.* New Haven, CT: Yale University Press, 1979.

Fisher, Leonard Everett. *The Oregon Trail.* New York: Holiday House, 1990.

Hill, William E. *The Santa Fe Trail, Yesterday and Today.* Caldwell, ID: Caxton Printers, 1992.

Magoffin, Susan Shelby. *Down the Santa Fe Trail and into Mexico: The Diary of Susan Shelby Magoffin, 1846–1847.* Lincoln: University of Nebraska Press, 1982.

McNeese, Tim. *Western Wagon Trains.* New York: Crestwood House, 1993.

Murphy, Dan. *Santa Fe Trail: Voyage of Discovery.* Las Vegas NV: KC Publications, 1994.

Murray, Robert A. *The Bozeman Trail: Highway of History.* Boulder, CO: Pruett Pub. Co., 1988.

Penner, Lucille Recht. *Westward Ho!: The Story of the Pioneers.* New York: Random House, 1997.

Sanford, William R. *The Santa Fe Trail in American History.* Berkeley Heights, NJ: Enslow Publishers, 2000.

Santrey, Laurence. *The Oregon Trail.* Mahwah, NJ: Troll, 1985.

Simmons, Marc. *Following the Santa Fe Trail: A Guide for Modern Travelers.* 2d ed. Santa Fe, NM: Ancient City Press, 1986.

Stewart, George R. *Ordeal by Hunger: The Classic Story of the Donner Party.* 1936. Reprinted, Boston: Houghton Mifflin, 1960.

Web sites

DiPasquale, Connie, and Susan Stafford. *Orphan Trains of Kansas.* [Online] http://raven.cc.ukans.edu/carrie/kancoll/articles/orphans/ (accessed April 12, 2000).

The End of the Oregon Trail [Online] http://www.teleport.com/~eotic/index.html (accessed April 12, 2000).

OCTA: Oregon-California Trails Association. [Online] http://www.octa-trails.org (accessed April 12, 2000).

Sources

Holliday, J. S. *The World Rushed In: The California Gold Rush Experience, An Eyewitness Account of a Nation Heading West.* New York: Simon and Schuster, 1981.

Peters, Arthur King. *Seven Trails West.* New York: Abbeville Press, 1996.

Place, Marian T. *Westward on the Oregon Trail.* New York: American Heritage, 1962.

Roscoe, Gerald, and David Larkin. *Westward: The Epic Crossing of the American Landscape.* New York: The Monacelli Press, 1995.

Schanzer, Rosalyn. *Gold Fever! Tales from the California Gold Rush.* Washington, DC: National Geographic Society, 1999.

Trails West. Washington, DC: Special Publications Division, National Geographic Society, 1979.

The Gold Rush

6

"It was a clear cold morning I shall never forget," wrote James Marshall in his diary on January 24, 1848 (as quoted in Rosalyn Schanzer's *Gold Fever!*). "My eye was caught with the glimpse of something shining in the bottom of the ditch. I reached my hand down and picked it up; it made my heart thump, for I was certain it was gold. Then I saw another piece. Putting one of the pieces on a hard river stone, I took another and commenced hammering. It was soft and didn't break; it therefore must be gold." With these words, carpenter James Marshall recorded his discovery of the mineral that would change California from a sleepy Mexican territory into the fastest-growing state in the rapidly expanding United States of America. Within six months of Marshall's discovery, word had spread that there was gold throughout the streams and hills of central California. It wasn't long before thousands of gold-hungry prospectors poured in from all over the world in what is now known as the great California gold rush.

The gold rush lasted just a few years, but it dramatically changed the lives of the individuals involved, the state, and the nation. Some who set out for California with hopes of instant riches never even made it to their destination; they died on the arduous journey west. Of the thousands who arrived in California, only a few struck it big in the goldfields. Many more built new lives providing services in the rapidly growing city of San Francisco. Migrants who were African American, Chinese, or Hispanic faced discrimination as white settlers took control of the state. The rapid migration of people to California also forced the growing United States to confront once again the issue of whether slavery should be allowed in new states.

California before the rush

California had offered riches to its inhabitants long before the discovery of gold on the American River. With its mild climate, its vast and fertile interior valleys, and an abundance of game, the country we now know as California supported a large native population. Historians estimate that before contact with the Europeans, some three hundred thousand native people lived in the area. These Indians organized themselves into more than one hundred different tribes, each with a distinct culture and traditions. All benefited from an environment that provided them with the best diet of any native population on the continent.

An early American settler in California observed: "The Indians were very well formed, robust, handsome people. They were partly tattooed, and wore ornaments of bone and beads. They used bows and arrows and were very expert fishermen. They gathered acorns, roots, and grass-seed." Though acorns were a staple food, Indians also hunted for game and caught salmon in the many streams that led to the Pacific Ocean. Indians living along the coast built their cone-shaped homes from the bark of the huge redwood trees that lined the shore. Those living inland built sturdy structures from a reed called "tule." Others built homes from palm fronds or cedar logs. Native Americans surely noticed the glittering gold nuggets lying in the streambeds, but they did not find value in the soft metal. They measured wealth differently. Some tribes valued woodpecker scalps. Others favored dentalium shells. Still others measured wealth in woven baskets or chunks of obsidian (a hard, black stone valued as a cutting tool). Instead of trading in money or gold, the Indians traded with the goods they found valuable.

Blessed with ample land and food, California's native peoples found little reason for conflict. This peaceful life began to change in 1769, when Spanish missionaries arrived on the California coast and set out to convert the natives, whom they called Diggers, to Christianity. Spaniards had visited California as early as 1602, when a fleet of Spanish galleons led by Sebastián Vizcaíno put ashore after seeing a pack of bears devouring a whale carcass. The Spaniards met a group of people they described as "generous Indians, friendly to the point of giving whatever they had." Vizcaíno named the bay Monte Rey but did not stay to settle the area. In fact, contact with the Spanish—who were busily colonizing lands to the south, in Mexico—remained limited until the missionaries arrived.

Mission life

Beginning in 1769, the Spanish sought to extend their empire northward into California. They began building missions (church-based districts), pueblos (villages), and presidios (forts) beginning in the south of the territory in San Diego and extending north all the way to San Francisco Bay. The primary goal of the Spanish missionaries who occupied the twenty-one missions in California was to convert the natives to Christianity. According to Father Francisco Palou, "We rejoiced to find so many pagans upon whom the light of our holy faith was about to dawn." And dawn it did, as missionaries baptized nearly fifty-four thousand Indians in the first decades of their work. By the turn of the nineteenth century they had gathered nearly the entire population of California Indians south of San Francisco Bay into their missions.

At first the Indians embraced the Spanish missionaries and the bands of soldiers and citizens that accompanied them. They hoped that the Spaniards would bring improved trade and spiritual power. But they soon discovered that the Spaniards wanted more than to save their souls. The soldiers who accompanied the missionaries wanted to become rich, and many claimed large plots of land for themselves, driving off the native peoples and forcing some Indians to work as slaves. But it was the missionaries who truly changed Indian

life. Not only did they convert the indigenous peoples to Christianity, but they also sought to convert them to a European way of life. Neophytes (newly baptized Indians) were taught a variety of skills in the missions. They learned to be weavers, brick makers, farmers, and vaqueros (cattle drivers, or cowboys). But they did so against their will, becoming slaves to their supposed saviors. The baptized Indians could not leave the missions, and they were severely disciplined for misbehavior.

"The cost of this wholesale transformation of Indian life was horrifying," writes historian Richard White in *"It's Your Misfortune and None of My Own": A New History of the American West.* Some Indians escaped the tyranny of the missions and fled into the wilderness. Others living in remote mountain valleys had little contact with the Spaniards. But for the majority of the Indians, the damage was done. Of the sixteen thousand Indians baptized by missionaries in their first decade, more than nine thousand died. By 1817, 90 percent of the mission Indians had died from disease or abuse. By the end of the gold rush, the entire Indian population had declined to just thirty thousand people, down from three hundred thousand before European contact.

The Californios

Those who benefited most from the Spanish occupation of California became known as the Californios (descendants of the original Spanish settlers). When California was under Spanish rule, trade and land access were controlled by the missions and by Spanish governors. But as Spain's influence declined, some Californios began to establish large ranches, called ranchos, and to trade with the Americans who were beginning to arrive in the West and with traders traveling up and down the coast. In 1821 Mexico declared its independence from Spain. In 1834 the Mexican government ended the dominance of the missions and granted large tracts of land to the Californios. The Indians received little from the breakup of the missions, and they remained subject to the control of the wealthy landowners. The richest of the Californios laid claim to large areas of land. Their ranchos were tended by the first cowboys, called vaqueros. But not all Californios were wealthy. Many worked on the ranchos of the wealthy landowners or tended smaller ranches of their own.

Wealthy Californio Mariano Vallejo (1808–1890) remembered the days when he and his peers dominated California society (quoted by Guadalupe Vallejo in *Century Magazine*): "We were the pioneers of the Pacific coast, building towns and Missions while General [George] Washington was carrying on the War of the Revolution. We often talk together of the days when a few hundred large Spanish ranches and Mission tracts occupied the whole country from the Pacific to the San Joaquin." The Californios organized great ranching empires and became rich selling cowhides to Russian, English, French, and American traders who stopped in at California ports. The Californios traded their hides for manufactured goods, bright cloth, jewelry, tobacco, furniture, and a wealth of other goods that they could not produce themselves. They also developed a rich cultural life centered on the ranchos, with fiestas, bullfights, and rodeos providing the entertainment. The wealthy families lived lives of leisure, and the ranchos employed many vaqueros. Sadly, the rancheros (ranch owners) also forced many of the remaining Indians and lower-class Mexicans to perform the lowest jobs on the ranch. For the wealthy, life in California was good; for the rest, it was a struggle.

The discovery of gold

Settlers from around the world began to arrive in California in the late 1830s and early 1840s. Some of the first American settlers reached California via overland trails in the fall of 1841. These frontiersmen and farmers settled in the Sacramento Valley, the vast and temperate valley that lies inland from San Francisco Bay. Keeping themselves separate from the Californios who lived along the coast, the settlers pursued farming and small-scale ranching. Another group of Americans arrived in 1846. Led by a printer named Sam Brannan, these 238 men, women, and children (who were members of a growing religious group known as Mormons) landed in a sleepy seaside town called Yerba Buena. Some of the band remained in the town, which would soon change its name to San Francisco, and Brannan started a newspaper, the *California Star*. The rest ventured out into the Sacramento Valley, where they settled near a place known as Sutter's Ranch. When the Mexican-American War (1846–48) broke out, these settlers sided with the U.S. Army and hoped that they would become the new base of power in the territory. The United States claimed California and the other southwestern territories following the Mexican-American War.

John Augustus Sutter (1803–1880; see box on p. 113) had arrived in California from Switzerland in 1839 with the dream of creating a farming empire. After attaining Mexican citizenship, he received a land grant of nearly 50,000 acres in the Sacramento Valley. Sutter built an adobe fort near the south bank of the American River and called his settlement New Helvetia. (Helvetia is another name for Switzerland.) By 1848 Sutter's Fort had become a center of trade and communications, and new settlers were arriving every day. In addition to the fortress, Sutter had built an inn, a granary (a grain storehouse), and a retail store. He had plans to build several mills powered by the many streams that flowed out of the

mountains surrounding the valley. Sutter appointed carpenter James Marshall to oversee the construction of a sawmill in the Coloma Valley, about 45 miles from Sutter's Fort on the south fork of the American River.

On the morning of January 24, 1848, Marshall was surveying work on the mill when he spotted something sparkling in the river. Mill construction had disturbed the

Sutter's Mill, in the Sacramento Valley, California. *(© Bettmann/ CORBIS. Reproduced by permission.)*

earth around the riverbed, and the moving water had washed away the gravel and sand to reveal what appeared to be gold. Picking out a few small nuggets, he ran back to the mill workers and shouted, "Boys, I believe I have found a gold mine." The men soon discovered more of the gleaming, soft metal, and Marshall decided that he must present his find to Sutter. Together the two men tested the mineral. It *was* gold. Marshall returned to the mine, and he and the workers dug for more gold when they were not working on the mill. Sutter hoped that he could keep Marshall's discovery secret. But word soon spread: there was gold on the American River.

A group of Mormons working on a flour mill discovered a second mine, which became known famously as Mormon Island. With this discovery gold fever spread through Sutter's settlement. According to J. S. Holliday, author of *The World Rushed In: The California Gold Rush Experience,* "Sutter could not hold his workers. The flour mill stood unfinished, hides rotted in the warehouse. All his plans depended on a staff of assistants, field workers, carpenters, and tanners. Suddenly they were gone, with plans of their own." Sutter's experience would be repeated across California and, within a year, across the nation. Once people heard of the gold, they quickly left their meager-paying jobs and rushed to the goldfields to pursue the possibility of instant wealth.

Word of gold in the Sacramento Valley had reached San Francisco by March, but most viewed the rumors with suspicion. That ended on May 12, 1848, when Sam Brannan returned from a trip to Coloma brandishing a bottle full of gold dust. "Gold! Gold! Gold from the American River!" Brannan shouted to all who would listen. One hopeful miner recorded his thoughts: "A frenzy seized my soul.... Piles of gold rose up before me.... castles of marble, thousands of slaves ... myriads of fair virgins contending with each other

John Sutter owned Sutter's Mill in California, where gold was first discovered in 1848, starting the California gold rush. *(Courtesy of the Library of Congress.)*

John Sutter

No man is more closely associated with the California gold rush than John Sutter is. It was at Sutter's Mill that the first gold was discovered in California. But Sutter failed to profit from the discovery, instead becoming one of the many casualties of the gold rush.

Johann August Sutter was born in the German village of Kandern on February 15, 1803. He was expected to follow in the tradition of his father and grandfather and work in the local paper mill, but Johann hoped for better and wandered about searching for meaningful work. Newly married in 1826, Sutter settled into a dry-goods business that his mother-in-law helped him start, but his mismanagement soon led to financial disaster. Faced with imprisonment for failing to pay his debts, Sutter left his wife and children and headed to America in the summer of 1834.

In America, Sutter called himself Captain John A. Sutter, a veteran of the Royal Swiss Guards. He impressed many with stories of his exotic European life and endeared himself to several wealthy Americans. Around 1846, Sutter arrived in Yerba Buena, California, carrying an ample supply of (borrowed) money and glowing letters of recommendation. Seeing the wide-open valleys, Sutter imagined himself the master of a vast empire. By 1847 he had secured a land grant of fifty thousand acres and had begun to build a settlement at the confluence (meeting) of the Sacramento and American Rivers. When the land beneath him changed hands from Mexico to the United States, Sutter proudly declared himself an American and continued to build his inland empire.

In 1848, a terrible disruption came into Sutter's dreams of landed wealth: gold was discovered on his property. His employees began to abandon their work to pan for gold in the mountain streams, and soon his land was flooded with gold-hungry prospectors who took whatever gold they could find, regardless of who owned the land. Sutter mismanaged his way out of a potential fortune again and again and was eventually tricked out of his remaining land holdings in the town of Sacramento by newspaperman Sam Brannan. He lived out his life on his farm on the Feather River, an aging alcoholic with little to show from the gold rush except his stories.

for my love—were among the fancies of my imagination.... in short, I had a very violent attack of the gold fever." Hundreds of San Franciscans packed up their belongings and headed inland. Almost overnight the bustling seaport was transformed into a ghost town.

Gold fever

News traveled slowly in the nineteenth century. It took several months for people in San Francisco, barely a hundred miles away, to hear of the discovery of gold in the Sacramento Valley. By the summer other westerners—Hawaiians, Oregonians, Mexicans, and Latin Americans—caught wind of the discovery and set out for California. Late in 1848 the *Oregon Spectator* reported, "Almost the entire male population has gone gold digging in California." By July 1848, the number of gold seekers stood at two thousand; by October they reached five thousand; and by year's end they numbered eight thousand. But there were more to come. Many of the first Californians to reach the goldfields—the '48ers—wrote letters to relatives in the East. These letters, filled with boasts of vast treasure troves, were often dismissed as rumors, but they were confirmed in July when copies of Sam Brannan's special edition of the *California Star* reached Missouri. Other papers reprinted the story, creating a buzz in cities throughout the settled East. Still, many refused to believe the stories until they received some official confirmation. That confirmation came on December 5, 1848, when President James K. Polk (1795–1849) told Congress that "the accounts of the abundance of gold in that territory are of such extraordinary character as would scarcely command belief were they not corroborated by authentic reports of officers in the public service." Polk's message left no room for doubt: there was gold in California.

The news now spread through the United States like wildfire, and the trickle of emigration turned into a steady flow. The *New York Herald* reported at the time that "the great discovery of gold has thrown the American people in a state of the wildest excitement. Gold can be scooped up in pans at the rate of a pound of pure dust a scoop. 'Ho! For California' is the cry everywhere." Similar announcements appeared in newspapers across the country, accompanied by letters home from miners. One such letter boasted that a Missouri carpenter had dug more gold in six months than a mule could pack; others bragged of men finding thousands of dollars worth of gold in a matter of days. At a time when wages were as low as two dollars a day, such riches sounded like heaven on earth. Men sold their belongings and their businesses to raise enough money to travel to California; others simply dropped what they were doing and headed west, figuring they would live off the land

until they found their fortune. One eastern minister, the Reverend Walter Colton, complained that his congregation and town, beset with greed, simply vanished: "The blacksmith dropped his hammer, the carpenter his plane, the mason his trowel, the farmer his sickle, the baker his loaf, and the tapster his bottle. All were off for the mines, some on horses, some on carts, and some on crutches, and one went in a litter," (as quoted in Rosalyn Schanzer's *Gold Fever!*).

By July 1848, the number of gold seekers in the Sacramento Valley stood at two thousand; by October there were five thousand; and by year's end they numbered eight thousand. *(Reproduced by permission of Archive Photos, Inc.)*

Getting there

By the spring of 1849, many easterners were planning to head west. They had a choice: they could travel overland on one of several known trails, or they could book passage on boats that would take them through the Isthmus of Panama or around South America and north to San Francisco. Neither journey was easy or inexpensive. The sea journey could take from four to nine months and cost several hundred dollars. The overland journey could be completed in four months and, for adventurers already in the Midwest, made more sense. Though there were no fixed costs for the overland journey, historians estimate that travelers typically spent six hundred to seven hundred dollars on the trip. It is estimated that between twenty-five thousand and thirty thousand people took the overland routes to California in 1849, and another forty-four thousand came in 1850. Whether they came by land or by sea, for the people known as the '49ers, getting there was more than half the battle.

Those traveling overland to California had their choice of two fairly well established routes: the southern Santa Fe Trail across land recently acquired from Mexico, with various branches leading to southern California, or the better-known Oregon-California Trail, whose southern branch led directly to the now-famous Sacramento Valley. The trails began at the major outfitting towns of Independence and St. Joseph, Missouri. There were guidebooks available for both routes, but while such books might help travelers avoid some problems, they could hardly prepare travelers for the difficulties that lay ahead. (See Chapter 5 for more information about the trails.)

As spring came to Missouri, masses of gold seekers gathered in tent cities on the banks of the Missouri River, waiting for the right time to set off on their journey. The emigrants (as they called themselves, for they were leaving their country behind) gathered themselves into traveling parties to better survive the journey. When the grass had grown long enough to feed the livestock and the spring rains had slowed, the travelers crossed the river and set off on their journey. In all, twenty-five thousand to thirty thousand men and women set off across the country in 1849 to join those seeking their fortune in the goldfields of California.

"The whole country was under water"

That season, sixty-two hundred wagons, more than twenty thousand people, and close to sixty thousand pack animals set off on the Oregon-California Trail; the Santa Fe Trail was nearly as congested. Though they were eager to cross the distant mountains before the winter snows set in, the emigrants struggled across trails left muddy by heavy rains. One traveler, J. H. Beadle, wrote (as quoted in *Gold Fever!*): "The whole country was under water. The mud was thicker and stickier every day; but the men kept a-hoopin' and swearin' and I never seed men so crazy to git on." Despite these difficulties, they pushed on across hundreds of miles of flat prairie. The travelers gathered around campfires at the end of a long day of travel, ate their biscuits and dried meat, and joined in songs such as "Sweet Betsy from Pike":

> Oh do you remember sweet Betsy from Pike
> Who crossed the wide prairie with her lover Ike?
> With two yoke of oxen, an old yellow dog,
> A tall Shanghai rooster and one spotted dog.

The gold seekers packed all their belongings into covered wagons that were roughly nine feet long and four or five feet wide. Most wagons were loaded down with all that was needed to start a life in a new place: bedding, dishes, clothes, and food; tools for mining, farming, and repairing the wagons; and guns and ammunition. Some of the travelers brought chickens, which swung in cages from the back of the wagon. The entire wagon was covered with a heavy canvas, waterproofed with linseed oil. If women and children were traveling with the party, they sometimes slept in the wagon. Mules or oxen pulled the wagons. Gold seekers grew accustomed to a boring diet that consisted primarily of biscuits and bacon, washed down with strong coffee. They hunted or fished when they could and gathered wild berries or greens to supplement their diet.

Legend has it that wagon trains crossing the prairie were under constant attack from marauding bands of Indians, but in truth the Sioux, Cheyenne, and other prairie tribes felt little need to disturb the bands of people who passed across their land. A more pressing danger was disease, especially cholera. Cholera is an acute intestinal infection that causes violent vomiting, fever, chills, and diarrhea. As the sickness swept through the camps, it sometimes killed travelers in a matter of hours. Those who survived were severely weakened.

Crossing the mountains

As the wagon trains reached present-day Wyoming, the flat prairies gave way to the more difficult terrain of the

 **Levi Strauss**

The gold rush made fortunes for many, and some of those who got rich actually did so by finding gold. But many others acquired their riches by providing services and products to miners flush with a little bit of gold. Levi Strauss, the inventor of jeans, was one such merchant.

Levi Strauss was born in Buttenheim, Bavaria (Germany), in 1829 and moved to New York City with his family when he was eighteen. In New York he joined his half brothers in the dry-goods business. When masses of people began heading west, Strauss saw an opportunity. In 1853 he opened a West Coast branch of his brothers' business and began selling work clothes to miners, who were notoriously hard on clothes. Strauss became a respected businessman and a prominent local philanthropist, but he did not become famous until 1873, when he and Jacob Davis attached rivets to a pair of pants.

Jacob Davis was a Reno, Nevada, tailor and a customer of Strauss's. One of Davis's customers kept ripping out the pockets of the pants Davis made, and Davis came up with the idea of reinforcing the stress points with metal rivets. He was eager to patent the idea, but he didn't have the sixty-eight dollars he needed to file for the patent. Davis asked Strauss to be his partner, and the two received patent #139,321 on May 20, 1873. Their work pants—which we now call blue jeans—soon became famous among workingmen for their comfort and durability, and they remain America's most popular pants, imitated throughout the world.

rising mountains. Many belongings that had seemed essential on the prairies were discarded as the mules and oxen strained to pull wagons up and down the steep mountain trails. Parties began to split up once they crossed South Pass. Some took the Mormon Trail toward Salt Lake City to restock before continuing westward. From Salt Lake City, some took the Old Spanish Trail toward Los Angeles, a route that promised refuge from snow. But most travelers stayed on the Oregon Trail to the north of the Great Salt Lake, looking for the California Trail that would take them down through present-day Nevada and across the Sierra Nevada Mountains into California.

By late summer or early fall, emigrants on the California trail found themselves following Nevada's Humboldt River, a sluggish stream that ends in a barren valley known as the Humboldt Basin. The travelers next had to cross the dreaded Forty-Mile Desert, with scorching heat, no food or water, and sand so deep that it threatened to swallow up oxen and wagons. And still the journey was not over, for the high and rocky Sierra Nevada Mountains had to be crossed before the snow started to fall. The mountains were hot and dry by day and freezing cold by night.

In the Sierra Nevadas, the Native Americans posed a real threat to the wagon trains. The Indians would steal the livestock and supplies from wagon trains, leaving some emigrants unable to continue their journey. The travelers were weary from the journey. In a letter to his wife quoted in *The World Rushed In,* emigrant William Swain described his weary fellow travelers as "living caricatures of the human species, some of them mounted on poor, dusty looking mules, others on miserable looking worn down horses, all dressed in dusty, ragged clothes, as most of us are." The trip got easier after the wagons crossed the last mountain pass and began to travel down into the Sacramento Valley. Some travelers never made it that far, having perished along the trail (see Chapter 5).

Travel by sea

For those who chose to travel to California by sea, the journey was no less arduous. Most sea travelers, called argonauts, chose the shorter passage across the Isthmus of Panama, a narrow strip of land joining North and South America. The first part of the trip was pleasant and relatively fast—it took only about three weeks to travel from New York City to Chagres, Panama. Then travel became more difficult. Gold seekers set off on canoes up the Chagres River through a torrid jungle. After a three-day trip, they reached Cruces, where they packed their belongings onto mules for a twenty-mile trip to Panama City on the Pacific coast of Panama. From there the argonauts booked a passage north to San Francisco. It was not an easy journey, but it all went well one could make it from New York to San Francisco in fifty-one days. For most, it took much longer.

The Panama crossing was both the most difficult and the most interesting part of the journey. The jungle was hot and humid, and many travelers became infected with diseases such as malaria and cholera. For those who remained healthy, however, travel through the jungle was an exotic adventure. Jennie Megquier, who traveled west with her husband, recalled, "The air was filled with the music of birds, the chattering of monkeys, parrots in any quantity, alligators lying on the banks too lazy to move," according to *The Gold Rush* author Liza Ketchum. With thousands of gold seekers pouring out of the jungle, Panama City soon became clogged with people seeking passage northward. Some travelers had to wait for weeks and pay a premium price to board an overcrowded ship.

Other argonauts opted for the long journey down the length of South America, around Cape Horn, and back north. The 18,000 mile journey took as long as nine months. It was, writes Linda Jacobs Altman in *The California Gold Rush in American History,* "a route for the stout of heart and strong of stomach." Argonauts had to endure terrible storms at sea, cramped and unsanitary conditions, spoiled food, and mind-numbing boredom.

Whichever route they took, the argonauts ended their journey in the growing city of San Francisco. By 1849 the harbor was filled with as many as five hundred boats, many of which were simply abandoned by crews eager to reach the goldfields. Enterprising merchants turned some boats into floating hotels and stores. San Francisco had become, almost overnight, a boomtown, with bars, gambling houses, restaurants, shops, shipping offices, and banks open twenty-four hours a day. Lodging was scarce, however; there were few hotels or rooms for rent, and the city was growing so fast that it looked like one large construction site. Jennie Megquier wrote, "It is the most God-forsaken country in the world," according to Ketchum. Most argonauts saw the wisdom of pushing on to the goldfields.

Whether they came by sea or by land, from the United States or from China, Nicaragua, or Europe, gold seekers who came to California in 1849 quickly put the difficulties of their journey behind them and set to their real work: looking for gold.

In the goldfields

Beginning in the summer and fall of 1848, hundreds and then thousands of men (there were few women) poured

into the California interior in search of gold. The first men took to the American River, but that area soon became so crowded that prospectors looked to the north and south, along the Feather, Yuba, and Tuolumne Rivers. In the end the entire western slope of the Sierra Nevadas proved to contain some gold.

The first miners met with some spectacular successes. On the Feather River, seven miners panned out 275 pounds of gold in two weeks; on the Yuba, another group found seventy-five thousand dollars' worth of gold in just three months. In an area known as Dry Diggings (later as Hangtown), a miner could find from a few ounces to five pounds of gold per day. The true stories of men barely able to carry all the gold they dug out soon led to fantastic stories about ever-larger claims that must exist just around the bend of the next river.

Once word spread that an area might contain gold, miners rushed to the region to stake their claim. Miners staked a claim when they decided on a patch of land or riverbed that they wanted to work on. Such claims were often informal, and "jumping claims" (taking over another man's site) often led to fights. The first miners found their gold simply by sifting the bottom of the streambed, allowing the current of the water to wash away the dirt and gravel and leave the gold. Bayard Taylor, quoted in *Gold Fever!*, described his first encounter with men panning for gold: "When I first saw men carrying heavy stones in the sun, standing nearly waist-deep in water, and grubbing with their hands in the gravel and clay, there seemed little temptation to gold digging; but when the shining particles were poured out lavishly from a tin basin, I confess there was a sudden itching in my fingers."

As the first claims were played out, miners resorted to more labor-intensive methods of attaining gold. They shoveled soil into rockers (boxes set on curved feet that allowed them to sift the soil) and washed the excess material away, or they diverted streams and built canals to bring water to their "dry diggings." Soon, even more labor- and capital-intensive forms of mining came into play. Hydraulic mining forced pressurized water into beds of gravel, causing the ground to disintegrate and leaving a residue of gold. Quartz mining required heavy equipment to break the gold free from the quartz. By the time these latter methods were being used, the majority of the gold seekers had moved on in search of easier riches.

The mining camps

As particular areas were discovered to have gold, camps sprang up overnight to accommodate miners who had staked claims. Enterprising merchants set up tent stores and charged the men exorbitant rates for food and supplies. An egg cost a dollar—a half-day's pay. So did a slice of bread, and it cost another dollar for butter. Food was scarce, and those selling it often ended up with more money than the prospectors. Prostitutes were fairly prevalent in the camps. The slightly more proper dance-hall women offered entertainment and were beloved by the miners. Popular entertainers Lola Montez and Lotta Crabtree gained widespread renown for their dancing and singing, and both enjoyed an independence unavailable to women in the civilized East.

Because the mining camps and cities of California formed so quickly and haphazardly, they had to do without some of the luxuries of civilized life. One such luxury was law enforcement. Mining camps were lawless places filled with greedy men, many of whom were outcasts from civilized society. There was nothing to keep such men from taking whatever they wanted except the threat of revenge. Miners fought hard to maintain their claims. Many carried weapons, and it was not unusual for a thief to be killed for "jumping" another man's claim. Violence was so common in the mining camps that barroom fighting might well be considered one of a miner's principal forms of recreation.

Vigilante justice

The "established" town of San Francisco was known for its violence. As a port city, San Francisco saw a rapid influx of immigrants from around the world. Some countries, such as Nicaragua and Australia, dispatched convicts to California just to clear their prisons. One group from Sydney, Australia, was known as the Sydney Ducks. Violent career criminals, the Sydney Ducks conducted a reign of terror on the city streets that was capped by a particularly brutal robbery of a retail store in 1851. The San Francisco business community was finally prompted to take action, forming a citizens' committee, called the Committee of Vigilance, to try the offenders and to drive other criminals from the city.

Vigilante justice (justice dealt out by citizens who take the law into their own hands) became the primary form of justice in gold rush country, as in much of the West. Such justice could be extremely harsh. After three suspected criminals were quickly tried, found guilty, and hanged, Dry Diggings became known as Hangtown. A storekeeper in Sonora, California, counted four dead in that town in the third week of

A miner digs for gold during the California gold rush.
(Reproduced by permission of Archive Photos, Inc.)

A sheep corral doubles as a hotel in California during the gold rush. *(© Bettmann/ CORBIS. Reproduced by permission.)*

June and six killed in the second week of July. All miners learned to watch their backs and had to be willing to use force to protect their interests. But it was foreigners and minorities who suffered the most abuse and violence as competition in the goldfields increased.

A diverse country

Even before the gold rush began, California was home to a variety of people. U.S. settlers, Indian tribes, and Californios all lived there. But the gold rush brought a diversity of people that was astonishing. Mexicans and Chileans were some of the first to arrive after the discovery of gold. Soon miners from European countries—especially the United Kingdom, Germany, and France—came to seek their fortune. Chinese immigrants began arriving in 1850, lured by calls for laborers if not by gold; by 1855 the Chinese population in

California had reached twenty-five thousand. And, of course, American settlers poured into California in vast numbers. Among them were African Americans who hoped that in this new land they might find opportunities unavailable to them in the East.

Who would wield power in this wild land? This question was answered early in the gold rush years by those seeking to make California a state. Political leaders and businessmen felt that California's rapidly growing population and wealth qualified it for immediate statehood without going through the initial stage of territorial government first. They managed to find enough delegates to call a constitutional convention in the fall of 1849 and send two senators-designate to petition the U.S. Congress for statehood in early 1850. The senators—John C. Frémont and William Gwin—found themselves in the middle of a pitched debate between the North and the South over whether slavery should be legal in new states. The Compromise of 1850 allowed California to join the United States as a free state; in return, the South was offered the Fugitive Slave Act of 1850, which allowed slave owners to travel into free territory to capture runaway slaves. On October 18, 1850, news of California's statehood reached San Francisco, and the city exploded in celebration. Though miners professed not to care, they would soon use their "rights" as white citizens to dominate the gold rush in ways they could not have before.

As competition for gold heated up, miners sought any advantage to exclude others from access. In April 1850, the California legislature passed a law that required every miner not from the United States pay a tax of twenty dollars a month. Less formal and more brutal forms of discrimination exacted a higher toll on foreign miners. Though some Native Americans profited by acting as guides or laborers, the majority were run off their lands or literally hunted for sport. In the Bloody Island Massacre of 1850, hundreds of Pomo Indian men, women, and children were ruthlessly slaughtered by white forces led by Captain Nathaniel Lyon after two American Indians sought revenge for the murder of a relative. In the southern mines, all Spanish-speaking people—whether from Mexico, Chile, or California—were lumped together as "greasers" and attacked. Many of these people had staked out some of the earliest claims, but they were run off regardless.

Chinese miners, who worked together to develop some of the most prosperous claims, were stoned, their houses burned, and their long braids (called queues) cut off. The *San Francisco Bulletin* reported, "White men are not usually hanged for killing Chinamen." This kind of brutality and violence was generally tolerated by the authorities. Sadly, white Americans were determined to ensure they had first claim to "their" country's gold.

Though foreigners were routinely discriminated against, many still found ways to build a life in gold country. The Californios landowners largely succeeded in their legal actions to reclaim their land—though such actions didn't help the many landless Mexicans and Californios. The Chinese proved adept at smuggling their earnings past tax agents, and when it proved difficult to work in the goldfields, they often opened successful businesses, including laundries. (Unlike American men, Chinese men had no inhibitions about doing laundry.) The Native Americans fared worst: their population dwindled to less than thirty thousand by 1860.

Modern Robin Hood

One Mexican exacted his revenge on his oppressors by becoming a modern Robin Hood. A peaceful young man named Joaquin Murieta ventured to California seeking gold in 1848. Within months of his arrival, his brother was lynched by a mob that hated Mexicans, his wife was raped and murdered, and Murieta himself was publicly beaten for a crime he did not commit. Enraged, Murieta became a desperado who ambushed his enemies, stole gold from white miners, and gave his takings to those who had been wronged. Murieta soon became a legend, and nearly every crime in southern California was attributed to him. When he was finally hunted down and murdered in 1853, his head was bottled in alcohol and displayed around the state.

Gold rush legacy

The violence and lawlessness that came to characterize California during the gold rush can perhaps be explained by the difference between gold seekers' dreams and reality. Of the thousands and thousands of prospectors who ventured

into the goldfields, very few got rich. Most made a small strike, spent it, and then struggled to make a living in the diminishing claims. By 1858 the gold rush was over, and only those with enough money to invest in heavy machinery were still digging for gold. Miners still infected with gold fever moved on to other gold rushes: Nevada's Comstock Lode, the Fraser River in British Columbia, Pikes Peak in Colorado. But the world seemed to have learned a lesson from the gold rush of 1849, and none of these later gold rushes gained the worldwide attention that the first one did.

Many returned home from the goldfields defeated, but many more settled in the mining towns and made a new life in California. For some, the gold rush brought riches in forms other than gold nuggets: Levi Strauss (see box on p. 118) got his start as a dry-goods retailer (selling clothing and textiles) in San Francisco (and we still buy his Levi's jeans today); butcher Philip Danforth Armour supplied miners with meat and founded a meatpacking business in the East that

While the population of California was quite diverse during the gold rush period, most minorities faced severe discrimination. These Chinese immigrants are being harassed upon arrival in San Francisco. *(Courtesy of the Bancroft Library, University of California.)*

still operates; John M. Studebaker built wagons for miners and brought his earnings back to Indiana, where his company became renowned for making quality automobiles in the next century.

For many the gold rush brought opportunities they would not have had elsewhere. Young men without prospects in the East started new lives in California. African Americans found a society freer and more open than the one they had left behind. And the few women who ventured westward with the miners enjoyed far more independence than women in the East did.

California itself was utterly transformed by the gold rush, going from a quiet Mexican territory to a rapidly growing and thriving American state within just a few years. The United States was also changed by the gold rush and the admission of California as a state. Suddenly, the young nation stretched from the Atlantic to the Pacific. The vast area between Kansas and California was now traversed regularly by settlers and travelers, and many began to settle in the western territories that would become Arizona, New Mexico, Colorado, Nevada, and Wyoming. By 1869 a transcontinental railroad made transportation from one coast to the other relatively easy. The gold rush also created a romantic myth about California that persists into the present day: for many Americans, California is still the promised land.

For More Information

Books

Collins, James L. *Exploring the American West*. New York: Franklin Watts, 1989.

Groh, George W. *Gold Fever*. New York: William Morrow, 1966.

Jackson, Donald Dale. *Gold Dust*. Lincoln: University of Nebraska Press, 1982.

Lewis, Oscar. *Sutter's Fort: Gateway to the Gold Fields*. Englewood Cliffs, NJ: Prentice-Hall, 1966.

Marks, Paula Mitchell. *Precious Dust: The American Gold Rush Era: 1848–1900*. New York: William Morrow, 1994.

McCall, Edith. *Gold Rush Adventures*. Chicago: Children's Press, 1980.

McNeer, May. *The California Gold Rush.* New York: Random House, 1962.

Stein, R. Conrad. *The Story of the Gold at Sutter's Mill.* Chicago: Children's Press, 1981.

Web sites

"Gold Rush Chronicles." *California's Gold Discovery.* [Online] http://comspark.com/goldminer-mall/chronicles/index.html (accessed April 13, 2000).

Gold Fever! The Lure and Legacy of the California Gold Rush. [Online] http://www.museumca.org/goldrush/fever01.html (accessed April 13, 2000).

The Museum of the City of San Francisco. *1849 California Gold Rush.* http://www.sfmuseum.org/hist1/index0.1.html#gold (accessed April 13, 2000).

Sources

Altman, Linda Jacobs. *The California Gold Rush in American History.* Springfield, NJ: Enslow Publishers, 1997.

Holliday, J. S. *The World Rushed In: The California Gold Rush Experience, An Eyewitness Account of a Nation Heading West.* New York: Simon & Schuster, 1981.

Ketchum, Liza. *The Gold Rush.* Boston: Little, Brown, 1996.

Schanzer, Rosalyn. *Gold Fever! Tales from the California Gold Rush.* Washington, DC: National Geographic Society, 1999.

Vallejo, Guadalupe. "Ranch and Mission Days in Alta California." *Century Magazine* (December 1890).

Van Steenwyk, Elizabeth. *The California Gold Rush: West with the Forty-Niners.* New York: Franklin Watts, 1991.

White, Richard. *"It's Your Misfortune and None of My Own": A New History of the American West.* Norman: University of Oklahoma Press, 1991.

Winning the West:
Indian Wars after 1840

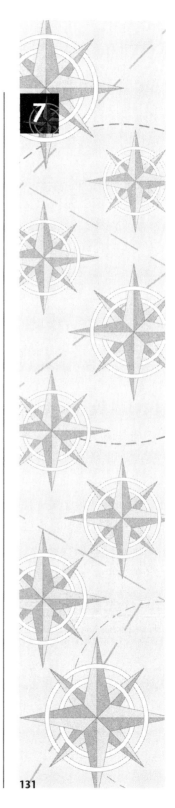

At the turn of the eighteenth century the territory east of the Mississippi River seemed like enough land for the growing U.S. population for generations to come. Early explorers had indicated that much of the land west of the Mississippi was either too arid or too mountainous to serve a nation of farmers. In fact, many maps depicted the area west of the Mississippi as the Great American Desert. But wars and the discovery of gold in the West soon led to a hunger for expansion. Settlers who had ventured into Texas (before the territory became a state) found themselves at odds with the Mexican governors of the territory. Eventually Americans joined the dispute, fighting a war with Mexico that earned the United States a vast territory, including present-day Texas, New Mexico, Arizona, Nevada, and California. (See Chapter 4 for more information about the Mexican-American War.)

The western lands acquired from Mexico in 1848 might well have remained relatively uninhabited and unvisited were it not for the California gold rush of 1849, which drew many thousands of gold seekers across the country to settle in California. Within a few years, the United States had added vast tracts of western land and a new state on the shores of the Pacific Ocean. Finally, an 1846 treaty with the British gave the Americans unimpeded control of the present-day states of Idaho, Oregon, and Washington. And, many Americans thought, why shouldn't they spread across the entire continent? Throughout the 1830s and 1840s there developed a national fervor for building the nation until it reached from coast to coast. This fervor was known as manifest destiny—the belief that it was God's intended plan for the Americans to control a vast empire stretching from the Atlantic to the Pacific. Manifest Destiny meant the end of what remained of the American Indians' traditional way of life.

In the years after 1840, many thousands of Americans moved out into the trans-Mississippi West. Those who made it as far as California and Oregon were rarely bothered by the Native Americans who lived in the region. But the miners, ranchers, and farmers who settled in the vast territory between the Mississippi and the Pacific faced strong resistance from the many Indian tribes that claimed this region as their own. In the Southwest, the Navajo and Apache raided mines and ranches and stopped wagon trains crossing their desert landscape. On the prairies, Sioux and Cheyenne warriors who had happily let wagon trains pass through took offense when whites began to claim the land and kill the buffalo that had sustained the Indian tribes for so long. The American settlers and soldiers who faced these tribes encountered resistance unheard of in the history of Indian removal (see Chapter 2). The difficulties of simply moving across the vast western landscape, combined with the ferocity of Indian tribes, made the final removal of the Indian threat a long and arduous process. It took until 1890 for the United States to finally conquer the people whose land it had so ruthlessly stolen.

Indians of the Southwest

The Indians of the American Southwest—the Pueblo, Zuni, Navajo, Apache, Hopi, Yavapai, Mojave, Yuma, Pima, and Papago tribes, among others—had already dealt with white conquerors for centuries when Americans began to encroach on their lands. An army of Spanish invaders had ventured north in search of gold in 1540, conquering a Zuni tribe with the help of guns—something never before seen by the Indians. Francisco Vásquez de Coronado (c. 1510–1554) and his men were not the first to search the Arizona and New Mexico deserts for gold, nor would they be the last. As the Spaniards colonized Mexico, they also extended their influence north into the Rio Grande Valley. Though the Pueblo tribes living in what is now New Mexico eventually came to terms with the Spanish and Mexican colonizers, the Apache and Navajo never accepted foreign rule and waged war against the Spanish and Mexican governments for nearly 150 years. Thus, when American traders and soldiers sought to extend their influence into the Southwest in the 1830s and 1840s, they faced tribes with a long history of resisting colonization.

At first the Navajo embraced the Americans, for the new arrivals had succeeded at what the tribes had tried to do for years: they had defeated the Mexicans. The Navajo assumed that the Americans would keep Mexicans from settling on their land and stealing their sheep. Moreover, the Americans and the Navajo shared a common enemy: the Apache. The Navajo soon found that they were badly mistaken, for the conquerors believed that first claim to the land went to white Christians, known now as New Mexicans. In the eyes of the whites, the vast rangelands the Navajo used to graze their sheep and horses were going to waste. The whites thought the land should be used more productively—and by them.

Navajo resistance

In the late 1840s, however, it appeared that whites and Navajo might still live peacefully together. The Navajo respected the power of the white forces and wanted to avoid hostilities, and the Americans saw no great need to drive these Indians from their desert lands. However, some tribe members resented white settlements on traditional Indian lands and showed their resentment by stealing horses and belongings from these settlements. Because the Navajo chiefs who had signed peace treaties were unable to control the thieves, whites felt that the treaties were being ignored and called for more protection from the U.S. Army. Beginning in

1851 they got what they asked for: the army began a long war against the Navajo.

Tensions between the army and the Navajo escalated quickly after the army constructed Fort Defiance in eastern Arizona in 1851, squarely in Navajo grazing territory and near religious shrines. When one Navajo turned his cattle and horses out onto the land, the fort's commander ordered sixty of the animals shot, and the Navajo stepped up their attacks on white settlements as a result. Emboldened by the lack of a strong army response, they attacked more and more frequently. On April 30, 1860, a force of one thousand warriors led by chiefs Manuelito and Barboncito attacked Fort Defiance directly, killing a number of soldiers before being driven from the fort. No longer able to overlook isolated Indian raids, after 1860 the army was determined to destroy the Navajo.

The man put in charge of the assault, Colonel Edward Canby, divided his army of New Mexican and Pueblo volunteers and Ute scouts and dispersed them across the landscape to hunt down and kill the Navajo. For months Canby's forces searched, wearing out their horses and nearly killing themselves with thirst. In all, they killed just thirty-four Navajo. The Navajo had proved that they were masters of the desert landscape, and the army needed a new strategy. Canby camped his tired army in the middle of the Navajo grazing lands, keeping the Indians from returning to care for their crops and livestock. By winter the Navajo were ready to make peace. In exchange for promises that Navajo raids would end and that thieves would be stopped, the Americans closed Fort Defiance and moved their base to Fort Fauntleroy. For months this treaty brought peace to the region. But the coming of a new commander ended that peace.

A line in the sand

Colonel James Henry Carleton was, in the words of historians Robert Utley and Wilcomb Washburn, "an imperious, flint-eyed martinet with rocklike fixity of purpose." His purpose was no less than the utter defeat of the Navajo people, and within a few years, he had achieved his goal. In June 1863, less than a year after he took command of army forces in the region, he declared that the Navajo had until July 20,

1863, to report to a forty-square-mile reservation in southern New Mexico known as Bosque Redondo. After that day, every Navajo not on the reservation would be considered an enemy and be hunted down ruthlessly. When the deadline passed without a single Navajo having entered the reservation, Carleton set out to keep his word.

At the time, twelve thousand Navajo lived in a region that stretched from central New Mexico to the western border of present-day Arizona, an area riddled with canyons and valleys that were as familiar to the Navajo as the backs of their hands. Yet Carleton masterminded a campaign designed to crush the Native Americans' will to resist. Carleton entrusted well-known scout and Indian fighter Kit Carson (1809–1868) to lead his campaign. According to Utley and Washburn, "For six months, in summer and winter, [Carson's force] marched ceaselessly, burning hogans [Navajo houses], killing Navahos where they could but always keeping them on the run." The soldiers burned crops, slaughtered sheep and horses, and destroyed villages. Eventually Carson trapped a huge number of Navajos in Canyon de Chelly, a steep-sided canyon in which the Navajo had traditionally taken refuge. They would find no refuge in January 1864, as the soldiers moved relentlessly up the canyon, capturing nearly six thousand Navajo in the process. The captives were marched southeast to Bosque Redondo, with many dying along the way. The Navajo resistance was broken; Carleton had kept his promise.

The Apache

The Apache were a small tribe, numbering about eight thousand people scattered across present-day Arizona and New Mexico. They were not skilled farmers, nor did they maintain vast herds of sheep like the Navajo. They built few lasting villages and lived in some of the most desolate areas of the American West. Yet they proved to be one of the most formidable tribes American forces ever faced. Skilled thieves, the Apache harassed white settlers and travelers from the moment the whites set foot in the West. Able warriors, the Apache were fearless on the attack and difficult to track. Warriors were known to travel seventy miles on foot in a single day, and it was believed that an Apache could virtually merge into his surroundings to avoid discovery. For nearly forty years, the Apache resisted American attempts to uproot them from their desert homes.

When Americans began settling in the former Mexican territories in the 1850s, they soon began to complain about the terrors visited upon them by the Apache. Moreover, the few roads, including the Gila Trail, that stretched across the desert passed directly through Apache territory and were frequent targets for attack. Military leaders decided that the Apache menace must end. The first major campaign against the Apache was led by Colonel James Carleton, the notorious Indian-hater who had broken the Navajo (see p. 134). Carleton showed the Mescalero Apache (as this band of the tribe was known) no mercy. He told his men, according to historian Don Nardo, that "the men are to be slain whenever and wherever they can be found. The women and children may be taken prisoner." Carleton eventually forced the Mescalero to surrender and moved them to the Bosque Redondo reservation in southern New Mexico.

The remaining Apache learned from the Mescalero's defeat and would not take on U.S. forces directly. Instead, separate bands of Apache conducted guerrilla warfare against the American forces, attacking small bands of isolated soldiers, killing settlers in distant locations, and generally making life miserable for Americans in the region. These bands of Apache tended to follow strong leaders, several of whom became famous for their skill in alternately terrorizing and evading their white enemies. The most noted of the Apache chiefs were Cochise and Geronimo (1829–1909).

Cochise

Cochise (c. 1812–1874) had once signed a treaty with Americans allowing the Overland Mail service to travel across Indian lands through what became known as Apache Pass. Cochise's tolerance ended in 1861 when a lieutenant at Fort Buchanan named George Bascom called Cochise in to answer to charges of kidnaping a settler's children and stealing his livestock. Cochise escaped from the prison he was thrown in, but Bascom held Cochise's family as hostages. Cochise began a series of raids on mail routes, capturing hostages whom he hoped to trade for his family members. When no trade was forthcoming, the Apache tortured and killed their hostages. Bascom retaliated, killing Cochise's adult nephews (though releasing his wife and children) and the war was on. For years thereafter Cochise led Apache warriors in an attempt to drive the white people from the Indians' land. For a time the Apache made travel between Santa Fe, New Mexico, and El Paso, Texas, nearly impossible.

In the mid-1860s American military leaders tried to make a treaty with Cochise and other prominent Apache chiefs, but the Native Americans wanted nothing to do with the reservations the white men offered. Raids continued into the 1870s, to such an extent that Arizona and New Mexico were deemed unfriendly places for whites to settle. Cochise took the largest share of the blame, even if he was not personally involved in many of the attacks. In the early 1870s, General George Crook received permission to chase the Apache into Mexican territory, where they had often hidden from U.S. forces. Tiring of a life on the run, Cochise surrendered to Crook after receiving promises that he and his people would be treated fairly. When it was clear that Crook planned to place the Apache on a reservation, however, Cochise escaped and continued fighting. Finally, in 1872, forces led by General Oliver O. Howard promised Cochise, now in his sixties, that the Apache would be moved onto land of Cochise's choosing. Cochise accepted—and died two years later, still waiting for the U.S. government to honor its promise. For the most part, Apache resistance ended, though Geronimo's small band kept up the fight into the 1880s (see box on p. 139).

Apache chief Cochise.
(Reproduced by permission of The Granger Collection, New York.)

Blood on the Plains

Well after California had attained statehood in 1850 and Oregon had been settled, and even after the present-day

Apache chief Geronimo fought against white settlement in the West until 1886. *(Reproduced by permission of UPI/Bettmann.)*

states of New Mexico and Arizona began to receive substantial numbers of white visitors, one area remained largely undeveloped. The Great Plains—which included the present-day states of Nebraska, Kansas, Oklahoma, North and South Dakota, Montana, Wyoming, and parts of Colorado and Idaho—was a land of dry, rolling prairies and harsh winters. It was crossed over by many but settled by very few. Up until the 1850s, it was populated almost entirely by Indian tribes such as the Sioux and Cheyenne, who had lived there for centuries, making their living from the land and from the buffalo that roamed it. These tribes were seminomadic, following the herds of buffalo on the horses that they had learned to ride so well. But as Americans discovered new deposits of gold in Colorado and Montana, and as settlers proved willing to commit themselves to farming and ranching in the area once known as the Great American Desert, the peaceful life of the Plains Indians changed. For thirty years, they fought to defend their way of life, but in the end they too were defeated.

The Plains Indians felt the pressure of white expansion as early as the 1700s, when Sioux tribes driven out of the East by white settlement eventually settled in the Great Plains. When the Oregon Trail began to see substantial travel in the 1840s, settlers crossed land controlled by the Sioux, Cheyenne, Arapaho, and Crow tribes but were rarely disturbed. The Plains Indians felt little threat from those who were just passing through, and an 1851 treaty helped secure the travelers' safe passage. In fact, the army felt so secure about the territory that they withdrew regiments from forts in Wyoming and Idaho. The easy relations between whites and Indians began to deteriorate in 1854, when a dispute over a wandering cow convinced an army officer that he needed to teach the Indians a lesson. The officer, John L. Grattan, led thirty men to the camp of the Brule Sioux to demand that they turn over the supposed cow thief; when they met with resistance, the troops opened fire, killing the Sioux chief and a number of other Indians. The Sioux warriors struck back, killing all but one soldier.

As with most Indian attacks—no matter how justified—this one was met by an overwhelming response. Colonel William S. Harney marched on a Sioux village near Blue Water Creek in Wyoming and launched an attack that left eighty-five Sioux dead and led to the capture of seventy prisoners. Many Indians, including a young warrior named Crazy Horse, now believed that there could be no peace with the whites. Events in Colorado soon confirmed their views.

The Sand Creek Massacre

Soon after gold was discovered near Pikes Peak in Colorado in 1858, American legislators created the Colorado Territory. In order to facilitate white settlement, the government tried to negotiate a treaty that would place the Cheyenne and Arapaho tribes on a small plot of land in southeastern Colorado. The tribes either rejected or ignored the treaty and continued to roam the prairies and the foothills of the Rocky Mountains. Finally, territorial governor John Evans encouraged white citizens "to kill and destroy, as enemies of the country, wherever they may be found, all ... Indians," according to Nardo. And he appointed a notorious Indian-hater, John M. Chivington, to lead the militia and drive the Indians out of Colorado.

In late November 1864, Chivington's force of seven hundred men neared the camp of Black Kettle, an Indian chief

Geronimo

By the mid-1870s, just one branch of the Apache tribe continued to resist white rule: the Chiricahua, led by Geronimo (1829–1909). Though they had been settled on the San Carlos reservation in eastern Arizona in the early 1870s, Geronimo and his followers left the reservation in 1874 when conditions there proved miserable. Well into the 1880s Geronimo led his warriors on frequent attacks on white settlements. Several times during these years Geronimo was captured, only to escape again.

By the early 1880s Geronimo had become a legend, his exploits widely reported in the eastern newspapers. Determined to catch and hold the elusive Indian, Brigadier General Nelson A. Miles (1839–1925) led a force of five thousand soldiers to capture Geronimo and his band of followers, which included about thirty-five warriors. It took them five months to trap Geronimo in Skeleton Canyon, Arizona, on September 3, 1886. Geronimo was moved to a reservation in Florida and later became something of a celebrity, appearing at the St. Louis World's Fair in 1904 and in President Theodore Roosevelt's inaugural parade in 1905. Already he had become a quaint reminder of the Wild West.

who had actually agreed to the terms of the treaty. Surprised that an army was approaching his camp, Black Kettle raised two flags: an American flag and a white flag of peace. But Chivington ordered his men to attack the camp, and they did so brutally. The five hundred Indians in the camp—mostly women and children—defended themselves as best they could, but the soldiers ripped through the camp. One member of Chivington's forces, quoted in Utley and Washburn's *Indian Wars,* remembered the battle: "They [the Indians] were scalped, their brains knocked out; the men used their knives, ripped open women, clubbed little children, knocked them in the head with their guns, beat their brains out, mutilated their bodies in every sense of the word." In all, two hundred Cheyenne were killed, and Chivington's men, clutching Indian scalps, rode into Denver boasting of their victory. The message to Indians was clear: they would receive no mercy from the white men. (Later congressional and military investigations into the Sand Creek Massacre decried the incident, but Chivington was never punished.)

The war escalates

Throughout the late 1860s, Indian attacks on white outposts and wagon trains increased—and so did white attacks on Indians. By the 1870s, Sioux, Cheyenne, Arapaho, Oglala, Tetons, Hunkpapas, and other tribes in Montana, Wyoming, and South Dakota believed that if they joined together they might be able to repel the white invaders. Savvy Indian chiefs such as Red Cloud (1822–1909), Crazy Horse (c. 1842–1877), and Sitting Bull (c. 1831–1890) began to school their warriors in more sophisticated methods of fighting. Rather than leaving battle strategies entirely up to the individual warriors, as was traditional, Indians began to orchestrate their actions. They sent small parties of decoys out to attract white forces into ambushes. They also instituted disciplined charges of warriors. Already fierce fighters, with these new methods the Native Americans became even more dangerous.

Yet all the gains in Native American strength were matched by changes in the U.S. Army. For years the army forces in the West had been a ragtag bunch of relatively undisciplined soldiers. But beginning in the late 1860s, a new kind of soldier and general took the field. Commanders such

as Philip Sheridan (1831–1888) and George Armstrong Custer (1839–1876) had learned a great deal during the recent Civil War (1861–65), and they commanded soldiers who had become hardened to the blood and trauma of battle.

Black Hills battles

U.S. soldiers and Indian warriors met in dozens of battles and skirmishes across the wide Plains region, with neither side gaining a decisive advantage. Eastern newspapers even mocked the American forces for their inability to capture the relatively small bands of Indians who were causing so much trouble. The final collision between the two forces came in the Black Hills of South Dakota. Sacred ground to many of the Plains tribes, the Black Hills had been protected by many treaties over the years. But General Custer led an expedition into the Black Hills in 1874 to support those who believed there might be gold in the region. When gold was found, tens of thousands of fortune seekers and settlers moved into this sacred territory. The Indians had no choice but to respond.

In the winter of 1875, thousands of Indians from a number of tribes began to gather on the banks of the Little Bighorn River in southern Montana. There they planned their strategy for the defense of the Black Hills, ignoring or never learning of the army's threat to hunt down and kill any Indians found off the reservations. For its part, the U.S. Army planned a major attack on the tribes for the spring of 1876. Three contingents led by Generals George Crook, John Gibbon, and Alfred Terry and George Custer would converge on the Indian camp and put an end to the threat.

The Battle of Little Bighorn

As the U.S. troops approached the Indian camp at Little Bighorn, Custer grew overeager. Always impetuous, Custer ignored his orders to wait for the remaining forces and marched his 675 men forward, hoping for a moment of glory if his men alone defeated the Indians. Dividing his soldiers into three groups, Custer and his commanders attacked on the morning of June 25, 1876. The first group to meet the Indians, 280 men led by Major Marcus Reno, faced attack from many hundreds of Sitting Bull's Hunkpapas band of Sioux. Though they fought valiantly at first, the troops were soon overwhelmed and were forced to retreat. Digging into a nearby hill, Reno's men were reinforced by 125 troops led by Captain Frederick Benteen. As they fought they became aware that more and more Indians were heading off in another direction. Something was drawing the Indian attack away.

That something was an attack on the other side of the camp, this time by a band of 267 men led by Custer himself. Three groups of Indians responded to this attack—Cheyenne under Lame White Man, Hunkpapas under Gall, and Oglala under Crazy Horse—and they soon surrounded Custer's men on all sides. According to Nardo, "Thousands of Indians took part in the bloody assault, during which most of the soldiers dismounted and separated into small groups. Here, Crazy Horse's new battlefield strategy worked brilliantly. The Indians attacked in well-coordinated waves, overwhelming the

troops. In the space of about forty-five minutes, Custer and all of his men were killed."

Aware that even more troops were on their way, the remainder of the Indians abandoned their village and prepared to fight again. When the remaining soldiers came upon the battlefield, they discovered Custer's dead army. At the center of the group of bodies was a core of white officers who had surrounded General Custer and fought to the bitter end. This final standoff, which ended in the death of all the soldiers, has become famous as Custer's Last Stand. The remaining troops thus bore witness to the carnage of the greatest Indian victory ever over white forces. It was the high point for the Indian alliance, and it called forth a devastating response.

The end

Following the Battle of Little Bighorn, the Indians separated into smaller units and were hunted down by Generals

An American Indian lies dead on the battlefield of Wounded Knee, the last major battle of the Indian wars. *(Reproduced by permission of the Corbis Corporation [Bellevue].)*

Terry and Crook. Sitting Bull and his band escaped into Canada; Crazy Horse was hounded by soldiers until 1877, when he finally surrendered and led his people onto a reservation. Other tribes were slowly rounded up and led to reservations as well. Their spirit had been broken by the white soldiers' never-ending pursuit and the continuing stream of white settlers who claimed Indian land as their own. By the 1880s there seemed to be no land left to them but the reservations.

Indians on the reservations lived lives of poverty and squalor. The lands given to them were generally inferior: farms failed, there was not enough land to support extensive grazing of livestock, and the herds of buffalo had nearly been exterminated. Indians lived off the supplies given to them by the Indian agencies that managed the reservations.

On the Plains reservations, a religious movement known as the Ghost Dance predicted that magical powers would allow the Indians to gain back all their land from the whites. Determined to squash even this limited resistance, the army isolated a band of 350 Sioux, hoping to arrest suspected Ghost Dance leaders. Gathered by Wounded Knee Creek in South Dakota, the Miniconjou Sioux were preparing to give up their weapons on December 29, 1890, when a weapon was accidentally discharged. Suspecting that they were being attacked, the soldiers opened fire on the camp. "The clash at Wounded Knee was a horror of murderous fighting," wrote Utley and Washburn. "Soldiers and Indians faced each other at close range and shot, stabbed, and clubbed one another." The army finally opened fire with its Hotchkiss guns, which fired fifty bullets a minute. Soon the Indians were routed. Approximately three hundred of the Sioux had fallen in one of the worst massacres in the long history of hostility between whites and Indians; only twenty-five soliders lost their lives. It was the last major battle of the Indian wars. Within a year and without much more bloodshed, the remaining Indians had moved to the reservations and the Indian wars were over.

Conclusion

For the better part of the nineteenth century, Indians and whites faced one another over a divide of misunderstand-

ing and mutual hatred. Believing in the superiority of their way of life, white Americans laid claim to any Indian lands that suited them and, when faced with Indian resistance, attacked with scarcely a trace of remorse. Most whites thought that it was inevitable and necessary that Indians be removed; they justified their actions by their belief that it was their destiny to populate and domesticate the continent. This led the whites to break treaties and promises and slaughter innocent people. Though we now find these actions morally questionable if not downright reprehensible, they allowed America to quickly attain and control the vast territory now known as the United States.

For their part, the Indians were ill equipped to deal with the endless assault of the white man. Long accustomed to intertribal warfare among peoples of roughly equal strength, most Indians never suspected that the whites could bring so many soldiers into battle. Attacks that might have

Chiricahua Apache prisoners, including Geronimo (first row, second from right), outside the railroad car transporting them to a reservation. Whites believed that it was their destiny to populate and domesticate the continent, and they used this belief to justify their treatment of Native Americans. *(Courtesy of the National Archives and Records Administration.)*

scared off an enemy tribe only brought down the wrath of large white armies. With radically different ways of living on and understanding the land, Indians could not grasp the white man's desire to possess land and mistakenly entered into treaties they had no intention of obeying. In the end, these factors, combined with the Indians' smaller population, inferior technology and weaponry, and lack of resistance to white diseases, meant that Indians were doomed to be victims in the onslaught of westward expansion.

For More Information

Books

Drinnon, Richard. *Facing West: The Metaphysics of Indian-Hating and Empire Building.* Minneapolis, MN: University of Minnesota Press, 1980.

Hook, Jason. *American Indian Warrior Chiefs: Tecumseh, Crazy Horse, Chief Joseph, Geronimo.* New York: Firebird Books, 1990.

Lawson, Don. *The United States in the Indian Wars.* New York: Abelard-Schuman, 1975.

Morris, Richard B. *The Indian Wars.* Minneapolis, MN: Lerner Publications, 1985.

Nardo, Don. *The Indian Wars.* San Diego, CA: Lucent Books, 1991.

Prucha, Francis Paul. *The Sword of the Republic: The United States Army on the Frontier, 1783–1846.* New York: Macmillan, 1969.

Rogin, Michael Paul. *Fathers and Children: Andrew Jackson and the Subjugation of the American Indian.* New York: Vintage Books, 1976.

Utley, Robert M. *Frontier Regulars: The United States Army and the Indian, 1866–1890.* New York: Macmillan, 1973.

Utley, Robert M. *Frontiersmen in Blue: The United States Army and the Indian, 1848–1865.* New York: Macmillan, 1967.

Utley, Robert M., and Wilcomb E. Washburn. *Indian Wars.* Boston: Houghton Mifflin, 1987.

Waldman, Carl. *Atlas of the North American Indian.* New York: Facts On File, 1985.

Web sites

Documents on American Indian Wars. [Online] http://www.hillsdale.edu/academics/history/Documents/War/19Ind.htm (accessed April 13, 2000).

National Indian Wars Association. [Online] http://www.indianwars.org/contents1.htm (accessed April 13, 2000).

Schultz, Stanley K. "Which Old West and Whose?" *American History 102.* [Online] http://us.history.wisc.edu/hist102/lectures/lecture03.html (accessed April 13, 2000).

Sources

Axelrod, Alan. *Chronicle of the Indian Wars: From Colonial Times to Wounded Knee*. New York: Prentice Hall, 1993.

Brown, Dee. *Bury My Heart at Wounded Knee*. New York: Holt, Rinehart & Winston, 1970.

Morris, Richard B. *The Indian Wars*. Minneapolis, MN: Lerner Publications, 1985.

Nardo, Don. *The Indian Wars*. San Diego, CA: Lucent Books, 1991.

Utley, Robert M., and Wilcomb E. Washburn. *Indian Wars*. Boston: Houghton Mifflin, 1987.

Westward Expansion and Indian Culture

8

It has long been argued that the process of western expansion helped form the American character. Such arguments hold that white Americans were hardened and strengthened as they moved westward across the continent, carving communities out of the wilderness. But it must be remembered that westward expansion had equally momentous consequences for the peoples who already occupied the land. These people, known as Indians, Native Americans, or American Indians, experienced the westward expansion of European and American settlers as a four-hundred-year assault on their culture, their land, and their very lives. In this assault, Europeans and Americans used war, enslavement, and disease to wrest control of the continent from its native inhabitants.

The common culture of trade

The end result of the centuries-long conflict between whites and Indians was the devastation of traditional Native American culture. But in the middle of the eighteenth century the population of whites and Native Americans was fairly evenly balanced. The tribes of the eastern seaboard had largely been defeated and driven westward by the expanding British colonies. However, there were a number of tribes in the trans-Appalachian region (the area between the Appalachian Mountains and the Mississippi River) and in the present-day Midwest that had established stable relationships with the French traders and soldiers who occupied the area. The French, at least, did not wish to conquer the Indians; they wanted to trade with them. For years French fur traders plied the woods and plains of America, trading knives, blankets, tools, and kettles for the Indians' beaver furs. Later, English and colonial American traders also began trading with Native American tribes. Years of contact with European and colonial American fur traders reshaped Indian culture. By the eighteenth century, Native Americans had a great deal of experience in dealing with white people, and they had incorporated white goods, guns, and horses into their cultural life.

Trade between whites and Native Americans encouraged other forms of cultural interaction. Many white traders married Indian women and were embraced by the women's tribes as family members. Whites and Indians traveled together on exploring and hunting missions, learning each other's language and way of life. But for all that they shared, there still existed a great cultural divide between the two peoples. In trade, for example, white traders sought to obtain as many furs as possible for the least amount of goods, and they were willing to bribe or trick Native Americans into an unfair exchange. Such traders believed the purpose of economic exchange was to protect their own interests and maximize their profit. The Native Americans had very different views. For them, exchanging goods was a way of cementing a friendship or an alliance. Friends, it was assumed, would look out for each other. Since white traders had so much more than they did, Native Americans often wondered why their friends did not give away more goods.

French-Canadian trader Pierre-Antoine Tabeau, quoted in *The Native Americans,* expressed his surprise at the Indians' view of trade:

> The Arikaras [a tribe in North Dakota] look upon the whites as beneficent spirits who ought, since they can, to supply all its needs and it looks upon the merchandise, brought to

the village, as if destined for it and belonging to it…. [I]t is a principle with them that he who has divides with him who has not. "You are foolish," said one of the most intelligent seriously to me. "Why do you wish to make all this powder and these balls since you do not hunt? Of what use are all these knives to you? Is not one enough with which to cut the meat? It is only your wicked heart that prevents you from giving them to us."

The fur trade helped maintain a general peace among the French, Native American, English, and colonial American peoples who occupied the North American continent, but that peace was only secure as long as no one of the powers felt strong enough to force its will on the others. For the first half of the eighteenth century, the relatively even balance of power kept a fragile peace, punctuated by occasional bloodshed as one group or another felt it necessary to claim new land or defend old. In the 1750s, however, a series of conflicts shattered this delicate balance and set the stage for white-Native American relations to change dramatically.

The end of Native American power

The French and Indian War (1754–63) was the first signal to the Native American tribes that the balance of power was shifting. The French, who had long been allied with the major midwestern Indian tribes, were defeated by the British and in 1763 gave the victorious British and Spanish vast tracts of American land, including most of the Ohio River Valley and the region that later became known as the Louisiana Territory (the area between the Mississippi River and the Rocky Mountains). Native American tribes were shocked at the French defeat and appalled that the French believed they could give away land to which they held no real claim. The Shawnee, according to Richard White in *The Native Americans,* demanded to know "by what right the French could pretend" to give away this land. The Native American tribes despaired that they now must deal solely with the English and their aggressive colonists, neither of whom had ever treated the Indians with cordiality or respect.

The next major setback for Indian peoples came with the American victory in the Revolutionary War (1776–83). Forced to choose sides in the conflict between the British and the colonists, the most powerful Native American tribes sided with the British. Cherokee, Iroquois, and Algonquian warriors all fought alongside the British, and to great effect. Had the war been decided based on the battles supported by Indian warriors in the west, the British would surely have won. But the British were defeated in the east, and with their forces stretched thin, they conceded defeat and granted full control of the contested lands to the Americans in 1783.

No longer impeded by British rule, which had limited westward expansion of the colonies, the Americans began moving out into the fertile trans-Appalachian region. Any Indian resistance to white encroachment was interpreted as hostility, and Americans became determined to drive the "uncivilized" and "hostile" Indians from the land. American settlers in the region were defended by a variety of military expeditions. Native American tribes (with the continued backing of the British, who hoped to maintain the fur trade in the Midwest) succeeded at mounting a credible resistance. But a third war, the War of 1812 (1812 14), finally drove the British from the U.S. interior and smashed any hopes the Native Americans had of unifying to resist the white advance. After 1814, Native American tribes were left to defend themselves against a powerful nation increasingly determined to control the land from the Atlantic to the Pacific Ocean. Each tribe adjusted to the march of westward expansion in its own way, but all eventually succumbed to the drive of the Americans to conquer the land. The following pages look at the way three tribes—the Iroquois, the Sioux, and the Navajo—dealt with the pressures of westward expansion.

The Iroquois

Occupying most of present-day western New York, the five tribes that made up the Iroquois—the Mohawk, Oneida, Onondaga, Cayuga, and Seneca—had long ago established a peace among themselves that made them one of the most influential Indian nations in the East. Legend has it that the five tribes so loved war that they could not give it up. Indeed, warfare was the primary means by which men gained status and moved into positions of leadership. But the tribes had recognized that war between them was too destructive. Over a period of years (perhaps as early as the fifteenth century), wise leaders from the five tribes realized the benefits of joining the tribes into the Iroquois Confederacy. The five tribes agreed to fight one another no more and to direct their warriors' energies toward the many enemies that lived to the north, east, and south.

The first Europeans to confront the Iroquois found them a powerful force indeed. Both French and Dutch traders had to contend with the Iroquois, who controlled the fur-rich country south of Lake Ontario. The Iroquois resisted any alliances with the French, who had often sided with enemy tribes, and instead negotiated treaties with the Dutch and later the English. The whites benefited from the furs the Iroquois trapped in their streams and woods, while the Iroquois enjoyed and then came to depend on the goods they acquired from the white men, including cloth, metal goods, farm tools, axes, firearms, and ammunition.

The Iroquois had not abandoned war when they began to interact with Europeans. Even as white diseases decimated their population in the seventeenth century, the Iroquois stepped up their warfare on other Native American peoples, taking many hostages to rebuild their tribe. Armed with European weapons, the Iroquois were more formidable than ever. By the middle of the seventeenth century, the Iroquois had defeated the Huron, the Wyandot, and the Erie and emerged as the most powerful tribe in the region. Only the French—with their superior numbers, weaponry, and organization—were strong enough to defeat the Iroquois, and they did so late in the century. Realizing that they could not stand against the French forces, the Iroquois leaders attempted instead to maintain neutrality, playing the French off the English, who had taken over control of the colony of New York from the Dutch in 1664. This neutrality endured through most of the eighteenth century, allowing the Iroquois to rebuild their communities and their population.

Fighting in the white man's wars

The neutrality of the Iroquois lasted only until the French and Indian War (1754–63). During this conflict between the French and the British over control of the American interior, the tribes of the Iroquois Confederacy were divided. Eastern tribes like the Mohawk supported the British, while

Iroquois leader Joseph Brant. The Iroquois established a peace among themselves that made them one of the most influential Indian nations in the East. *(Reproduced by permission of the Bettmann Archive.)*

the western Seneca fought alongside the French. When the English won the war, they occupied the French forts and were generally less accommodating to the Indians than the French had been. Resenting English dominance, the Seneca rebelled in 1763 and 1764 and were severely reprimanded, losing claim to much of their land.

With the coming of the Revolutionary War in 1776, the Iroquois were again forced to take sides. Again, some warriors allied themselves with the British while others fought with the colonists. In some battles, Iroquois fought against Iroquois. The British and their Iroquois allies so terrorized colonists in western New York that in 1779 General George Washington (1732–1799) ordered Major General John Sullivan to lead his forces into Iroquois country. Sullivan's campaign wiped out nearly every major Iroquois village and laid waste to crops and farmland. The Iroquois, led by warriors Joseph Brant, Kayengkwaahton (also known as "Old Smoke"), and Cornplanter, fought back fiercely and reclaimed many of their tribal lands. However, when British forces surrendered in 1783, they ceded to the Americans all of the Iroquois land.

In negotiating the treaties that followed the end of the war, the hostile Iroquois tribes at first insisted that they had not been defeated, but the superior strength of the U.S. Army persuaded them to back down. Signed under protest, these treaties banned the Iroquois from much of western New York and Pennsylvania and from all of Ohio. Many of the Iroquois retreated into Canada to live on the Grand River Reservation (also known as the Six Nations Reserve) on the north shore of Lake Erie. Their leader, Joseph Brant (1742–1807), recognized that the reservation could not provide enough land to support the men's major activity—hunting—and urged men to take up the agricultural work that had traditionally been left to women. Though Brant's plan to turn the tribe into farmers eventually worked, for years after the war the loss of morale on the reservation bred drunkenness, violence, and family instability.

The Navajo

The Navajo peoples of present-day New Mexico and Arizona were affected very differently by westward expansion than the eastern tribes were. In fact, the advance of the Americans was not the first time they had dealt with a foreign nation encroaching upon their tribal lands—Spain was the first to colonize the desert Southwest, beginning in the late sixteenth century. Because of their geographical location and culture, the Navajo resisted the depopulation faced by other more closely spaced tribes and did not experience cultural annihilation. At the end of the twentieth century, the Navajo had the largest population of all native peoples and were thriving in the land claimed long ago by their ancestors.

Archaeologists believe that the Navajo moved into the Southwest from far northwestern Canada and Alaska more than five hundred years ago. Unlike other native peoples, the Navajo did not live in large tribes but rather in small bands that claimed membership in larger clans. Though they recognized similarities with their fellow Navajo, they did not follow a single leader. Perhaps because of this, the Navajo proved adept at borrowing cultural customs from the Native American tribes that already lived in the Southwest. From the Hopi and the Pueblo they learned how to raise crops in the harsh desert landscape and how to construct dwellings. When they came into contact with Spaniards in the seventeenth century, they quickly acquired horses, sheep, and cattle. The Navajo depended upon sheepherding as the basis of their economic life into the twentieth century. The Navajo traced their family connections through their mothers, and women, men, and children all gathered food and tended sheep. Navajo religious beliefs focused on *hozho,* a complex term that combines balance, beauty, harmony, and goodness.

The Navajo's loose organization and their ability to thrive in the harshest desert landscapes left them relatively untouched by Spanish colonization. While the large Pueblo communities along the Rio Grande became bases for Spanish missionaries and soldiers, the Navajo remained secluded in the more remote parts of northwestern New Mexico and northeastern Arizona. When the Pueblo revolted against the Spanish in 1680 and were later attacked, many of them moved into Navajo lands. The Navajo adopted many Pueblo customs, including their agricultural methods—especially the raising of corn.

The American menace

The Navajo's contact with American colonists and soldiers began after the United States acquired present-day New Mexico and Arizona from Mexico at the end of the Mexican-American War (1846–48); this contact brought conflicts and hardship the tribe had never before endured. At the first meeting between American officials and Navajo representatives, a false accusation of horse theft ended in violence when white soldiers shot and killed seven Navajo. The survivors of the meeting spread word of the invaders' hostility. Navajo leader Manuelito, the son-in-law of one of the dead, vowed to avenge his relative's death and spoke for those who wished to resist white settlement. Other Navajo leaders wanted peace, but no Navajo leader could speak for the whole tribe. Even when Navajo tribes made treaties with the Americans, other Navajo felt no obligation to comply.

In the early 1850s, the U.S. Army announced its intention to dominate Navajo lands with the construction of Fort Defiance in the middle of traditional Navajo grazing lands. Minor skirmishes between Indians and soldiers heightened tensions, and in April 1860 Manuelito and another Navajo leader named Barboncito led one thousand warriors in a major attack on Fort Defiance. Though they nearly succeeded in taking the fort, the Indians were eventually driven back. This and other attacks convinced American leaders that they must drive the Navajo from their lands, and Colonel James Carleton took charge of this task in the fall of 1862.

Carleton selected legendary trapper and explorer Kit Carson (1809–1868) to lead the roundup of the Navajo and announced that every Indian who did not surrender and relocate to the reservation he had selected would be killed. But few Navajo surrendered to Carleton's bullying. Most disappeared into the hills and mountains, eluding capture for half a year and wearing out many American soldiers in the

Canyon de Chelly, where thousands of Navajo retreated after a nearly successful attack on Fort Defiance. Kit Carson tracked down nearly six thousand Navajo in Canyon de Chelly and forced them to surrender. (© CORBIS. Reproduced by permission.)

process. Eventually, however, thousands of the Navajo gathered in a network of canyons and rivers in an area of present-day Arizona known as Canyon de Chelly. Carson's men tracked the Navajo there and relentlessly burned their fields, poisoned their wells, and killed many, including women and children. These actions forced the surrender of nearly six thousand Navajo early in 1864. The Navajo were marched to Fort Defiance, and though many escaped during the journey and hid in the isolated canyons of northern Arizona, many more learned that they would be sent to a reservation far from their home.

The Long Walk

On March 6, 1864, the soldiers at Fort Defiance gathered twenty-five hundred Navajo refugees and started them on a long trek past the borders of their homeland to the reservation of Bosque Redondo near Fort Sumner in east-central

New Mexico. This was the Long Walk, a part of Navajo history still remembered with great sorrow and bitterness. Many people died or were killed on that journey. The army had not supplied enough food, but the Indians were forced to continue marching despite hunger and cold. Those who were too sick, weak, or old to keep up were killed or left behind.

By the time the group reached the Rio Grande, the spring melt had flooded the river, making it very treacherous to cross. The Indians tried to get across any way they could, but many were swept away and drowned. At the end of their ordeal they arrived at the wasteland that was to be their new home. The Bosque Redondo reservation, which Carleton had promised would be a garden of Eden, was nothing but a desolate, barren flatland with no means of support for the Indians. Carleton had not provided enough food or supplies for the inhabitants of the remote reservation, nor had he considered how difficult it would be for the exiles to become self-supporting as farmers on such a worthless piece of land.

A people united

For all the horror of life on the reservation, the Navajo's time at Bosque Redondo had one positive effect: it helped them realize their unity as a tribe. Slowly, the Navajo came to recognize that their interests would be best served if they acted in unison. By 1868, after four miserable and devastating years at Bosque Redondo, a group led by Barboncito negotiated with the Americans for their release. Offered land alongside the other tribes living in Indian Territory (in present-day Oklahoma), Barboncito replied, according to *The Navajos* author Peter Iverson, "I hope to God you will not ask me to go to any other country than my own." Eventually, the Navajo signed a treaty that granted them 3.5 million acres of their original land in northeastern Arizona and northwestern New Mexico. The U.S. government also agreed to supply the Navajo with fifteen thousand sheep and goats and five hundred cattle. In return, the Navajo agreed to end their hostilities and to allow the construction of railroads through their land. In the early morning hours on June 18, 1868, more than seven thousand Navajo began their six-week journey home from exile.

Returned to the land they loved, the Navajo rebounded from their subjection like no other Indian tribe in America. Their population grew, and their sheep herds grew even faster. By the late 1870s the Navajo petitioned for an expansion of their reservation. The land granted to them was the first of many additions, and by the twentieth century the lands controlled by the Navajo had nearly tripled from their original reservation. Sheepherding continued to be a major element of Navajo life, but with increased contact with white Americans in the twentieth century, the Navajo also began to profit from the sale of traditionally designed rugs, jewelry, and pottery. In the late twentieth century a significant proportion of the Navajo still spoke their native language and followed traditional cultural customs. Living in a desert land that whites did not covet, this Indian tribe managed to survive westward expansion intact.

The Plains Indians

Their land was known on the white man's maps as the Great American Desert. Stretching from the Mississippi River on the east to the foot of the Rocky Mountains on the west, and from the Canadian border all the way south to Texas, the land roamed by the Plains Indians was a vast prairie, dry in the summer, windblown and cold in the winter. It was a land of waving grasses and millions of buffalo, antelope, and prairie dogs. Long after tribes in the rest of the country had been either exterminated or forced onto reservations, the inhabitants of the Plains lived independent of the white man's laws. The Sioux (the largest of the Plains tribes, containing many smaller clans), Crow, Cheyenne, Pawnee, Comanche, and many others spoke different dialects and had different cultural customs, but they shared common cultural traits. They hunted for buffalo; were often nomadic, traveling to where the hunting was good; and preferred war to life on the reservation. These tribes clung to their ways even in the face of an unprecedented onslaught of white attacks against the native peoples.

Prior to the arrival of Europeans in the Americas, Plains tribes had engaged in small-scale agriculture and had hunted on foot—a difficult task when hunting thousand-pound buffalo. These Native Americans lived in tepees (or tipis), conical structures that consisted of long poles joined together at the peak and wrapped in buffalo hides. They moved their tepees by means of travois (pronounced truh-VOY), a simple vehicle consisting of a net or blanket supported by two long poles, which were often pulled by their dogs. Their limited mobility changed dramatically after 1680, when various Native Americans came into possession of horses brought into the country by the Spanish.

The horse transformed Plains culture, allowing tribes to move long distances across the prairies and, most important, allowing them to rely on buffalo for the majority of their food supply. Warriors embraced the horse as a fighting companion, as revealed in this comment by Crow chief Plenty Coups, quoted in *500 Nations:*

> My horse fights with me and fasts with me, because if he is to carry me in battle he must know my heart and I must know his or we shall never become brothers. I have been told that the white man, who is almost a god, and yet a great fool, does not believe that the horse has a spirit. This cannot be true. I have many times seen my horse's soul in his eyes.

Plains culture changed again in the late seventeenth and eighteenth centuries, when eastern tribes fleeing the expansion of the British colonies began to move into the trans-Mississippi region. The increased competition for hunting grounds and for buffalo led to warfare between the tribes, and over time the Plains Indians became skilled warriors, often attacking from their swiftly moving horses. The Sioux tribes were especially known for their skills as warriors. The most populous of the Sioux peoples, the Dakotas, may have numbered as high as twenty-five thousand members. They were an athletic tribe, with high cheekbones and prominent noses. They wore bright war paint when going to battle and were known for their lavish headdresses adorned with feathers, which commemorated their feats of daring. For years, popular illustrations of Indians always pictured a Dakota Sioux; it was this tribe that was depicted on the old Indian-head penny and nickel.

The white invasion

When whites first began to move across the Plains in the 1830s, Plains Indians noted their passage with interest but no great concern. After all, these small bands of travelers

An engraving of buffalo hunting on horseback. The Plains Indians had many uses for the buffalo; they used various parts for food, clothing, tools, and shelter. *(Courtesy of the Library of Congress.)*

were just passing through, not disturbing Indian hunting grounds or staking claim to Native American land. As the traffic increased in the 1840s and 1850s, carrying travelers to gold claims and fertile land in the Far West, the white presence became a problem. As Alvin M. Josephy Jr. explains in *500 Nations:* "Although the Americans made no critical demands on the tribes for cessions of Great Plains territory, their increasing traffic drove away game, destroyed wild-food

Using the Buffalo

The Plains Indians depended on the buffalo not only for food but also for a variety of other uses. The hides of buffalo calves provided swaddling for newborn babies, while the thick hides of adult buffalo were sewn together to make the coverings for the giant tepees the Indians used for shelter. Hides were also used to make clothing, moccasins, bags, and other items. Buffalo bones were used to make tools such as scrapers, knives, and cooking utensils; rib bones were used as runners for sleds. Even buffalo dung was used, for fires.

Buffalo products also had less pragmatic uses. Skulls, horns, and decorated hides were used in ceremonies and for ornamentation. Other parts of the animal were used to make rattles and drums, dolls and toys, and shields.

Many stories about the American West have turned out to be myths or exaggerations, but this one is true: the Indians used every last bit of the buffalo that they killed.

gathering grounds, polluted water sources, and spread measles, whooping cough, and other dread sicknesses among the Indians. Then in 1858 and 1859, gold discoveries on the South Platte River at the foot of Colorado's Rockies started a stampede of whites across the buffalo-hunting grounds of the Cheyenne, Arapaho, Sioux, Kiowa, and Comanche Indians."

The effects of this encroachment cannot be overemphasized. Disease nearly exterminated some tribes. The Mandan tribe saw its population decrease from thirty-five hundred to less than two hundred after a smallpox epidemic. Richard White, writing in *The Native Americans,* described the last moments of Mandan chief Four Bears': "The whites, whom, he said, 'I always considered as Brothers [have] turned out to be my Worst Enemies.' He did not fear death, but it was too much 'to die with my face rotten that even the Wolves will shrink in horror at seeing Me.'" In the late 1850s and early 1860s, army troops determined to protect settlers and travelers tried to herd various Native American tribes onto reservations or toward Indian Territory in present-day Oklahoma—ignoring previous treaties that granted the Indians free access to the land in exchange for permitting white passage through the country.

In the early 1860s Indian leaders were divided over whether they should make peace with the white invaders or oppose them. When the primary proponent of peace, Black Kettle, and his people were ruthlessly slaughtered in the Sand Creek Massacre of 1864 (see Chapter 7), those who wanted to make war had even more reason to do so. Following the end of the Civil War (1861–65), the Indians had no choice but to fight, for top U.S. military leaders had set their sights on removing the Indian "threat" from the southern Plains.

Though the military scored victories against the Kiowa, Comanche, Cheyenne, and Arapaho, perhaps the most damage to Plains Indian life was inflicted in the early 1870s by buffalo hunters. According to Josephy, "In 1871, an eastern tannery had developed a method to produce superior leather from buffalo hides.... The price of buffalo hides had shot up, and almost overnight the southern plains had filled with hide hunters, killing buffalo by the hundreds of thousands. It was an obscene period. Between 1872 and 1874, the hunters ... slaughtered almost four million of the great beasts...." By the mid-1880s the buffalo population had been reduced from some thirty million to fewer than one thousand. "A bond of spiritual understanding between Native Americans and the buffalo, going back thousands of years, had been ripped apart," according to Josephy. Deprived of their primary source of food, many Native Americans had no choice but to go onto the reservations and accept government rations. The Indians of the southern Plains had been defeated—but the northern tribes remained, and they were unifying for a showdown with white forces.

War on the northern Plains

The contest for the northern Plains began, as in the south, following the massacre of Black Kettle's people in 1864. Sioux, Cheyenne, and Arapaho, determined to avenge the murders, terrorized white settlers and travelers along the Platte River, a main byway on the Oregon Trail (see Chapter 5). They set fire to ranches, burned whole towns, and ripped down miles of telegraph wire, making communication and travel across the prairies tremendously difficult. Army troops led by General John Pope (1822–1892) attempted to defeat these tribes in battle, but Pope could never find enough Indians or achieve a decisive military victory. In fact, Lakota warriors led by Red Cloud (1822–1909) proved so successful at interrupting movement along the Bozeman Trail through Wyoming and Montana that the army decided to evacuate its forts in that part of the country. In the late 1860s, it seemed as if the northern Plains tribes might successfully defend their land.

Lakota warriors led by Red Cloud made travel on the Bozeman Trail through Wyoming and Montana almost impossible. *(Courtesy of the National Archives and Records Administration.)*

A variety of treaties between the government and Indians barred white settlement on Native American lands and pledged that Indians would not disturb white travelers. But such treaties almost always failed: Native American tribes did not always accept the authority of treaty signers to bargain away their rights, and whites simply ignored the prohibitions on settlement. White settlers believed that American lands should be theirs for the taking, and they expected that the U.S. Army would support them if they ran into trouble. Most often they were right. The Treaty of 1868 guaranteed the Sioux the western half of present-day South Dakota, but when prospectors found gold in the Black Hills area—sacred ground to the Native Americans—settlers and miners poured into the region, protected by the might of the U.S. Army. In 1874 the army constructed a fort in the heart of the Black Hills, starting the confrontation that would end the Indian wars in the United States and devastate the northern Plains tribes.

With war in the wind, representatives of the U.S. government met with twenty thousand Sioux in 1875 to settle claims to the land. Tribal leaders railed against the government for its treachery. According to Josephy, Lower Yanktonai chief Wanigi Ska (White Ghost) told the white men:

> You have driven away our game and our means of livelihood out of the country, until now we have nothing left that is valuable except the hills that you ask us to give up.... The earth is full of minerals of all kinds, and on the earth the ground is covered with forests of heavy pine, and when we give these up to the Great Father we know that we give up the last thing that is valuable either to us or to the white people.

Hunkpapa Sioux leader Sitting Bull (c. 1831–1890) was more succinct: "We want no white men here. The Black Hills belong to me. If the whites try to take them, I will

Hunkpapa leader Sitting Bull warned American leaders that Native Americans would stand firm for their right to live in the Black Hills of South Dakota. *(Reproduced by permission of The Bettmann Archive.)*

fight." Negotiations broke down, and General Philip Sheridan simply ordered all the Sioux to report to their assigned reservations. No Native Americans obeyed Sheridan's order, and the war started.

For a time, the Plains tribes thwarted the army. Eastern newspapers mocked the efforts of the experienced white soldiers to capture a band of "savages." In late June 1876

The capture of Crazy Horse, drawn by Native American artist Amos Bad Heart Bull.
(Reproduced by permission of The Granger Collection, New York.)

some eight hundred troops led by General George Custer (1839–1876) attacked a Sioux encampment on the Little Bighorn River in Montana. Not suspecting the strength of the Sioux forces, Custer and his men were wiped out. It was the Sioux's greatest victory and perhaps the greatest victory the American Indians ever had. (See Chapter 7.)

Following the Battle of Little Bighorn the Indians separated into smaller groups but they were hunted down by Generals Alfred Terry and George Crook. Sitting Bull and his band escaped into Canada; Oglala Sioux chief Crazy Horse (c. 1842–1877) was hounded by soldiers until 1877, when he finally surrendered and led his people onto a reservation; he died a few months later. Other tribes were slowly sent to reservations as well. Their spirit had been broken by the white soldiers' never-ending pursuit and the continuing stream of white settlers who claimed Indian land as their own.

Forced onto reservations

Like other defeated Indian tribes across the nation, the Plains tribes were confined to reservations. Overcrowded and with poor land, the reservations were a miserable place to live for people accustomed to roaming freely across a great expanse of territory. In the 1880s many Indians on the northern reservations began to follow a new religion called the Ghost Dance, which promised to drive the white man from their land and return them to power. The communal dances and ceremonies scared the whites guarding the reservations, as did the presence of famous chiefs like Sitting Bull. For his alleged support of the Ghost Dance, Sitting Bull was arrested and murdered by the police in 1890.

Also in 1890, a group of Indians led by Miniconjou Lakota chief Big Foot hoped to escape the desperation on their reservation and join the Oglala reservation of Red Cloud. At the time, the U.S. Army was pursuing the arrest of Ghost Dance leaders. The U.S. Army's 7th Cavalry rounded up the weary travelers in late December 1890 and led them to Wounded Knee Creek. On the morning of December 29, the Indians were ordered to give up their weapons. When a gun was accidently discharged, the soldiers started a bloodbath like no other in Indian history. Surrounding the virtually defenseless Indians, the soldiers opened fire with their battery of Hotchkiss guns (primitive machine guns), killing hundreds of men, women, and children. Even those who tried to crawl away from the battle were shot and left to die in the snow. Oglala holy man Black Elk, quoted in *500 Nations*, said of Wounded Knee: "A people's dream died there. It was a beautiful dream.... The nation's hoop is broken and scattered. There is no center any longer, and the sacred tree is dead."

Conclusion

The massacre at Wounded Knee marked the end of meaningful Native American resistance in America. Of the hundreds of tribes and millions of Indians who had roamed the continent before the white men arrived, only thousands remained, herded onto reservations not of their choosing and forced to rebuild their cultures from the scraps that their white conquerors left them. America's native populations were the clear losers in the nation's westward expansion. The majority of Indians in America remain on their reservations. Many tribes experienced a resurgence in the late twentieth century, thanks to their opening of casinos and, in the Pacific Northwest, their success in protecting tribal fishing rights. But the fact that they remain isolated on reservations stands as a constant reminder of their defeat.

For More Information

Books

Ballantine, Betty, and Ian Ballantine, eds. *The Native Americans: An Illustrated History.* Atlanta, GA: Turner Publishing, 1993.

Fichter, George S. *How the Plains Indians Lived.* New York: David McKay, 1980.

Graymont, Barbara. *The Iroquois.* New York: Chelsea House, 1988.

Iverson, Peter. *The Navajos.* New York: Chelsea House, 1990.

Josephy, Alvin M., Jr. *500 Nations: An Illustrated History of North American Indians.* New York: Knopf, 1994.

Snow, Dean R. *The Iroquois.* Oxford: Blackwell, 1994.

Underhill, Ruth M. *The Navajos.* Norman: University of Oklahoma Press, 1956, 1989.

White, Jon Manchip. *Everyday Life of the North American Indians.* New York: Indian Head Books, 1979.

Web sites

Georgia College and State University. *Ina Dillard Russel Library Special Collections: Native American Resources.* [Online] http://library.gcsu.edu/~sc/resna.html (accessed April 6, 2000).

The Navajo Central.org Website. [Online] http://navajocentral.org/home page.htm#language (accessed April 6, 2000).

"Pueblo Indians and Revolts." *New Mexico History.* [Online] http://www.rr.gmcs.k12.nm.us/dNMhist.htm (accessed April 6, 2000).

Sacred Beings: Buffalo and Deer, Sustainers of Life. [Online] http://www.cmcc.muse.digital.ca/membrs/fph/rodeo/rodeo63e.html (accessed April 14, 2000).

Sheppard, Donald E. "Native American Conquest: Early American History for Teens." *New Perspectives on the West.* [Online] http://www.pbs.org/weta/thewest/wpages/wpgs000/w010_001.htm (accessed April 14, 2000).

Wounded Knee. [Online] http://msnbc.com/onair/msnbc/TimeandAgain/archive/wknee/?cp1=1 (accessed April 6, 2000).

The Wild West

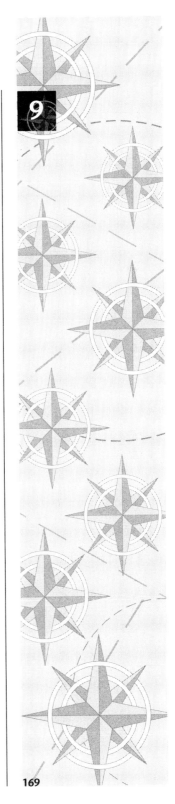

The 150-year-long conquest of the American West was one of the most colorful eras of American history. From the moment that small bands of settlers set out across the Appalachian Mountains in the 1750s to the closing of the frontier around 1890, Americans sprawled and fought their way across thick forests, vast prairies, and soaring mountains, claiming as their own lands once inhabited by Native American tribes, or by Spanish or Mexican settlers, if they were inhabited at all. Fierce battles with Native Americans, protracted wars with the British and the Mexicans, and the sheer difficulty of taming the wilderness shaped the expanding American nation. But when people today think of the "Wild West," they do not think of land claims, wars, or early conflicts with Native Americans in the forested East. Instead they think of gunfights in dusty western towns, masked outlaws holding up trains, cowboys on horses, and stalwart lawmen protecting law-abiding citizens. The Wild West has been romanticized, but it is based in fact. In this chapter, we will explore the real-life Wild West.

Guns and lawlessness

Guns and lawlessness were a part of the frontier experience from the very beginnings of westward expansion. From the moment that settlers began moving across the Appalachians and into the Ohio Valley, the gun was an essential tool. The settler's rifle was a guarantee that he would never go hungry—and a means of fending off the Native Americans.

Yet the real Wild West experience is defined not by battles with Indians or claiming land, but by the competition among settlers for access to and control of the riches of the western landscape. Beginning with the California gold rush of 1849 and 1850 and continuing through the cattle booms of the 1860s and 1870s, a number of booms drew people westward in search of easy money and excitement. Many of the people who participated in these booms were law-abiding citizens and hard workers who valued integrity and honesty. But among them were also cheaters and outlaws, degenerates who escaped old problems in the East and created new ones in the West. Horse thieves, claim jumpers, cattle rustlers, and cold-blooded killers, these western outlaws were despised by upright citizens of the West, and they contributed to the most colorful conflicts in the long history of western expansion. These conflicts occurred in mining camps and cattle towns, on wagon trains and in saloons, and among outlaws and lawmen.

The gold rush

One of the first and the most dramatic of the western booms occurred in 1849 and 1850 in the Sacramento Valley of California. In January 1848 James Marshall discovered gold at Sutter's Mill on the American River. Word of his discovery brought prospectors first from throughout the territory (soon to become a state) and then from throughout the world. Camps sprang up overnight near areas where gold was discovered to accommodate miners who had staked claims. Enterprising merchants set up tent stores and charged the men exorbitant rates for food and supplies. Food was scarce, and those selling it often ended up with more money than the prospectors.

These mining camps were among the first American boomtowns. Because they formed so quickly and haphazardly, many of them did not have any established law enforcement. Mining camps were often filled with outcasts from civilized society who took whatever they wanted and were curbed only by the threat of revenge. Miners struggled to maintain their claims. Many carried weapons, and it was not unusual for a thief to be killed for "jumping" another man's claim. Violence was common in the mining camps, with fighting on streets and in the barrooms. Contributing to the bawdy atmosphere of early mining towns were the prostitutes who entertained the men for money.

Even the "established" town of San Francisco was known for its violence. As a port city, San Francisco saw a rapid influx of immigrants from around the world. Some countries, such as Nicaragua and Australia, dispatched convicts to California just to clear their prisons. One group from Sydney, Australia, formed a gang known as the Sydney Ducks.

View of Deadwood, South Dakota in 1876. The boomtowns of the West attracted all types of people in search of a fresh start, easy money, and excitement. *(Reproduced by permission of Archive Photos, Inc.)*

Violent career criminals, the Sydney Ducks conducted a reign of terror on the city streets that culminated in a particularly brutal robbery of a retail store in 1851. The San Francisco business community was finally prompted to take action, forming a citizens' committee, called the Committee of Vigilance, to try the offenders and to drive other criminals from the city. Vigilante justice (justice dealt out by citizens who take the law into their own hands) became the primary form of justice in gold rush country, as in much of the West. (See Chapter 6 for more about the gold rush.)

The cowboy frontier

The classic hero of the American West is the cowboy. Historian Walter P. Webb described this heroic figure in *The Great Plains:* "There is something romantic about him. He lives on horseback as do the Bedouins [an Arabian desert tribe]; he fights on horseback, as did the knights of chivalry; he goes armed with a strange new weapon which he uses ambidextrously [with both hands] and precisely; he swears like a trooper, drinks like a fish, wears clothes like an actor, and fights like a devil. He is gracious to ladies, reserved toward strangers, generous to his friends and brutal to his enemies. He is a cowboy, a typical Westerner." This is the cowboy of legend, who populated dime novels and romantic films.

For all the glory and romance attached to the image of the cowboy, his job was as low and gritty as can be imagined: he herded cattle. The first cattle to arrive in the New World came to Mexico with the Spanish in the 1500s, and under Spanish rule cattle raising became an important way of life for many Mexicans. In 1821, after Mexico won its independence from Spain, it offered free land to Americans if they would settle in Texas and become Mexican citizens. Writes Albert Marrin in *Cowboys, Indians, and Gunfighters: The Story of the Cattle Kingdom:* "Americans poured into Texas by the thousands. They were a mixed lot, people from all walks of life. Some were shady characters anxious to keep a step ahead of the law. If one day the sheriff was looking for someone, the next he might find G.T.T. (GONE TO TEXAS) chalked on the front door." Taking advantage of Mexican laws granting 4,438 acres of land to cattle ranchers, the new

Mining camps and boomtowns had difficulty enforcing laws. Justice was often dealt out by citizens who took the law into their own hands. *(Courtesy of the National Archives and Records Administration.)*

Texans (who were mainly from the South) brought their herds of cattle along with them.

The British breed of cattle introduced by the Texans soon mingled with the wild Spanish cattle that roamed Texas to form a breed known as the Texas longhorn. Writes Marrin: "The longhorn was an amazing beast. Lanky and swaybacked, with big ears and long legs, it varied in color from black to red, yellow, white, and spotted. It weighed from eight hundred pounds for youngsters to twice that for ten-year-olds.... [Its horns] measured three to five feet from tip to tip." The longhorn was extremely durable, capable of protecting itself on the open range, finding grass in the most hostile climates, and locating water where men could find none. Cowboys claimed that the longhorn was also the meanest animal on earth, and stories abounded of longhorn bulls rampaging and killing men. One story told of a longhorn that attacked and nearly defeated a squad of American soldiers.

Before the Civil War (1861–65), many Texans owned cattle but few got rich from it. After the Civil War, however, the situation changed. Rising beef prices in the Northeast created a demand for cheap meat, a demand that had not existed before the war. Railroads built during the war made it possible to ship beef from the Midwest. Suddenly cattle that were worth four dollars in Texas were worth forty dollars if they could be brought to northern markets. The only problem facing cattle ranchers was how to get the cattle to market. Their answer was the cattle drive, in which cowboys herded thousands of cattle north to railheads (points on a railroad where traffic stops) in Kansas. From there the cattle could be shipped east and money could pour into the pockets of Texans. And so the cattle boom began.

The cattle boom

In 1866, ranchers across Texas hired tough young men to ride out onto the range (open, unfenced grasslands) and bring all the cattle marked with the rancher's brand back to the ranch to ready them for the drive north. By spring some 260,000 cattle in dozens of herds began to move northward toward Sedalia, Missouri, which was at that time the western terminus of the railroad. Driving a herd of cattle across prairies and rivers was difficult, but the cowboys' troubles increased as they entered Indian Territory (present-day Oklahoma). Indians demanded ten cents a head for the cattle to cross their land and threatened to frighten the cattle into stampedes if the fee was not paid. Even worse, farmers in Missouri and Kansas, fearful of a disease carried by Texas cows, stopped whole herds at the border and threatened to shoot any cattle or cowboys who crossed.

(Kansas farmers later passed laws forbidding Texas cattle from entering the settled portions of the state.) Finally, armed Kansas ruffians known as jayhawkers demanded payment from the cowboys and were ready to kill man and beast to get it. In the end the first cattle drive was a bust: of the 260,000 cattle that started out, only 35,000 cattle reached the railheads.

Though many ranchers saw their dreams of riches die on the cattle drive of 1866, one man saw an opportuni-

Cowboys are often portrayed as heroes of the Wild West, and though their lives are often romanticized, herding cattle was a difficult, dangerous, and dirty job. *(Courtesy of the National Archives and Records Administration.)*

The Cattle Drive

Working as a cowboy on a cattle drive was one of the most difficult, dusty, and dangerous jobs a man could have. Leading the drive was the trail boss, whose job it was to plan the route, find water, locate campsites, and lead his cattle north. The trail boss also helped select a work crew, hiring one cowboy for every 250 to 300 head of cattle; this meant that a typical herd of 2,000 to 3,000 longhorns would require eight to twelve cowboys. These cowboys looked after the animals on the long journey north, riding alongside and behind the herd, keeping them moving and preventing them from breaking into a dangerous stampede. One of the most important members of the crew was the cook, often known as the Old Lady. Usually an older cowboy, the Old Lady woke before the rest to prepare meals and stayed up late to clean up after dinner. A good cook kept the cowboys happy with good "grub," tended wounds, and took care of other domestic duties. He was the second-highest-paid member of the crew behind the trail boss. The lowest-paid member of the crew was the wrangler, a younger cowboy who looked after the herd of workhorses.

A herd on the trail moved about ten miles a day. Leading the way was the trail boss and the Old Lady with his wagon. To the side rode most of the cowboys, who kept wandering cattle from separating from the rest of the herd. Bringing up the rear, and eating the dust of several thousand shuffling cattle, were the drag men. Cowboys joked that the drag was where a cowboy learned to curse.

ty. Joseph M. McCoy, an Illinois livestock dealer, realized he could not solve the problems posed by Indians or the weather, but he thought he could help the cowboys avoid crossing settled territory and provide them with a secure railhead: a town from which they could ship their cattle to the East. Taking advantage of a Kansas law that allowed Texas cattle into the unsettled western half of the state and of the westward-reaching arm of the Kansas Pacific Railroad being built across the state, McCoy located a shabby little collection of buildings known as Abilene and declared that this would be the destination of the next cattle drive. McCoy set about creating a town, hauling in lumber and building an office, a hotel, a barn, and massive holding pens. McCoy even sent men south to promote the new town. Though the cattle drive of 1867 was small, all thirty-five thousand cattle

Cowboys faced many dangers on the trail. Depending on the spring rains, the rivers they had to cross could be raging torrents or pits of quicksand. The cattle had to be coaxed into the water, and if they were spooked the entire herd might panic and turn back, or drown themselves swimming in circles. Prairie fires were another danger, for they sometimes swept so quickly across the plains that neither cattle nor cowboys could get out of their path. Tornadoes, hailstorms, and lightning strikes also posed dangers, but the worst threat of all was the stampede. Skittish animals, longhorns sometimes bolted when alarmed, and the panic of one could set the whole herd into flight. If all three thousand cattle charged at once, there was little that could stop them, so cowboys were constantly on the lookout to prevent a stampede from starting. The worst stampedes occurred at night, when a lightning strike or a sharp noise might alarm the herd and send them charging into the blackness. The cowboys had to wake quickly, mount their horses, and charge after the herd, unable to see any perils that might lie in their way. Stampedes killed cows and men by the dozens on the trails north.

At the end of the five-hundred- to eight-hundred-mile journey lay civilization—or so the small cow towns of western Kansas seemed to men who had seen only one another for weeks on end. The cattle were sold, the men were paid, and the cowboys could explore the pleasures of a cow town.

brought to Abilene were sold, and word spread that the market was open once more.

Abilene boomed in the coming years. In 1868, about 75,000 cattle arrived in the town after following the Chisholm Trail northward from Texas. In 1869 the number grew to 350,000, and in 1871, 700,000 cattle passed through Abilene on their way to market. Soon other towns began to bustle with the growing cattle boom. According to Laurence I. Seidman, author of *Once in the Saddle: The Cowboy's Frontier, 1866–1896,* the Salina, Kansas, *County Journal* reported on the impact of Texas cattle on the area: "The entire country east, west, and south of Salina down to the Arkansas River and Wichita is now filled with Texas cattle. There are not only 'cattle on a thousand hills' but a thousand cattle on one hill and every hill. The bottoms are overflowing with them and the water courses with this great article of traffic. Perhaps not less than 200,000 head are in the State, 60,000 of which are within a day's ride of Salina, and the cry is 'still they come!'"

The wild life of a cattle town

The cattle boom changed Abilene considerably. Soon the town was crowded with traders, railroad men, and ranchers, all flush with the cash that flowed through the cattle trade like water. And it was crowded with cowboys, eager for some fun after weeks of grueling labor on the trail. In his autobiography, *We Pointed Them North,* cowboy Teddy Blue Abbott explained what he and other cowboys were after:

> "I was looking for fun, and that I believe was the case with nine-tenths of them. They were wild and reckless, it is true, and to understand that you would have to know the kind of life they led. They were not like those city fellows with a saloon on every corner. They didn't get to drink very often. They were out there for months on end, on the trail or living in some cow camp, eating bad food, sleeping in wet clothes, going without everything that means life to a man ... and when they hit the bright lights of some little cow town, they just went wild."

Fresh off the trail, cowboys galloped through town on their horses, riding up on the wooden sidewalks and shooting holes in water barrels just for kicks. Some spent their newly claimed money on fancy clothes and a new hat; others went to church. But most tied off their horses and made their way to the center of any cow town: the saloon. Bellying up to the long bar that stretched the length of the room, a cowboy could enjoy a whiskey or—if it was a small town—a variation of rotgut, raw alcohol diluted with water and flavored with whatever the bartender had on hand. Some cowboys gambled at one of the many gaming tables scattered throughout the room; the less experienced hands might well be taken in by a cardsharp (a cheater who took advantage of unskilled players). Poker was the cowboys' favorite game, though others played keno, chuck-a-luck, or faro. Other cowboys sought out dance partners in nearby dance halls. After weeks on the trail, the cowboys thought even the homeliest dance-hall women looked good; for seventy-five cents a man could dance with a woman for ten minutes. For a little more money, he might take her down the hall to one of the tiny, private bedrooms for more intimate attention.

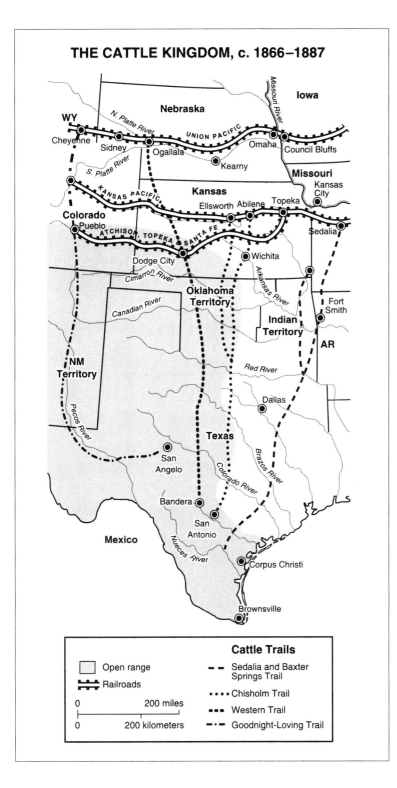

THE CATTLE KINGDOM, c. 1866–1887

Iowa

Nebraska

Missouri River

N. Platte River

WY

Cheyenne

Sidney

UNION PACIFIC

Ogallala

Omaha

Council Bluffs

S. Platte River

Kearny

Missouri

Kansas Pacific

Kansas

Kansas City

Colorado

Ellsworth Abilene

Topeka

Pueblo

ATCHISON, TOPEKA & SANTA FE

Sedalia

Dodge City

Wichita

Cimarron River

Oklahoma Territory

Arkansas River

Canadian River

Indian Territory

Fort Smith

AR

NM Territory

Red River

Pecos River

Dallas

Texas

San Angelo

Colorado River

Brazos River

Bandera

San Antonio

Mexico

Nueces River

Corpus Christi

Brownsville

Cattle Trails

☐ Open range

▦ Railroads

0   200 miles

0   200 kilometers

– – Sedalia and Baxter Springs Trail

•••• Chisholm Trail

••• Western Trail

–•– Goodnight-Loving Trail

Map of the Cattle Kingdom, showing the major cattle trails. *(Reproduced by permission of The Gale Group.)*

Dancing Cowboys

The Best of the American Cowboy quotes Abilene's founder, Joseph McCoy, describing the uproarious behavior of cowboys in a dance hall:

> Few more wild, reckless scenes … can be seen on the civilized earth than a dance-house in full blast in one of the many frontier towns. To say they dance wildly … is putting it mild. The cowboy enters the dance with a peculiar zest, not stopping to [remove] his sombrero, spurs, or pistols, but just as he dismounts from his cow-pony so he goes into the dance. A more odd, not to say comical, sight is not often seen than a dancing cowboy; with the front of his sombrero lifted at an angle of fully forty-five degrees; his huge spurs jingling at every step or motion; his revolvers flapping up and down like a retreating sheep's tail; his eyes lit up with excitement and liquor, he plunges in and "hoes it down" at a terrible rate, in the most approved yet awkward country style; often swinging his "partner" clear off the floor for an entire circle, then "balance all" with an occasional demoniacal yell. After dancing furiously, the entire "set" is called to "waltz to the bar," where the boy is required to treat his partner, and, of course, himself also, which he does not hesitate to do time and again.

The boom in Abilene brought settlers into the region, which meant that the quarantine line for Texas cattle also moved westward. By 1871 Abilene was forced to give up the cattle trade, and other towns farther west took up its joys and its burdens. Newton, Kansas, served the cattle trade for just one year; Ellsworth, Kansas, welcomed cows to town from 1871 to 1875, as did Wichita from 1872 to 1876. Dodge City, Kansas, however, holds the record for the longest-lasting cow town, for it served the cattle trade between 1877 and 1885. Between 1866 and 1885 some eight million longhorns traveled the trails north to Kansas from ranches across Texas and throughout the Great Plains. "In just one generation," writes Marrin, "the cattle kingdom spread from Texas to Oklahoma, Kansas, Nebraska, the Dakotas, Montana, Wyoming, Nevada, Utah, Colorado, Arizona, and New Mexico. At its height, this cattle kingdom covered an area of 130 million acres. It changed a nation's eating habits. Never before, in the entire span of human history, were so many people able to have meat on a regular basis."

After 1885 a number of factors led to the end of the cowboy era. The increased settlement of Kansas finally led to the closing of the cattle towns, and expanding railroad lines meant that ranchers could usually find closer places to drive their cattle, if they had to drive them at all. Huge blizzards that struck the Plains in 1886 and 1887 killed off cattle by the thousands, proving that cattle couldn't just be left to fend for themselves. Finally, farmers claimed increasing amounts of western land, and ranchers were forced to purchase and fence land for their cattle. Men who were once cowboys now became farmhands, but the legend of the cowboy lives on still in the novels, films, and television shows that celebrate those tough and fiercely independent men.

Cowboys and killers

Cattle towns, like mining towns and railroad camps across the West, were rough places, filled with men tough enough to endure the difficult life they had chosen, or desperate enough to make a new life in the Wild West. Though it is clearly an exaggeration to say that the West was filled with tough guys and desperadoes, it certainly claimed a larger proportion of hard and colorful characters than had ever been seen in American history. The tough guys of the West—gunfighters, bank and train robbers, cattle rustlers, and marshals and lawmen—have become legendary giants, and their exploits fill many books. The following sketches offer just a glimpse of those characters and incidents that made the West wild.

Wes Hardin

Perhaps the most brutal and prolific killer in the history of the West was Wes Hardin (1853–1895). Born John Wesley Hardin in Texas, he was a teenager when the South was defeated in the Civil War. Hardin took the loss hard and vowed that he would carry out his revenge on any Northerner who crossed his path. His career as a killer began at age fifteen when Hardin killed an ex-slave with whom he had argued. Believing that the Union soldiers who came to arrest him would not treat him fairly, Hardin ambushed and killed the three men. He then took off for the West, where he learned to gamble and further honed his skills as a killer. Joining a cattle drive in 1871, Hardin killed seven men while on the trail. Not yet twenty, he had become one of the most feared gunmen in Texas.

Though Hardin tried to settle down with a wife on a farm, his killing of two lawmen and a gambler led to his capture and imprisonment in Gonzales, Texas. Hardin soon escaped, holed up with relatives, and took part in an obscure family feud that lasted for some years. But Wes Hardin had advanced to the top of the list of most-wanted criminals in Texas and could have no peace in that state, so he changed his name and headed to Florida. Tracked down by Texas Rangers, Hardin was captured and sentenced to twenty-five years in prison. Serving time in the prison in Huntsville, Texas, Hardin studied theology and law. Upon his release in 1895, he went to El Paso to practice law but soon found that he preferred gambling and drinking. He was sitting in a saloon on the night of August 19, 1895, when gunman John Selman walked through the door and shot Hardin through the back of the head. The murderous Hardin had killed forty men in his lifetime and was one of the least romanticized of the western outlaws.

The fistfighting marshal

By June 1870 the cattle center of Abilene was badly in need of a marshal who could bring some semblance of order to a town plagued by hundreds of brawling cowboys. It found such a marshal in Tom "Bear River" Smith, a former New York policeman who had made a name for himself breaking up a riot in Bear River, Wyoming. Marrin describes him as a "solid, muscular man with blue-gray eyes and a soft voice [who] didn't smoke, drink, gamble, or use foul language." Smith wore guns but preferred not to use them. Instead, he confronted lawbreakers with two weapons they were not used to: his fists.

"Smith's first act," writes Marrin, "was to post signs in the saloons and gambling houses: ALL FIREARMS ARE EXPECTED TO BE DEPOSITED WITH THE PROPRIETOR." This rule didn't sit well with ruffians who were used to wearing their guns wherever they went. One such cowboy named Big Hank came up to Smith and asked, "Are you the man who thinks he's going to run this town?" Smith stared him down and demanded that he hand over his guns. When Big Hank refused, Smith flattened him with a hard right to the jaw, took his guns, and ordered him out of town. "Big Hank meekly obeyed," relates Marrin, "never again to set foot in Abilene. He had been totally humiliated." Southerners, it seemed, believed that fighting with one's fists was ungentlemanly. "Being punched in the face, knocked into the dirt, and disarmed was the worst indignity a cowboy could suffer. Smith had used a 'secret weapon' cowboys did not understand. And that in turn added to his reputation as a lawman."

Tom "Bear River" Smith went on enforcing the law in his newfangled way throughout the summer, and he succeeded in ridding the town of gunfighting. But his fists were no defense against the ax a disgruntled farmer used to chop off Smith's head when Smith came to arrest him one night in November 1870. Smith's tombstone calls him "a fearless hero of frontier days who in cowboy chaos established the supremacy of law."

The Fence Cutter's War

For years Texas ranchers had allowed their cattle to roam the open range, sending cowboys out to sort the cattle by brands when it came time for the spring roundup. This system worked well in a territory where there simply wasn't enough wood or rocks to build fences and where public lands were free for use. In the late 1870s, however, forward-thinking ranchers began using a new invention—barbed wire—to enclose lands, reserve precious water sources for their cattle, and cut down on the number of cowboys they needed to hire. Little did these ranchers know that they would soon spark a war between those who had the money to fence and those who did not.

Putting up fence was a rich man's game. It required land and money to buy the fencing. According to *The Book of the American West* contributor Wayne Gard, the Frying Pan Ranch spent some thirty-nine thousand dollars erecting a four-wire fence around a pasture of 250,000 acres in 1882. But what troubled the non-fencing cattlemen most was that the fencers were enclosing public water sources and keeping others from grazing cattle on public land. By 1883, when a drought made good grazing land scarce, small ranchers and homesteaders began to pressure lawmakers to ban the fencing of public lands. When they received no government assistance, they banded together in small groups with names like Owls, Javelinas, or Blue Devils and, under the cover of night, began to tear down the offending fences. "In Tom Green County," writes Gard, "night workers cut nineteen miles of fence on the ranch of L. B. Harris. The Fort Worth *Gazette* reported that they piled a carload of Harris' wire on a stack of cedar posts and lighted a $6,000 fire." Other ranchers received similar treatment. The Fence Cutter's War was on.

In 1883 fence cutting was reported in half the counties in Texas. Many fence cutters left ominous notes promising that fencers would meet an early end if they kept on enclosing land. Fencers replied in kind, posting signs that fence cutters risked their lives if they touched another fence. Though there was no loss of life in the Fence Cutter's War, the effects were dramatic. Newspapers estimated that losses from the war totaled twenty million dollars, and settlers moved away from areas where the hostilities were fiercest. Finally, in 1884 the state legislature passed laws forbidding the fencing of government lands and established fines for those involved in fence cutting. Fencing soon became the norm, in Texas and elsewhere. The fence cutting wars were at an end.

The end of the Wild West

When the West was wild, it was wild indeed. Gunfighters disrupted growing towns with their seemingly random violence, and armed bandits sometimes made travel difficult and costly. Lawmen—some former criminals themselves—attempted to keep the peace but sometimes did so with violence of their own. Violence was a regular part of life in the West, which had few laws or authorities. But this violent, unrestrained period of western history did not last very long. Prior to the Civil War, violence had never been perceived as an epidemic. After the war, however, the cowboy era brought hundreds of young, aggressive men into the frontier, where they clashed with the thousands of settlers who began pouring out into the western territories. Conscientious, solid citizens were trying to civilize the West, and they found the lawlessness of cowboys and other western characters a real threat. For example, the Cheyenne, Wyoming, *Daily Leader* declared, "Morally, as a class, cowboys are foulmouthed, blasphemous, drunken, lecherous, utterly corrupt. Usually harmless on the plains when sober, they are dreaded in towns, for then liquor has an ascendancy over them." The Wild West, which thrived between roughly 1866 and 1890, seemed so wild because the rudeness and violence of the frontier clashed with the sensibilities of an encroaching civilization.

By 1890 the forces of order had largely triumphed in the West. Towns across Kansas barred the cattle trade and rid themselves of the wild cowboys. No longer able to live the free life of the cowboy, many men returned to farms and to the civilizing influence of families. Railroads stretched across the continent, bringing settlers to once-remote areas. With the settlers came churches, civic organizations, family life, and, perhaps most important, law and order. In 1893 historian Frederick Jackson Turner (1861–1932) noted something that was probably obvious to many in the West: the frontier was closed, and the West was no longer wild.

For More Information

Books

Dary, David. *Seeking Pleasure in the Old West.* New York: Knopf, 1995.

Dykstra, Robert R. *The Cattle Towns.* New York: Knopf, 1968.

Glass, Andrew. *Bad Guys: True Stories of Legendary Gunslingers, Sidewinders, Fourflushers, Drygulchers, Bushwhackers, Freebooters, and Downright Bad Guys and Gals of the Wild West.* New York: Doubleday, 1998.

Granfield, Linda. *Cowboy: An Album.* New York: Ticknor & Fields, 1994.

Horan, James D. *The Authentic Wild West: The Outlaws.* New York: Crown, 1977.

Landau, Elaine. *Cowboys.* New York: Franklin Watts, 1990.

Rainey, Buck. *Western Gunfighters in Fact and on Film.* Jefferson, NC: McFarland, 1998.

Rosa, Joseph G. *The Taming of the West: Age of the Gunfighter, Men and Weapons on the Frontier, 1840–1900.* New York: Smithmark, 1993.

Savage, Jeff. *Cowboys and Cow Towns of the Wild West.* Springfield, NJ: Enslow, 1995.

Steckmesser, Kent Ladd. *The Western Hero in History and Legend.* Norman: University of Oklahoma Press, 1997.

Web sites

The American West: A Celebration of the Human Spirit. [Online] http://www.americanwest.com (accessed April 14, 2000).

The Great American Gold Rush. [Online] http://pwa.acusd.edu/~jross/goldrush.html (accessed April 14, 2000).

Internet Resources about Black Cowboys and Pioneers. [Online] http://danenent.wicip.org/lms/themes/cowboys.html (accessed April 14, 2000).

Ranch-Hands and Rangers: The Cowboy West. [Online] http://www.library.csi.cuny.edu/westweb/pages/cowboy.html (accessed April 14, 2000).

Sources

Abbott, E. C. "Teddy Blue," and Helena Huntington Smith. *We Pointed Them North: Recollections of a Cowpuncher.* Norman: University of Oklahoma Press, 1955.

Adams, Ramon F., ed. *The Best of the American Cowboy.* Norman: University of Oklahoma Press, 1957.

Altman, Linda Jacobs. *The California Gold Rush in American History.* Springfield, NJ: Enslow Publishers, 1997.

The Book of the American West. New York: Julian Messner, 1963.

Forbis, William H. *The Cowboys.* New York: Time-Life, 1973.

Marrin, Albert. *Cowboys, Indians, and Gunfighters: The Story of the Cattle Kingdom.* New York: Atheneum, 1993.

O'Neil, Paul. *The Frontiersmen.* New York: Time-Life, 1977.

Seidman, Laurence I. *Once in the Saddle: The Cowboy's Frontier, 1866–1896.* New York: Facts On File, 1991.

Van Steenwyk, Elizabeth. *The California Gold Rush: West with the Forty-Niners.* New York: Franklin Watts, 1991.

Webb, Walter Prescott. *The Great Plains.* New York: Grosset & Dunlap, 1931.

Religion and the West

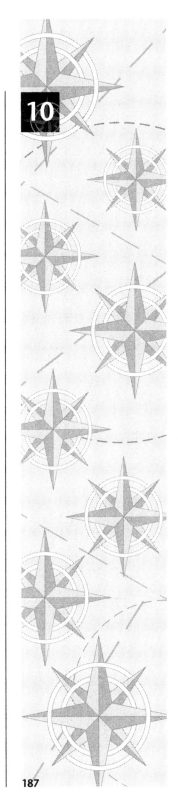

Religion had a significant impact on the settling of the West. Religious beliefs shaped how many Americans thought about the frontier and its possibilities. Some believed their religion would "civilize" the West, saving it from evil forces, and they ventured out into unknown areas to save souls. Others' religion caused them to seek refuge in the West as they were forcibly chased from the "civilized" East. The West became a vast testing ground for how tolerant America would become. The effects of religion on the West can best be understood by describing the experiences of three groups: the Native Americans, the Protestants, and the Mormons.

The first missionaries

By the early nineteenth century all Native Americans had had some degree of contact with Europeans. While there were certainly instances of pleasant, respectful meetings between Native Americans and Europeans, the majority of their interactions led to the eventual decimation of the Native Americans. Some early interactions with Europeans gave Native

Americans cause to be wary of them. In 1598 Spain granted all of present-day New Mexico to Juan de Oñate (pronounced Wahn day Own-YAH-tay; c. 1550–1630) to found a colony. Oñate terrorized the Pueblo inhabitants of the Southwest, brutally and forcibly converting them to Catholicism. If Native Americans dared to resist, they were attacked by the Spanish army. In the early 1600s, Oñate ordered an entire town burned when Native Americans denied the advance of the Catholic friars (members of a religious order). The resulting attack killed five hundred men and three hundred women and children. Oñate sentenced the survivors to twenty years of labor, a sentence made all the more difficult when Oñate ordered that each man over twenty-five years old have one foot severed.

The Pueblo nation of New Mexico revolted in 1680, drove the Spanish colonists from their land, and reached an agreement with Spain. Over the next twelve years, as they held the Spanish at bay, the Pueblo tried to rid their lives of Spanish influence, shunning European goods and holding ceremonies to "unbaptize" Catholic converts. Never again did the Spanish so brutally try to impose their religion and culture on the Pueblo.

In 1769 missionary Father Junipero Serra and a Spanish army established the first of what would become twenty-one missions along the coast of California. Serra directed the soldiers to round up the native peoples and bring them, by force if necessary, to the missions. Unable to leave the missions, the native Californians were converted to Christianity and severely disciplined for resistance. Once baptized, the Native Americans essentially became slaves to the missions and were trained to work in its fields, lay bricks, make shoes and saddles, or provide other necessities for the mission.

Native American religious traditions

Over the years, as contact with other cultures increased, Native Americans struggled to account for the changes in their spiritual beliefs. There were many different Native American religious beliefs and practices, so it is difficult to do more than generalize about common features of Native American religion and how it changed with the press of westward expansion.

Though many Native American groups identified themselves as "the real people," who had a special relationship with their creator, they did not oppose other groups' assertions of similar claims. Native American religions were diverse and adaptable and emphasized the interdependence of life. They blended ancient traditions with more recent practices to continually offer new ways to approach the sacred. Borrowing from others' practices or new experiences only enhanced Indian ceremonies and beliefs. In *The Invasion Within: The Contest of Cultures in Colonial North America,* James Axtell noted that in religious matters "purposeful change and adjustment was the only norm."

Although some Native American belief systems were based on pantheism, or worship of all gods, many added a Great Spirit as the most powerful of the many gods. There were different interpretations of the Great Spirit, but the description of an Osage Indian in 1925 provides a good common definition: "All life is wakan [spiritual power]. So also is everything which exhibits power, whether in action, as the winds and drifting clouds, or in passive endurance, as the boulder by the wayside. For even the commonest sticks and stones have a spiritual essence which must be reverenced as a manifestation of the all-pervading mysterious power that fills the universe." Others spoke of Wakanda, or Great Wakan, in the sense of a "supreme being." In addition, nature spirits provided guidance for understanding humans' place in the natural world. For many Indian cultures, relations with nature were just as important as human relations. These Indians believed that parts of nature, from birds to fish to rocks, were in some sense people—that is, ancestors of the human race. The Indians interpreted behavior in the natural world in human terms and used their interpretations to explain a wide range of natural happenings, from how night and day were divided to why dogs have long tongues.

The challenge of white contact

Despite the differences between the religious worlds of Europeans and Native Americans, there was no avoiding interaction. By the early nineteenth century, Native Americans had experienced dispossession of and removal from their lands. They had begun to feel that trade with white Americans and alcohol consumption were damaging their cultures. Defeat in battle and the white encroachment also undercut many native groups' confidence in the power of their traditional belief systems. Disease proved one of the most devastating attacks on the Indians' worldview. In 1837 smallpox nearly wiped out the Mandan tribe of North Dakota. Cholera, brought by settlers traveling the Oregon Trail a decade later, decimated the Lakota and the Cheyenne of the Great Plains. In the face of these disasters, Indians struggled to explain the terrible loss of life and their changing circumstances.

The Indians' response to Christianity, or what they called the "white man's medicine," was varied and often depended on local factors, including how a certain tribe experienced disease, defeat, or removal. Many groups initially seemed interested in the secrets of the Bible, or "Great Book," and were willing to convert in order to learn about what they saw as a potential source of power. When ancient ways seemed insufficient to deal with their changing situations, some Indians incorporated Christian rites and beliefs into their own practices. If the expected benefits did not materialize, some rejected the missionaries and turned hostile. Despite Indians' initial willingness to participate in Christian practices, they did not abandon their belief system. The Coeur d'Alenes, for example, were instructed by Jesuits (members of a Catholic religious order) during the 1840s. The Coeur d'Alenes honored the new "medicine" by building an impressive Renaissance-style church, without nails, in present-day Idaho. Yet they also reshaped Catholicism to suit their own traditions, developing a Christian war ethic that prescribed prayer before battle, forbade scalping and warfare on Sundays, and enlarged the meaning of charity to include killing in defense of the community.

Indian skepticism

While Native Americans adapted to the new ideas the whites brought, some aspects of the white man's religion puzzled them. One of the most disturbing trends Indians identified was the difference between how Christians behaved and what they preached. In his 1833 autobiography, Sauk leader Black Hawk decried this: "The whites may do bad all their lives, and then, if they are sorry for it when about to die, all is well? But with us it is different: we must continue throughout our lives to do what we conceive to be good." In a famous speech in 1828, Red Jacket of the Iroquois touched a sore point among Protestants with his comment on denominational divisions: "You say there is but one way to worship and serve the Great Spirit. If there is but one religion, why do you white people differ so much about it? Why do you not all agree, as you can all read the book? ... We also have a religion which was given to our forefathers, and has been handed down to us their children. We worship that way. It teaches us to be thankful for all the favors we receive, to love each other, and to be united. We never quarrel about religion."

Many Native Americans tried to counter the persistence of missionaries by arguing that Native Americans and whites were meant to believe differently. Black Hawk explained, "If the Great and Good Spirit wished us to believe and do as the whites, he could easily change our opinions, so that we would see, and think, and act as they do." But whether Native Americans accepted or rejected Christianity, the march of westward expansion took away Indians' ability to continue their traditions without acknowledging the impact of life with whites.

Tecumseh and the Prophet

One of the most important instances of Indian resistance to white encroachment was based on Indian religious beliefs. In 1794 General Anthony Wayne (1745–1796) defeated an Indian force drawn from several tribes, including the Shawnee, at the battle of Fallen Timbers (see Chapter 1). The resulting Treaty of Greenville in 1795 was meant to end Indian resistance to white settlement in much of present-day Ohio. The British continued to rally the Indians against the white Americans, however, and fighting continued through the War of 1812 (1812–14).

Indian resistance was based not only on Britain's support but also on the Shawnee religion. In 1805 a Shawnee named Tenskwatawa, or the Prophet (c. 1768–1834), began to have visions and used them to create a religious message grounded in resistance to white expansion. He preached moral reform and spiritual renewal through returning to old ways. The new religion revived old rituals and added some new ones that were rooted in Christianity, like the ceremony of confessing sins to Tenskwatawa. The Prophet traveled widely among the western tribes, and people from across the trans-Appalachian region (the area between the Appalachian Mountains and the Mississippi River) joined him.

Tenskwatawa's brother was Tecumseh (1768–1813), the war leader of the Shawnee. As the American government continued to pressure all the western Indians for more land cessions, Tecumseh tried to forge a union among Indian tribes based on the Prophet's teachings. Tenskwatawa's defeat at the Battle of Tippecanoe in 1811 dealt the religious revival a serious setback, and the religious movement gradually faded as American troops wore down the Indians. Tecumseh's eventual alliance with the British marked the beginning of the end for Native American resistance, as England acknowledged American control over the Great Lakes area in 1815.

Coping with white domination

After losing their land and livelihood and being confined to reservations, Native Americans sought new ways to cope with their dramatically changed lives. Many native religions began to be driven by the vision of an Indian utopia free of whites. In the early 1870s native prophets in California began preaching about the eventual reemergence of Indian culture and the defeat of whites. These prophets claimed that if "true believers" danced, prayed, and received visions of their dead relatives, fire or flood would purge the earth of whites and Indians would be free to live as they wished. These dances were called "ghost dances."

The most famous ghost dance was that of the Plains Indians in 1889, when the despairing Indians gathered to summon the destruction of whites and the revival of Indian life. Led by Paiute prophet Wovoka, these ghost dances would last for days. His followers would dance in circles, chant, pray, and fall into trances that revealed visions of the Indians' old world, a landscape alive with buffalo and free of whites. Stories of these ghost dances inspired similar gatherings in reservations across the Plains. Fearful of these ceremonies, whites asked the military for help. In 1890, when whites attempted to arrest the leaders of this religious rebellion, famous Sioux chief Sitting Bull was killed. Shortly thereafter, Seventh Cavalry troops rounded up a group of suspected Ghost Dance

Paiute prophet Wovoka (left) led the ghost dances of the Plains Indians. The dances were meant to bring fire or flood to purge the earth of whites and allow Native Americans to live as they had before whites came to North America. *(Reproduced by permission of the Granger Collection.)*

leaders (two-thirds of whom were women and children) near Wounded Knee Creek in South Dakota. As five hundred soldiers attempted to disarm the Indians, a gun misfired. Thinking they were being attacked, the soldiers opened fire on the almost defenseless Indians. In the end more than three hundred Sioux were slaughtered. Those who escaped were left to freeze to death in the surrounding hills (see Chapter 8). Though the Ghost Dance movement continued after the massacre at Wounded Knee, for many the killings marked the end of Indians' hope for a life without whites.

Protestant missionaries

For many, religion was the glue that held together civilized society. Westward expansion altered American society because new communities were often established without the social rules of the church to govern behavior. On the frontier, many Americans perceived a decline in public morality and

Native Americans preparing to perform a ghost dance.
(Reproduced by permission of The Bettmann Archive.)

civic-minded behavior and a rise in antisocial activities such as drinking, dueling, gambling, and prostitution. Some worried that if such tendencies were not curbed, the republic itself, based as it was on notions of responsible citizenship, was threatened with corruption and eventual extinction. Samuel Mills's reports from his travels west of the Alleghenies (part of the Appalachian Mountains) from 1812 to 1814 reinforced concerns about frontier communities without ministers, churches, or Bibles. In the capital of Illinois, Mills could not find one copy of the Bible. Mills's and others' expeditions influenced churches to start missionary projects to prevent heathenism from overtaking the new communities of the frontier and to bring Native Americans into the protecting fold of Christian civilization.

The desire to convert Indians was the initial draw for many missionaries. While the first missionary projects concentrated on the Indian populations nearest white settlements, missionaries soon set their sights farther west. When

four Indians from the Columbia Plateau (in present-day Washington, Oregon, and Idaho) came to St. Louis, Missouri, in 1831 to seek "the white man's book of heaven," Methodists, Presbyterians, and Jesuits turned their attention to the distant lands beyond the Rocky Mountains. But in 1847, Cayuse Indians, believing missionaries had started a devastating measles epidemic, massacred missionaries Marcus and Narcissa Prentiss Whitman and eleven others at an Oregon mission. Missionary projects in the region came to an abrupt halt.

Missionaries were not the only means of introducing religion to the newly formed communities of the West. Migrants carried their religious background with them to their new homes. In addition, churches reached out to the West with evangelizing programs.

One of the greatest triggers for religious evangelizing came with the discovery of gold in California in 1848. The gold rush prompted a vast migration: the California population rose

Illustration depicting the murder of Marcus and Narcissa Prentiss Whitman. They were killed by Cayuse Indians who blamed the missionaries for starting a measles epidemic among the Native Americans. (© *Seattle Post-Intelligencer Collection/Museum of History & Industry/CORBIS. Reproduced by permission.*)

Peter Cartwright was a Methodist preacher who preached on the American frontier for more than forty years. *(Courtesy of the Library of Congress.)*

from 14,000 in 1848 to 200,000 four years later and then to 380,000 in 1860. The sudden emergence of a makeshift society exclusively devoted to the accumulation of wealth captured the attention of the nation. One common image of California depicted it as a breeding ground for a creeping corruption that could infect the rest of the country. By the 1850s the Protestant establishment had become obsessed with California as the indicator of a need for evangelism. This new interest replaced their earlier enthusiasm for converting Native Americans.

Despite California's image as an unchurched wasteland, there were a few stalwart clergymen accompanying the 49ers, and they industriously established at least fifty small churches within a short time. In the early years of the gold rush, the letters and reports of the overworked ministers tell of an endless round of duties—marriages, funerals, care of the sick and dying—interspersed with street-corner and saloon evangelism. Methodist minister William Taylor exhorted daily on San Francisco's wharf to ensure that the first words heard by arrivals would be the Gospel.

Mormons

Indians were not the only inhabitants of America who were chased away from white settlements. Mormons also fled the persecution of the East. The Mormon church demanded that the Saints, as believers were called, display cleanliness, virtue, industry, and complete obedience to the church in return for assured salvation. As the Mormon community grew and prospered, outsiders became envious and suspicious of them. Soon hostility toward Mormons grew to a fever pitch, and they were forced to migrate farther and farther west in search of a secluded area where they could practice their faith.

Peter Cartwright, Methodist Preacher

Peter Cartwright (1785–1872) was a typical Methodist preacher of the trans-Appalachian West. In 1802, at age seventeen, Cartwright began riding into the rough areas of Kentucky, Tennessee, Ohio, and Indiana to preach. He became famous for his homespun sermons and for his ability to handle every situation that arose on his journeys. Unlike many in his profession, Cartwright was married and had nine children. In fact, his decision to move to Illinois in 1823 was prompted by family concerns, especially a desire to raise his seven daughters and two sons in a free state and to be able to purchase land for their future inheritance. Cartwright wrote that his first Illinois district in 1826 "commenced at the mouth of the Ohio river, and extended north hundreds of miles, and was not limited by the white settlements, but extended among the great, unbroken tribes of uncivilized and unchristianized Indians." He preached for more than forty years on the frontier and immortalized the old frontier and the "backwoods preacher" in his autobiography. He remembered:

> A Methodist preacher in those days, when he felt that God had called him to preach, instead of hunting up a college or Biblical institute, hunted up a hardy pony or a horse, and some traveling apparatus, and with his library always at hand, namely, Bible, Hymn-book, and Discipline, he started.... He went through storms of wind, hail, snow and rain; climbed hills and mountains, traversed valleys, plunged through swamps, swam swollen streams, lay out all night, wet, weary, and hungry, held his horse by the bridle all night, or tied him to a limb, slept with his saddle blanket for a bed, his saddle or saddle-bags for his pillow, and his old big coat or blanket, if he had any, for a covering. Often he slept in dirty cabins, on earthen floors, before the fires; ate roasting ears [corn on the cob] for bread, drank butter-milk for coffee, or sage tea for imperial; took, with a hearty zest, deer or bear meat, or wild turkey, for breakfast, dinner, and supper if he could get it.... This was old fashioned Methodist fare and fortune.

Source: Peter Cartwright, Autobiography of Peter Cartwright, the Backwoods Preacher, edited by W. P. Strickland (Cincinnati, OH: Hitchcock & Walden, 1868).

The Church of Jesus Christ of Latter-day Saints, known as the Mormons, originated in 1823 when a young Joseph Smith (1805–1844) had a vision of God and Jesus. Later Smith claimed he had been visited three times by the angel Moroni, who told him of golden plates containing the lost history of the Americas. Smith translated the plates to write the scripture of the "true" church. After eighteen months of writing, Smith published *The Book of Mormon* in 1830. The first gathering of the church took place in April 1830. The church was structured like others, except that

Smith claimed to have been endowed with divine power and declared that he had unquestionable authority to direct the Saints. Opposition to this new religion grew as people outside the church learned of the church's approval of polygamy (marriage to more than one person at the same time) and the union of religion and politics. Critics charged that polygamy defiled the Christian family and that the blending of religion and politics sullied the ideals of the newly democratic nation.

Despite hostility from outsiders, the Mormon religion prospered. Nearly two thousand Mormons had gravitated to Kirtland, Ohio, by 1835. Finding themselves unwelcome in Ohio, the congregation moved to Missouri in 1837. Hostility toward Mormons grew in Missouri until 1838, when warfare broke out. Smith was arrested on charges of treason, and the governor of Missouri declared the Mormons a blight to be exterminated. The Mormons fled to Illinois, where they secured a charter for their own city, which they called Nauvoo. They hoped to make Nauvoo into a safe place to live apart from non-Mormons. Soon they had built Nauvoo into the second-largest city in Illinois, with a population of more than ten thousand. By 1844, the Mormons prospered as merchants. Nauvoo included sawmills, flour mills, a tool factory, a foundry, a chinaware factory, and an unfinished temple. Illinois residents felt threatened by the growth of the town and felt jealous because they were shut out of Mormon commerce. Increasingly frustrated, they worked up an anti-Mormon hysteria and began to harass the Mormons. In the midst of this hysteria, the state governor ordered Joseph Smith and his brother Hiram to be arrested. Both were shot dead in 1844 by a group that stormed the jail where the brothers were held.

The promised land

Brigham Young (1801–1877) succeeded Smith as the leader of the church. But the troubles in Illinois did not end with Smith's death. In 1845 the Illinois legislature revoked the Nauvoo city charter. Young and others decided that the Mormons needed to find a secluded area to prosper and grow as a church. Young gathered the Saints to travel more than a thousand miles to the Salt Lake Valley in present-day Utah, an area Young did not think others would covet. Organizing the emigrant families into groups, Young prepared his follow-

Brigham Young and his
followers in a convoy of
carriages heading for Salt
Lake City.
(© Bettmann/CORBIS.
Reproduced by permission.)

ers to travel along what would become known as the Mormon Trail. Young's encouragement and good leadership made the first trek a tremendous success and strengthened the faith of many. Thereafter the Saints commemorated the parallels between their journey and that of the ancient Hebrews: like them, the Mormons had been led by a Moses through a wilderness to a promised land.

On April 14, 1847, the pioneer company left Winter Quarters (near present-day Omaha, Nebraska) in search of the Great Salt Lake Valley. By July 21, 1847, the first of the travelers reached the valley; within forty-eight hours a dam and irrigation ditches had been built and five acres of potatoes had been planted. Eight days after arriving, the Mormons had plowed fifty-three acres of land; planted forty-two acres of potatoes, corn, buckwheat, oats, and beans; plotted out a forty-acre temple; and made preliminary surveys for the city of Salt Lake. None of the first company perished on the trip to Salt Lake (except Young's horse, which was shot accidentally).

Some Must Push and Some Must Pull: The Best-Known of the Handcart Songs

1. Ye saints who dwell on Europe's shore,
prepare yourselves for many more

   To leave behind your native land for
sure God's judgment are at hand.

   For you must cross the raging main before the promised land you gain,

   And with the faithful make a start, to
cross the plains with your handcart.

   Chorus: For some must push and some
must pull, as we go marching up the hill;

   So merrily on our way we go, until we
reach the Valley-O.

2. The lands that boast of modern light,
We known are all as dark as night,
Where poor men toil and want for
bread,
Where peasant hosts are blindly led.
These lands that boast of liberty
You ne'er again would wish to see,
When you from Europe make a start
To cross the plains with your handcart.

3. As on the road the carts are pulled,
'Twould very much surprise the world
To see the old and feeble dame
Thus lend a hand to pull the same;
And maidens fair will dance and sing,
Young men more happy than the king,

And children, too, will laugh and play,
Their strength increasing day by day.

4. But some will say, "It is too bad,
The saints upon the foot to pad,
And more than that, to pull a load
As they go marching o'er the road."
But then we say, "It is the plan
To gather up the best of men,
And women, too, for none but they
Will ever travel in this way."

5. And long before the valley's gained,
We will be met upon the plain
With music sweet and friends so dear,
And fresh supplies our hearts to cheer;
And then with music and with song,
How cheerfully we'll march along,
And thank the day we made a start
To cross the plains with our handcarts.

6. When you get there among the rest,
Obedient be and you'll be blessed,
And in God's chambers be shut in,
While judgments cleanse the earth from
sin;
For we do know it will be so,
God's servant spoke it long ago.
We say it is high time to start
To cross the plains with our handcarts.

Source: B. A. Botkin, ed., A Treasury of Western Folklore *(New York: Crown, 1951).*

The handcart companies

By the end of 1848, five thousand Saints had traveled to Salt Lake City. Content that they had found their new Zion, or ideal community, the Mormons increased their missionary activities to invite all believers to Salt Lake and established the Perpetual Emigrating Fund (PEF) to aid the emigration of poorer converts. Of all the emigrants to travel the Mormon Trail, the handcart companies were the poorest and the most determined. Many of these travelers were penniless Scandinavians or Englishmen who jumped at the chance when the church offered to pay their way to America. When the converts arrived in Iowa City, Mormon organizers outfitted them with supplies and handcarts, which were much like large wheelbarrows—wooden boxes on two large wheels with two long shafts for pulling. Followed by a supply wagon pulled by oxen, handcart emigrants pulled their belongings an average of 10 to 20 miles a day on dry, flat land and much less when crossing rivers or trying to traverse sand or sticky mud.

The first of the handcart companies left Iowa City in June 1856, arriving in Salt Lake four months later. The fourth and fifth companies got a later start that would prove disastrous. The late start meant that the companies would have to brave high winter winds and freezing conditions at the end of their journey. And along the way, unforeseen hardships awaited them. The dry air of the plains shrank the green wood of their cart wheels, and some fell apart. Buffalo herds stampeded their cattle and oxen. Taking precious time to search for them, the companies only recovered part of their stock. Without the teams to pull the heavier supply wagons, the handcarts were weighted down with additional supplies, which slowed the companies' progress all the more. Hundreds of miles from Salt Lake, winter set in and rations were cut. People began to die. John Chislett, captain of a hundred in Handcart Company Number Four, is quoted in *Seven Trails West*: "Our old and infirm people began to droop, and they no sooner lost spirit and courage than death's stamp could be traced upon their features.... We soon thought it unusual to leave a campground without burying one or more persons."

Hearing about the handcart companies' troubles, Mormons in Salt Lake rallied to send rescue wagons along the trail, bringing food and comfort to travelers. Though the rescue efforts were generous and committed, the fourth and fifth handcart companies lost more than 200 of the original 1,076 travelers who had left Liverpool, England.

The tragedy did not stop others from pulling their loads to Zion. In the following four years, more than a thousand people pulled handcarts to Salt Lake. In all, one in ten handcart travelers died on the trail, and more died shortly after reaching the valley. The last handcart company traveled in 1860. Though the majority of believers traveled under easier conditions, the suffering and struggle endured by the handcart companies on the Mormon Trail suggested "that the true Mormon Trail was not on the prairie but in the spirit," according to Arthur King Peters in *Seven Trails West*. By 1870, more than eighty thousand Mormons had trekked to Salt Lake City, with six thousand dying on the way.

The Mormons had found their Zion and were successfully increasing their numbers to stave off their opponents. Almost a decade after Mormons reached Salt Lake and just as the first handcart companies were starting out from Iowa City, public outrage about Mormon polygamy and Brigham Young's authority over his followers caused President James Buchanan (1791–1868) to dispatch twenty-five hundred troops to destroy Salt Lake City. In 1858, the Mormons were prepared to defend their position. However, before the troops reached the city, Buchanan withdrew them and pardoned the Mormons. Instead of destruction, the army brought the Mormons monetary gain, as they bought supplies and provisions when they marched through the city. In *Seven Trails West* Peters credited the army's business as the origin of many Mormon fortunes. At the end of the twentieth century, the Mormons remained centered in Salt Lake City and continued to grow as a community; the church counts more than nine million people as Saints.

Conclusion

Religion played a strong hand in shaping the West: it was used as an oppressive force that tried to change native cultures; a tamer of immorality in newly formed communities; and a rallying cry to believers seeking a safe haven from the world. Many risked their lives to bring their religion to the frontier. In the end, the frontier struggles among those of differing religious beliefs helped secure the tradition of religious tolerance in America.

For More Information

Books

Monaghan, Jay. *The Book of the American West*. New York: Julian Messner, 1963.

Stegner, Wallace. *The Gathering of Zion: The Story of the Mormon Trail*. Salt Lake City, UT: Westwater Press, 1981.

Wexler, Sanford. *Westward Expansion: An Eyewitness History*. New York: Facts On File, 1991.

White, Richard. *"It's Your Misfortune and None of My Own": A New History of the American West*. Norman: University of Oklahoma Press, 1991.

Williams, Jean Kinney. *The Mormons*. New York: Franklin Watts, 1996.

Web sites

Heritage Gateways. [Online] http://heritage.uen.org/cgi-bin/websql/ index.hts (accessed April 14, 2000).

Kavanaugh, Thomas W. *Imaging and Imagining the Ghost Dance: James Mooney's Illustrations and Photographs, 1891–1893*. [Online] http:// php.indiana.edu/~tkavanag/visual5.html (accessed April 14, 2000).

"So We Die." *The West: Episode 2 1806–1848*. [Online] http://www.pbs. org/weta/thewest/wpages/wpgs100/w12_010.htm (accessed April 14, 2000).

Tecumseh. [Online] http://www.geocities.com/SouthBeach/Cove/8286/ warrior.html (accessed April 6, 2000).

Sources

Allison, Robert J. *American Eras: Development of a Nation, 1783–1815*. Detroit: Gale Research, 1997.

Axtell, James. *The Invasion Within:The Contest of Cultures in Colonial North America*. New York: Oxford University Press, 1985

Ballantine, Betty, and Ian Ballantine. *The Native Americans: An Illustrated History*. Atlanta, GA: Turner Publishing, 1993.

Botkin, B. A., ed. *A Treasury of Western Folklore*. New York: Crown, 1951.

Cartwright, Peter. *Autobiography of Peter Cartwright, the Backwoods Preacher*. Edited by W. P. Strickland. Cincinnati, OH: Hitchcock & Walden, 1868.

Josephy, Alvin M., Jr. *500 Nations: An Illustrated History of North American Indians*. New York: Knopf, 1994.

Mancall, Peter C., ed. *American Eras: Westward Expansion, 1800–1850*. Detroit: Gale Research, 1999.

Peters, Arthur King. *Seven Trails West*. New York: Abbeville Press, 1996.

Technology and the Making of the West

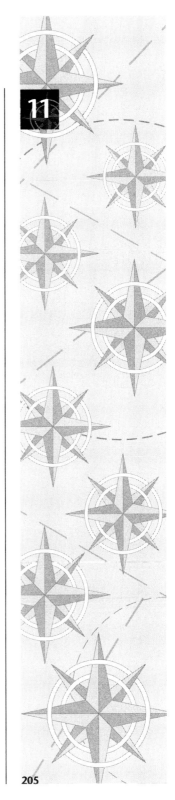

11

Moving west took daring and courage. People risked their lives to open the West to commerce and settlement, braving harsh climatic and geologic conditions to cross the country and secure the land. Technology helped ease some of the strain and, in some cases, ensured success. Canals, stagecoaches, and railroads made it possible for thousands of people to settle the West. Securing the land often meant defending the chosen spot against Indian attack; advances in gun design swayed the battles in favor of the white settlers. New technologies aided farmers and cattlemen in places where standard fencing materials were scarce. Once settled, people wanted to correspond with the loved ones they had left behind or keep abreast of news in other parts of the country. Technological advances increased the speed of correspondence from months to weeks and then to minutes. Each technological advance further opened the West and helped bind the growing country together.

The Erie Canal shortened the travel time from New York City to Buffalo from three weeks to eight days. *(Reproduced by permission of Archive Photos, Inc.)*

Canals

Traveling around America used to be quite difficult. During the colonial period, roads were primitive and rivers did not connect people to all the places they wanted to travel. By the Revolutionary War (1776–83), some had considered the benefits of creating man-made rivers called canals to connect natural waterways. As early as 1790, there were thirty canal companies working in the newly formed nation. The first canal made in America stretched 27 miles and connected the Merrimack River with Boston Harbor. Hundreds of canals were dug throughout America from the end of the Revolutionary War to the beginning of the Civil War in 1861. French statesman and historian Alexis de Tocqueville (1805–1859) noted that Americans had "changed the whole order of nature to their advantage," according to Russell Bourne in *Floating West.*

One of the most important canals was the 363-mile-long Erie Canal, which linked Rome, New York, to Buffalo,

New York. Interest in building a canal across New York started when the new state was still a British colony, but work did not begin until 1817. Part of the appeal of such a canal was the ease and speed of travel it would offer to people eager to reach the frontier lands of western New York and Pennsylvania.

Building canals was slow, difficult work. Surveyors first laid out the path of the canal and planned locks along the route to "level out" the distance. Much of the digging was done by Irish immigrants who had left their homeland because of the potato famine (widespread starvation brought on by a disease that destroyed potato crops). The Erie Canal used about three thousand Irish "bogtrotters" to dig the forty-foot-wide and four-foot-deep ditch. Spending their days shoveling, sometimes through swamps and bogs, the workers were paid between 37.5 and 50 cents per day if they had a set wage, or work crews of three men earned about 12.5 cents for each cubic yard of earth they moved. As work progressed, many native New Yorkers joined the crews, and innovations in digging soon helped the work go faster. Horses and oxen pulled plows to break up the dirt before workers began to dig. The animals were also used to pull dirt off the work area. Cables were strung over tall trees and attached to tree stumps so that a single canal worker could pull out a stump by turning an endless screw. Crews called "blowers" that cleared away rock, could use Dupont's Blasting Powder, a substance that ignited when and how it was supposed to, instead of the more unpredictable black powder.

The Erie Canal was completed in 1825, and within a year it had collected $750,000 in tolls. Much of the canal's success came from the speed it gave travelers. When people walked or rode wagons or stagecoaches, it took them a few weeks to get from New York City to Buffalo. But the journey took only eight days on the Erie Canal. The canal became the most-used route west in the 1830s and 1840s. By 1830, about one thousand people arrived in Buffalo daily, ready to head west to settle in Ohio, Michigan, Indiana, and Illinois. Not only was canal travel faster, but it was a cheaper method of shipping for merchants as well. Farmers in Buffalo who once paid one hundred dollars for a ton of freight to reach New York City in three weeks could now send the same material for ten dollars and it would reach its destination in eight days. The Erie Canal made Buffalo the busiest port on the Great Lakes.

The success of the Erie Canal started America's great canal-building era. Along the Atlantic Ocean, more than 800 miles of canals were completed during the 1820s. By the 1830s, 1,300 miles of canals were under construction, including the Chesapeake and Ohio Canal and the Pennsylvania and Maryland systems. By 1840, more than 4,000 miles of canals linked American towns.

Despite the popular enthusiasm for canal travel, which offered unheard-of leisure and speed, America's attention soon turned to railroads. Like canals, trains could take people where rivers could not. But trains offered travelers more speed and luxury, and railroads were quicker to construct. Though revenues on the Erie Canal topped five million dollars annually in 1862, by 1869 railroads were carrying more freight than canals were. The competition from railroads forced many canals to close, and the construction of some canals was abandoned altogether.

The stagecoach

Stagecoaches had carried travelers throughout the East from the time roads were wide enough to accommodate four wheels. By 1820 regular stagecoach service reached St. Louis, Missouri. But the dirt trails farther west had only been tackled by several two-wheeled wagons traveling west from Missouri in the 1820s and by one four-wheeled wagon, which made it to Fort Boise, Idaho, before falling apart in 1836. The first wagon train of emigrants left Missouri for California in 1836, beginning a large migration of people to the Oregon Country in the 1840s. Demand for overland passenger service soon became great enough to establish stagecoach service to the West.

Before the opening of transcontinental stagecoach lines, regional lines offered service in many areas throughout the West. By the mid-1800s stagecoach service was offered from Independence, Missouri, to Santa Fe, New Mexico; throughout the Willamette Valley in Oregon; and throughout the states of Texas and California. The routes offered people without livestock or the ability to travel on foot a way to get from place to place. The stagecoach lines of California, however, had a special purpose: they opened in response to the demands of gold rush miners, who would pay handsomely to transport gold and mail from the mines. James E. Birch, who had traveled to California from Rhode Island to seek his fortune in the mines, soon discovered he could make more money running a stagecoach line. He did very well carrying the miners' goods from mines near San Francisco to the city and newcomers to the mines. In the late 1840s and 1850s California was served by more than seven stagecoach lines.

Early stagecoaches offered a means of transportation for people who didn't own livestock or who didn't want to or weren't able to walk long distances. The coaches were not known for comfort. *(© CORBIS. Reproduced by permission.)*

The Overland Mail Company

In 1857 Congress, which was interested in establishing regular mail service between the Mississippi River and California, passed a post office measure. As the operator and owner of stage lines, steamships, and express companies in the East, John Butterfield knew the delivery industry well, and he won the contract to establish regular mail service in the West. Butterfield and his investors spent more than one million dollars to establish and grade roads, dig wells, and build stations every nineteen miles along the route. Under his efficient management, Butterfield's Overland Mail Company opened for service on September 16, 1858. The mail traveled from St. Louis to Tipton, Missouri, by train and was then transferred to stagecoach for the trip to San Francisco. Butterfield's line complied with the government's demand that service be "performed in good four-horse coaches and spring wagons, suitable for the conveyance of passengers, as well as the safety and security of the mails." But the twenty-four-day trip took a toll on passengers. In *Throw Down the Box!* George A. Thompson quotes Waterman Ormsby, a *New York Herald* reporter who was the first to ride the stagecoach line. Ormsby said of his trip, "I know what Hell is like, for I've just had twenty-four days of it!" Butterfield operated the Overland Mail Company for two and a half years until he retired.

"Dreary weariness"

Stagecoaches were not known for comfort. In *Getting There: Frontier Travel without Power,* Suzanne Hilton quoted one man's opinion about his stagecoach journey: "Dreary weariness comes over the coach-crowding passengers. The air gets cold. The road grows dusty and chokes you. The legs become stiff and numb. The temper edges. Everybody is overcome with sleep but can't stay asleep. Everybody flounders and knocks about against everybody else in helpless despair."

In addition to being uncomfortable, stagecoaches were vulnerable to attack. Robbers, called "road agents," stopped coaches, stole all the valuables, and sometimes killed passengers or drivers. Stagecoaches carrying bullion (bars of gold) from the mines were especially targeted. The most famous road agents were Black Bart (see box on p. 212), who terrorized stage lines in California, and Henry Plummer in Montana. But history has shown that the road agents' high jinks did not pay; thieves were generally either jailed or hanged for their efforts. Indians were another threat to stagecoach travel. Enraged by the further encroachment of settlers on their lands, the Sioux, Apache, and other tribes along the stagecoach lines attacked way stations and ran off horses.

The stagecoach kings

In 1861, Benjamin F. Holladay became one of the

Black Bart

Though many bandits and gangs robbed stagecoaches, Black Bart earned special recognition as a highwayman because he robbed so many people, never fired a shot, and proved so elusive to the law. Black Bart robbed twenty-eight California stagecoaches between 1875 and 1883. Always masked in a flour sack with eyeholes and carrying a shotgun, Black Bart would demand that the drivers "Throw down the box!" After he collected the treasure from the express box, Bart would leave on foot. Twice he left behind a message in verse. According to Jay Monaghan's *The Book of the American West,* the poem Black Bart left at his fourth robbery read as follows:

> I've labored long and hard for bread,
> For honor and for riches,
> But on my *corns* too long you've tred
> *You fine-haired sons of bitches.*
> Black Bart,
> The Po 8
>
> (Po 8 meant PoEight or Poet)

Soon Wells Fargo, California governor William Irwin, and the postal authorities collectively posted eight hundred dollars as a reward for Black Bart's capture and conviction. In 1883, detectives found a handkerchief with a laundry mark (a tag identifying a commercial laundry or cleaners), F.X.O.7, at the scene of a Black Bart robbery. This tag would prove to be the criminal's undoing. Wells Fargo detective J. B. Hume had long been on the lookout for evidence that would lead him to Black Bart. He ordered that San Francisco's ninety-one laundries be searched for the matching laundry mark. The search led him to C. E. Bolton. Thought to be the owner of a mine who lived in a nearby hotel, Bolton was a well-dressed man with a gray mustache and goatee. Detectives searched his room and found clothing with an identical laundry mark and poems in the same handwriting as those left at

most powerful stagecoach kings in the country when he purchased the entire Central Overland California and Pikes Peak Express and changed the name to the Overland Mail Company (the company contained portions of John Butterfield's now dismantled Overland Mail Company). Holladay intimidated his competition and consolidated other stagecoach lines into the Overland Mail Company. In 1866, Holladay sold his company to Wells, Fargo and Company for more than two and a half million dollars. Wells Fargo now owned every stage line of importance west of the Missouri River. By 1865, travelers could buy a $250 ticket on a stagecoach that left the Missouri River on Monday through Saturday to make the six-day trip to the Rocky Mountains. Stagecoaches suf-

Black Bart was a famous "road agent" or stagecoach thief who terrorized stage lines in California. *(Reproduced by permission of The Granger Collection, New York.)*

Black Bart's robberies. Bolton was soon convicted and was imprisoned at San Quentin on November 21, 1883.

Though Black Bart claimed while in jail that his name was Bolton and that he had been a captain in the Civil War, a Bible in his room in San Francisco was inscribed "Charles E. Boles, First Sergeant, Company B. 116th Illinois Volunteer Infantry, by his wife as a New Year's gift." Whether his name was Bolton or Boles will never be known. He was released from prison on January 21, 1888. Shortly thereafter some stage lines were held up, and rumors circulated that Black Bart was operating again. But soon the holdups and the rumors disappeared—as did any trace of Black Bart.

fered from competition with the Transcontinental Railroad when it was built in 1869. The stagecoach lines couldn't match the speed or the relative safety offered by the trains. Wells Fargo sold its stagecoach lines to another stagecoach company, Gilmer and Salisbury, in 1869. The latter company continued operation of the profitable lines, which offered service between outlying areas and the railroads, into the 1900s.

Railroads

Railroads were an efficient and quick method of transportation in the East long before a transcontinental railroad

Mary Fields

Mary Fields was the first black woman to deliver mail in the United States. Born a slave in Hickman County, Tennessee, Fields was granted her freedom when the Civil War ended in 1865. A letter from her old master's daughter and her best friend, Dolly Dunn, encouraged her to move near Cascade, Montana, where Dolly was a nun at the mission. A strong, capable woman who was good with horses and quick with a gun, Fields bested forty others for a job as the stagecoach driver on the difficult mountain trail between the St. Peter's Mission and Cascade, Montana. She was sixty years old when she got the job. Fields delivered the mail on time for eight years, battling bandits and once packing the mail on her back when the winter snow stopped her horses. After her retirement as Stagecoach Mary Fields, she opened her own laundry business. She was eighty-two when she was laid to rest.

was possible. By 1860, more than 30,000 miles of track connected the major cities of the East. Construction of a transcontinental railway was not delayed for lack of vision, however. As early as the Lewis and Clark expedition in 1804 (see Chapter 2), eastern entrepreneurs longed for a shortcut to Asian markets. In 1844 New York City merchant Asa Whitney even proposed that Congress sell him a strip of land running west from Wisconsin to the Pacific Ocean so that he could construct a railway to provide easy access to the riches of Asia. While Whitney's idea was met with interest, it ultimately failed because Congress could not decide which city should be the starting point for the railroad. For nearly two more decades interest in a transcontinental railroad remained high, but political lobbying between the North and the South over where to begin the line kept the project from being started.

When the Southern states seceded and the Civil War began in 1861, Congress was finally able to pass a bill that provided private corporations with federal land and government money to build the railway. Congress launched the construction of the transcontinental railroad with the passage of the Pacific Railroad Act on July 1, 1862. President Abraham Lincoln (1809–1865) signed the legislation and decided where the line would start. The railroad would stretch from Sacramento, California, to Omaha on the Missouri River in the Nebraska Territory. With government aid, the California-chartered Central Pacific company would lay the track from the west and the federally chartered Union Pacific company would construct the line from the east. In 1864 a second act was passed to provide more loans and land grants to the railroad effort.

A difficult journey

Over the years construction continued haltingly. During the Civil War, workers and materials were hard to secure. In 1863 work began in California. Charles Crocker led the laborers and hired ten thousand Chinese workers to help blast a passage through the Sierra Nevada Mountains. Chinese laborers made up four-fifths of the workforce and were paid two-thirds what white laborers were. By 1865 only forty miles of track had been laid westward from Omaha. In Nebraska, General Grenville M. Dodge added ten thousand men, mostly ex-soldiers and recent Irish immigrants. The laborers on both sides of the country suffered miserable conditions while working, sometimes in gale-force winds and snowstorms or hanging in baskets over rock faces. Hundreds died in the effort.

Even with the thousands of workers and hundreds of wagons continuously carrying materials to job sites, Indian attacks frequently delayed production. Indians viewed the railroads as a disaster. As the land was cleared, hunters slaughtered the buffalo on which the Indians depended. The transcontinental railroad split the buffalo country into two "herds" when it reached Cheyenne, Wyoming; the construction of the Kansas Pacific Railroad in 1868, the Santa Fe Railroad through Kansas in 1871, and the Northern Pacific Railroad through the Dakotas in 1880 threatened the Indians' way of life and dependence on the buffalo even further. Of the millions of buffalo found in the West in the previous decade, only 1,091 re-

Poster advertising the Union Pacific Railroad.
(©Bettman/CORBIS)

mained in 1887. Indians were displaced all along the route as land was claimed for the railroads.

The Central Pacific and Union Pacific fiercely competed with each other. By 1868, the Central Pacific was forging across the Nevada desert and the Union Pacific tackled South Pass, laying 5 to 10 miles of track a day. The crews were working so quickly that the graders actually passed each other. Congress finally ruled that the two roads would join at Promontory, Utah. On May 10, 1869, a ceremony celebrated the completion of the project. Officials from both companies and other guests assembled to watch the last spikes driven into the railroad ties: one silver spike from Nevada; one of gold, silver, and iron from Arizona; and two gold ones from California. When the two companies' engines met nose to nose, the telegraph carried the news across the nation, starting a series of celebrations from the East to the West.

The railroad mania

Passenger service began on the railroad five days after the golden spike was driven. From Omaha, the trip cost $111 for first-class tickets, which included private toilets and sleeping coaches called "Pullmans" and "Silver Palace Cars"; $80 for second-class seats, which were unreserved coach accommodations; and $40 for emigrant-class tickets that bought passengers seats in a car that had hard seats, bunks with straw-filled mattresses, a toilet, and a coal-burning stove. The dining cars were open to all. The scheduled trip took four days, four hours, and forty minutes, unless washouts, buffalo, train robberies, or Indians delayed the train.

The transcontinental railroad started what became a railroad mania that would only begin to lag after four other railroads reached the Pacific coast and the "Great Empire Builder" James J. Hill completed, without federal subsidy, his Great Northern Railroad, the fifth transcontinental railroad, in 1893. At the end of the Civil War in 1865, 3,272 miles of track had been laid west of the Mississippi River, and by 1890, 72,473 miles of track connected major areas of the West.

The railroads dramatically changed the economic viability of the West. The "iron horses" led to the development and economic prosperity of new towns, helping support the success of many farms and industries. Carrying passengers

The last spikes of the transcontinental railroad were driven in at the Golden Spike Ceremony on May 10, 1869. *(Reproduced by permission of Archive Photos, Inc.)*

more quickly and in greater comfort than other forms of transportation could, the railroads brought another economic bonus as well: tourism.

Guns

Aside from the devastating effects of disease on Native Americans when whites advanced across the continent, guns proved to be the biggest threat to the native tribes. Nearly a century before the first white settlers arrived in the West, the Spanish matchlock or hand cannon gave the Spanish invaders an advantage over the original North American inhabitants. Jay Monaghan's *The Book of the American West* noted that, "these early firearms not only paved the way for the winning of the West but became our first sporting weapons, bringing down game as well as humans."

When Lewis and Clark made their famous expedition west in 1804, they would fire their cannon or shoot a flying duck if they needed to impress or scare the Indians they encountered. But guns were not altogether new to Native Americans. Traders had supplied Indians with older versions of guns since about the seventeenth century. Cheaply constructed muskets and more expensive and well-made rifles, known as "trade guns," were manufactured especially for sale to Indians in the early 1800s. Native Americans also acquired other weapons as gifts or stole them. Over the years Indians became known for their ability to handle a gun on horseback, firing and reloading at full gallop. The Indian victory at Little Bighorn on June 25, 1876 (see Chapter 7), is often held up as the greatest display of Indians' ability with guns. By 1890 and the battle at Wounded Knee (see Chapter 7), Americans' possession of more advanced weaponry—in this case, the Hotchkiss guns that fired two-pound explosive shells—would end the days of Indians freely roaming the Plains.

The Texas pistol

Long before Wounded Knee, advancements in gun manufacturing gave Americans the advantage over Indian tribes in the West. One of the most revolutionary guns was the Colt revolver; inventor Samuel Colt (1814–1862) received a patent for a revolving pistol and revolving rifle in 1836. Unlike earlier muskets or rifles, revolvers could hold six shots. So many of Samuel Colt's guns were in Texas by 1839 that they became known as the "Texas pistol" or "Texas arm." In the early 1840s, Colt learned about machinery and the possibilities of mass production.

Colt made a deal with Eli Whitney, Jr. (son of the eighteenth-century inventor), to build machines that could produce weapons for a U.S. government contract Colt won

in 1846. Though Colt lost money on his contract with the government to manufacture one thousand six-shooters, he retained Whitney's machines. Colt soon added more machines with the help of Elisha K. Root, an excellent mechanic who designed nearly four hundred machines to mass-produce Colt's guns. A visitor to their factory was fascinated by the new machines, as quoted by David Freeman Hawke in *Nuts and Bolts of the Past:* "Each portion of the firearm has its particular section. As we enter ... the first group of machines appears to be exclusively employed in chambering the cylinders; here another is boring barrels; another group is milling the lock frames; still another is drilling them; beyond are a score of machines boring and screwing the nipples.... Here are the rifling machines ... now we come to the jigging machines that mortice out the lock frames." These machines were faster than people, but they were not precise. Though Colt bragged about the uniformity of his gun parts, historian David Hounshell reported that the parts "did not come close to being interchangeable," according to Hawke.

Though Colt's guns were among the most popular in the West, he was not the first to mass-produce guns. Since the early 1800s at Harpers Ferry Armory, John Hall had been mass-producing guns with such precision that "if a thousand guns were taken apart and limbs thrown promiscuously [casually] together in one heap they may be taken promiscuously from the heap and will all come out right," according to Hawke in *Nuts and Bolts of the Past.* Historian Merritt Roe Smith pronounced Hall's advances in precision manufacturing to be "one of the great technological achievements of the modern era," according to Hawke. By the 1840s, many small manufacturers were producing muskets and rifles with interchangeable parts.

Colt revolvers' ability to hold more than one shot was more important than interchangeability was in winning the West. Samuel Colt's 1849 .31-caliber pocket pistol became one of the most popular and longest-selling of his models. But the 1851 Navy Model and the 1860 Army Model, called "Navys" and "Armys," were to become the "standard sidearm out West till the advent of cartridge revolvers after the Civil War," according to Monaghan. Renowned explorer John C. Frémont (1813–1890) reportedly slept with two Colts near his head and a Colt rifle under his blanket. Famous scout Wild Bill Hickok (1837–1876) used a "Navy" Colt. The outcome of an Indian attack in 1841 confirmed the superiority of the revolvers. Frontiersman Kit Carson (1809–1868) and a small party used Colt Paterson eight-shot cylinder rifles and five- and six-shot Paterson revolvers to kill or wound about one hundred attacking Kiowa and Comanche warriors; Carson and his party lost only one man. In 1844 Colonel John Hays and fifteen Texas Rangers used Colt revolvers against an attack of eighty Comanche, killing forty-two of them. These and similar stories bolstered Colt's position in the marketplace.

Colt died in 1862. Root became president of the company but died three years later. By that time, the power of the gun had been firmly established in the West. Since then, technological advancements in weaponry have continued to influence territorial disputes around the world.

The Pony Express

When the United States was consolidated east of the Mississippi, communications between the states were fairly swift. But after the California gold rush drew many thousands of Americans westward, helping California become a state in 1850, it became extremely difficult to exchange mail and information with business associates, friends, and relatives who lived on the other side of the continent. There was simply no efficient way to get mail from one side of the country to the other. The railroads reached no farther than the Missouri River, and the telegraph lines stretched only to St. Joseph, Missouri. Ships that traveled around the tip of South America took six months to reach their destinations, though travelers who took the shortcut across the Isthmus of Panama might shorten the journey by a month. Overland travelers took nearly as long. Most people entrusted their mail to strangers, who promised that they would pass the mail on when they reached the other coast. By 1857, the Butterfield Overland Mail Company won a contract to carry U.S. mail on its stagecoaches traveling the overland trails, but the trip still took about twenty-five days. A better solution was needed.

By 1860, the country bubbled with the turmoil of the coming civil war. To keep the growing population of California abreast of the news, the country needed an express mail service. After a conversation with California senator William M. Gwin, William Russell persuaded his partners, Alexander Majors and William Waddell, to start a delivery service they called the Pony Express. Russell's ambitious plan was to deliver mail between Sacramento, California, and St. Joseph, Missouri, in ten days. Russell's partners were reluctant because they could see no way to make a profit from such an enterprise. Nevertheless, they agreed and quickly established a plan for the service to succeed.

In order for the Pony Express to deliver mail in ten days, it needed the fastest horses and the most committed riders. To beat the clock, riders would have to run their horses at top speed. But the horses tired quickly and had to be changed frequently. To supply fresh horses, the company built relay stations every 10 to 20 miles along the nearly 2,000-mile route. The riders would spend about two minutes at a station, just long enough to throw the *mochila* (the

Pony Express rider Frank E. Webner. Pony Express carriers had to ride their horses at top speed to deliver mail between Sacramento, California, and St. Joseph, Missouri, in ten days. *(Courtesy of the National Archives and Records Administration.)*

leather saddlebag that held the mail) over the back of a fresh horse and ride off again.

"Willing to risk death daily"

The route was difficult and dangerous. The riders spent long hours in the saddle and were sometimes threatened by hostile Indians, horse thieves, or unbearable heat or cold. Russell, Majors, and Waddell knew the kind of men they needed. Their help-wanted announcements read: "Wanted—young, skinny, wiry fellows not over eighteen. Must be expert riders, willing to risk death daily. Orphans preferred. Wages $25 per week." From the hundreds who applied, eighty were hired. William F. Cody (1846–1917) was the most famous of the riders. Cody joined the Pony Express when he was fourteen and holds the record for the longest ride without a break for sleep (384 miles). Cody later became famous as Buffalo Bill Cody, the leader of a traveling Wild West show.

Pony Express riders were admired for their skill and bravery. Many became local heroes when they reached towns. But even those who never saw a Pony Express rider were enthralled by the idea of men who would risk everything to speed the mail across the country. Writer Mark Twain (1835–1910) captured the public's fascination with the riders in *Roughing It,* which he wrote while traveling west by stagecoach:

> We had a consuming desire from the beginning, to see a pony rider; but somehow or other all that passed us, and all that met us managed to streak by in the night and so we heard only a whiz and a hail, and the swift phantom of the desert was gone before we could get our heads out of the windows. But now we were expecting one along any moment, and would see him in broad daylight. Presently the driver exclaims:
>
> "Here he comes!"

... [T]he flutter of hoofs comes faintly to the ear—another instant and a whoop and a hurrah from our upper deck, a wave of the rider's hands but no reply and man and horse burst past our excited faces and winging away like the belated fragment of a storm!

So sudden is it all, and so like a flash of unreal fancy, that but for a flake of white foam left quivering and perishing on a mail sack after the vision had flashed by and disappeared, we might have doubted whether we had seen any actual horse and man at all, maybe.

The end of the Express

After just eighteen months of faithful service, the Pony Express became obsolete. With the transcontinental telegraph line completed on October 24, 1861, messages could reach the West Coast in minutes. But the Pony Express had captured the hearts of Americans and lives on today in the legends of the men who would brave any perils to deliver the mail. Through harsh conditions, the Pony Express completed 308 runs and delivered 34,753 letters, losing one rider and one *mochila* along the way. An article at the time in the *Sacramento Daily Bee* summed up the public sentiment toward the orders to discontinue the service:

Farewell and forever, thou staunch, wilderness-overcoming, swift-footed messenger. For the good thou hast done we praise thee; and, having run thy race, and accomplished all that was hoped for and expected, we can part with thy services without regret, because, and only because, in the progress of thy age, in the advance of science and by the enterprise of capital, thou hast been superseded by a more subtle, active, but no more faithful, public servant.

The telegraph

Also known as the "talking" or "singing" wire, the telegraph came to the United States in 1843, when Congress passed a bill enabling Samuel F. B. Morse (1791–1872) to construct the first telegraph line between Washington and Baltimore. Morse had conceived of the telegraph much earlier, in 1832, and the first telegraph message was sent in 1838 after Morse coordinated his efforts with business associates Alfred Vail and Leonard Gale. The instant communication offered by Morse's system of wire taps (later called Morse code) inspired many entrepreneurs, who hastily built small local and regional telegraph systems. By 1851, fifty telegraph companies were operating in the United States. But by 1856, Hiram Sibley had begun consolidating the independent telegraph lines into his newly formed company, Western Union Telegraph Company. Between 1857 and 1861 other companies consolidated until the U.S. telegraph interests were held by only six systems.

By the beginning of the Civil War, commercial interests were keen to build a transcontinental telegraph line. To connect the eastern telegraph systems with the West, Congress passed the Telegraph Act of 1860, which granted the lowest bidder public lands and a yearly contract to operate a telegraph line connecting the East to San Francisco, California. Sibley won the contract and formed the Pacific Telegraph Company to start construction westward from Omaha, Nebraska, to Salt Lake City, Utah. Sibley sent his associate Jeptha H. Wade west to form the Overland Telegraph Company, which would handle construction eastward from Fort Churchill in the Nevada Territory (on the border of California) and extend the existing California lines to Salt Lake City. In July 1861, the Pacific Telegraph Company and the Overland Telegraph Company raised the first poles for the transcontinental telegraph line.

As the companies advanced, they set up new telegraph stations daily to keep in touch with Sacramento and Omaha. To bridge the distance not yet linked by wire, Western Union had made a special arrangement for Pony Express riders to carry messages between the two companies as they slowly worked toward each other.

By October 24, 1861, telegraphers sent the first message from San Francisco to Washington. The message from Chief Justice Stephen Field of California assured the recipient, President Abraham Lincoln, of California's loyalty to the Union. The *New York Times* is quoted in *Seven Trails West* as remarking that "the work of carrying westward the transcontinental telegraph line has progressed with so little blazonment [publicity], that it is with almost an electric thrill one reads the words of greeting yesterday flashed instantaneously over the wires from California." The coasts of the country, the article continued, are now "united by this noblest symbol of our modern civilization." Two days after that first message, the other U.S. express message service, the Pony Express, ended—a financial failure, but secure as a legendary part of conquering the West.

The stringing of telegraph wire across the country did not inspire the hero worship that the Pony Express riders did, but the telegraph was one of the most transforming technologies to influence the development of the West. The telegraph was the first American industry based on electricity and the first monopoly, and it turned a profit from the beginning. The telegraph's ability to send news from one coast to the other in a matter of minutes fostered the growth of news agencies and other commercial enterprises, and it revolutionized railroad operations. The telegraph remained one of the most important technologies in the development of social and commercial life in America until the emergence of the telephone and the radio in the late nineteenth and early twentieth centuries.

Barbed wire

Barbed-wire fencing revolutionized the practice of raising cattle in the West. Fencing was not new to cattlemen; fencing in other parts of the country had typically been constructed from stones, tree trunks, or any surplus material left after clearing the land. But the western prairies, stretching from Texas north to Canada, didn't have surplus building material. The western prairies were the ultimate grazing ground for livestock, a natural rangeland with few trees or rocks. Since the government owned the prairies, the rangeland and water for the cattle were free. Thinking that traditional methods of fencing their herds would be too expensive and too difficult to maintain, cattlemen instead hired cowboys to help herd their animals across the prairies from the lush natural grasslands to water. A culture of long, cooperative cattle drives came to characterize the prairies as cowboys drove herds to market. But cheap, easy-to-install barbed wire would soon change ranching forever.

At the De Kalb County Fair of 1873, three men saw a piece of wood with bits of wire sticking out of it that Henry M. Rose had made to control a "breachy" cow (a cow that

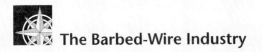

The Barbed-Wire Industry

Figures from 1874 to 1880 show the growth of the barbed-wire industry.

Year	Amount of Barbed Wire Made and Sold
1874	10,000 lbs.
1875	600,000 lbs.
1876	2,840,000 lbs.
1877	12,863,000 lbs.
1878	26,655,000 lbs.
1879	50,377,000 lbs.
1880	80,500,000 lbs.

Source: Walter Prescott Webb. Great Plains. (Boston: Ginn and Company, 1931).

tries to escape): lumberman Jacob Haish; hardware merchant Isaac Leonard Ellwood; and farmer Joseph Farwell Glidden, a man worried about raising his crops without the security of good, strong fencing. Ellwood remembered the day in *A History of De Kalb County, Illinois,* noting that "all three of us stood looking at this invention of Mr. Rose's and I think that each one of us at that hour conceived the idea that barbs could be placed on the wire in some way instead of being driven into the strip of wood." With Glidden's wire stretcher and barbed-wire design, which he patented in November 1874, farming on the prairie would soon change dramatically. Glidden and Ellwood became partners in The Barb Fence Company, and Haish became their first competitor with his own barbed-wire design. Their products were met with enthusiasm in the marketplace, and the barbed-wire industry grew rapidly.

The Homestead Act of 1862 and the railroads that came later moved many people onto the prairies. The cattle that had freely roamed the vast prairies were soon impeded by homesteaders (people who were granted ownership of land by living and working on it) who strung barbed fences around their newly acquired property. Sensing that their way of life was threatened, ranchers, who had up to this point worked out informal range rights among themselves, began to homestead as much property as they could. What they could not homestead they bought or leased. If they could not acquire the land, they sometimes fenced it anyway.

By the 1880s, cattlemen had realized that ringing their herds with barbed-wire fences allowed them to reduce their labor costs by employing fewer cowboys. It also gave them more control over their herds, keeping their prized bulls from wandering and impregnating competitors' cattle and allowing ranchers to rotate herds from pasture to pasture to prevent overgrazing. Barbed wire ended the old methods of ranching. Gone were the long trail drives that characterized the prairies from 1866 to 1880 (see Chapter 9). Cowboys no longer lived the rough-and-tumble life that fostered so many romantic visions. Instead of herding their boss's cattle over vast public prairie lands, they now worked more as traditional farmhands, drilling wells to provide water to pastures that did not border on streams and tending the fenced herds. The longhorn cattle, a hybrid of Spanish and British cattle, were soon bred out of existence as fencing was used to separate breeds and improve a cattleman's stock.

The Fence-Cutters War

As barbed wire changed the practice of ranching, conflicts erupted over its impact. Controversy over the improper and unfair use of barbed fencing provoked arguments over who had the right to use public lands. After erecting miles of fencing around public lands, the largest cattle-raising companies tried to secure leases to graze their animals on federal lands. By 1883, those opposed to fencing the open range had begun cutting barbed fences in a protest since labeled the fence-cutting wars (see Chapter 9). Texas ranchers were so evenly divided over the issue and so violent in their opinions that civil war seemed a real possibility. Texas governor John Ireland called out the Texas Rangers to protect the peace and held a special legislative session to solve the problem. Legislation regulating how and where fences could be erected on or near public lands curbed the fence cutting in Texas in 1884, and similar legislation soon eased tensions in other states. The impact of the laws was impressive: they ended the fence-cutting wars less than a year after the conflicts started and reinforced the patterns of ranching introduced by barbed-wire fencing. Nevertheless, the pain of the struggle was so great that fence cutting remained a felony in Texas at the end of the twentieth century.

Conclusion

Westward expansion would still have proceeded without the technological achievements described in this chapter, but it would have happened more slowly and in a very different way. Inventions helped determine the very shape of the West. The telegraph instantly connected Americans across thousands of miles; railroads killed some towns and gave birth to others; the gun quickly established the settlers' dominance over the country; and barbed wire created vast ranching empires. In the end, technology was one of many factors that contributed to the making of the American West.

For More Information

Books

Clifton, Robert T. *Barbs, Prongs, Points, Prickers, and Stickers: A Complete and Illustrated Catalogue of Antique Barbed Wire.* Norman: University of Oklahoma Press, 1970.

Moody, Ralph. *Stagecoach West.* New York: Crowell, 1967.

Voight, Virginia. *Stagecoach Days and Stagecoach Kings.* Champaign, IL: Garrard Publishing, 1970.

Webb, Walter Prescott. *Great Plains.* Boston: Ginn & Company, 1931.

West, Tom. *Heroes on Horseback: The Story of the Pony Express.* New York: Four Winds Press, 1969.

Web sites

Adventures of Wells Fargo. [Online] http://wellsfargo.com/about/stories/ (accessed April 14, 2000).

Everett, George. "Ex-Slave Mary Fields at Home in Montana Whether Working in a Convent or Managing a Mail Route." *Wild West.* [Online] http://www.thehistorynet.com/WildWest/articles/02963_text.htm (accessed April 14, 2000).

The History of the Erie Canal. [Online] http://www.history.rochester.edu/canal/index.htm (accessed April 14, 2000).

Riding on the Overland Stage: Mark Twain's Account. [Online] http://www.ibiscom.com/stage.htm (accessed April 14, 2000).

The West: The Grandest Enterprise Under God, 1868–1874. [Online] http://www.pbs.org/weta/thewest/wpages/wpgs100/w150_001.htm (accessed April 14, 2000).

When the Pony Express Was in Vogue. [Online] http://www.sfmuseum.org/hist1/pxpress.html (accessed April 14, 2000).

Sources

Boies, Henry L. *A History of DeKalb County, Illinois.* Evansville, IA: Whipporwill Publications, 1987.

Bourne, Russell. *Floating West: The Erie and Other American Canals.* New York: W. W. Norton, 1992.

Coe, Lewis. *The Telegraph: A History of Morse's Invention and Its Predecessors in the United States.* Jefferson, NC: McFarland & Company, 1993.

Dale, Rodney. *Early Railways.* New York: Oxford University Press, 1994.

Dicerto, Joseph J. *The Pony Express: Hoofbeats in the Wilderness.* New York: Franklin Watts, 1989.

Ferris, Robert G., series ed. *Prospector, Cowhand, and Sodbuster: Historic Places Associated with the Mining, Ranching, and Farming Frontiers in the Trans-Mississippi West.* Vol. 11. Washington, DC: United States Department of the Interior National Parks Service, 1967.

Hawke, David Freeman. *Nuts and Bolts of the Past: A History of American Technology, 1776–1860.* New York: Harper & Row, 1988.

Hilton, Suzanne. *Getting There: Frontier Travel without Power.* Philadelphia: Westminster Press, 1980.

Lauber, Patricia. *Cowboys and Cattle Ranching Yesterday and Today.* New York: Thomas Y. Crowell, 1973.

Laughlin, Rosemary. *The Great Iron Link: The Building of the Central Pacific Railroad.* Greensboro, NC: Morgan Reynolds, 1996.

McCallum, Henry D., and Frances T. McCallum. *The Wire That Fenced the West.* Norman, OK: University of Oklahoma Press, 1965.

McNeese, Tim. *America's Early Canals.* New York: Crestwood House, 1993.

McNeese, Tim. *America's First Railroads.* New York: Crestwood House, 1993.

Monaghan, Jay. *The Book of the American West.* New York: Messner, 1963.

Peters, Arthur King. *Seven Trails West.* New York: Abbeville Press, 1996.

Rennert, Vincent Paul. *Western Outlaws.* New York: Crowell-Collier Press, 1968.

Thompson, George A. *Throw Down the Box! Treasure and Tales from Gilmer and Salisbury the Western Stagecoach King.* Salt Lake City, UT: Dream Garden Press, 1989.

Van Der Linde, Laurel. *The Pony Express.* New York: Macmillan, New Discovery Books, 1993.

The Frontier and American Character

12

The frontier has long held a special place in the hearts and minds of Americans. Since shortly after the first colonies were founded on the Atlantic coast, the frontier has beckoned to settlers. The frontier was the wilderness just outside the civilized towns; it offered people an opportunity to strike out and succeed on their own. In Europe, a serf (a laborer who works the land and is owned by the lord who owns the land) could never think of leaving his allotted plot of land to rise from poverty, nor could a shopkeeper's son ever hope to run his own store before his father's death. But in America, a hardy immigrant could determine his or her own destiny on the unknown frontier.

To venture into the wilderness took daring and courage. Pioneers carried their belongings until they found a spot worth claiming. Whole families or groups of people gathered to venture out into the unknown with a wagon train of supplies. Forging their own way or following others' dusty tracks, pioneers braved Indian attacks and unknown environments to find a satisfactory plot of land. After trekking hundreds and sometimes thousands of miles, the pioneers built their homes and other necessary buildings, gathered and hunted the bounties of the new land or cleared fields for crops, and set about establishing the rules for their new life on the frontier. Each of these tasks made up the process of "frontiering." Despite the difficulties of frontiering—forging into unknown territory, battling hostile enemies, braving harsh weather, suffering countless dangers and possibly death in order to build a new life—pioneers displayed an untiring optimism that things would go their way.

Defining the frontier

By definition, the American frontier meant the vast unclaimed land west of white civilization. As whites spread westward from the Atlantic coast, the boundary of the frontier also moved farther west. As each group of pioneers carved out their spot on the frontier, communities soon developed around them. The land became "civilized" as pioneers forced Indians to move farther west, and the small settlements grew into thriving towns. The newly civilized land now bordered on the frontier.

From the first settlements at Jamestown in 1607, the process of frontiering was repeated for three hundred years until the entire continent was settled. For the first settlers, the West began at the edge of Massachusetts Bay or Chesapeake Bay. By the colonial period, civilization had reached the crest of the Appalachian Mountains. After the War of 1812 (1812–14) settlements civilized the land up to the banks of the Mississippi River. But it was not until the mid-1800s that large numbers of settlers ventured farther than the Mississippi River. These settlers arrived on the Pacific coast and, in 1850, established the state of California. From that point, on the frontier—the wild, unclaimed land—consisted of the Great Plains, the desert Southwest, and the Rocky Mountains.

Four centuries after the discovery of America, the frontier had disappeared. The hardiest fur traders and mountain men had explored and settled parts of the West long before the mass western emigrations demanded complete American control of the territory between the Atlantic and Pacific Oceans. While the fur traders and mountain men arrived first, and in some cases established American claims to territories, mass emigrations do more to illustrate the extraordinary pull of the frontier. Between 1800 and 1870, nearly half a million Ameri-

cans set out across the frontier. Trappers, traders, farmers, and families set out on a journey of discovery. The pioneers traveled across plains and deserts and over high mountain passes, taking a chance that there was a better life somewhere to the west. They endured weeks and even months of arduous travel in order to reach their destination and build the communities that defined the American West.

A pioneer cabin in the Yosemite Valley, California (c. 1855). *(By Currier and Ives. © Hulton Getty/Liaison Agency.)*

The call of the West

On the American frontier, as in few other places on earth, a person amounted to the sum of his or her skills and endurance. Without the established lines of ancestry and wealth that made up the social structure in Europe, success on the American frontier, with its wealth of natural resources and fertile lands, was open to anyone strong enough or courageous enough to master it. Never before had a society offered all its citizens the opportunity for success. In the

The Difficulties of Moving West

While traveling from Indiana over the Oregon Trail, pioneer Elizabeth Smith Geer recorded the hardships of emigration that shaped the character of many Americans. In November 1847, she wrote:

> It rains and snows. We start this morning around the falls with our wagons ... I carry my babe, and lead, or rather carry, another through snow, mud and water, almost to my knees. It is the worst road ... I went ahead with my children and I was afraid to look behind me for fear of seeing the wagons turn over into the mud ... My children gave out with cold and fatigue and could not travel and the boys had to unhitch the oxen and bring them and carry the children on to camp. I was so cold and numb. I could not tell by feeling that I had any feet at all ... I have not told you half we suffered. I am not adequate to the task.

Source: Schlissel, Lillian, ed. Women's Diaries of the Westward Journey. New York: Schocken Books, 1982.

American West, "all men were future 'gentlemen' and deserved this designation, all women were prospective 'ladies' and should be treated as such. 'With us,' one frontiersman stoutly maintained, 'a man's a man, whether he have a silk gown on him or not,'" writes Ray Allen Billington in Westward to the Pacific.

For many the unclaimed lands to the west represented the opportunity of a lifetime—a chance to take control of their lives, to strike it rich, to make their own rules, or to claim their own land. The gold rushes in California in 1849 and in Colorado in 1858 and the discovery of silver in Nevada in the mid-1800s lured people from the East and from all over the world. The overland trails guided settlers to the fertile lands of opportunity in the West.

Though some settled and began to "civilize" the frontier, others were intrigued by the vastness of the continent and the possible riches available ever farther west. Those who were not content to settle in one spot Billington labeled "men with the West in their eyes." These people would pick up at a moment's notice to move farther into the frontier in search of a better life. John Steinbeck (1902–1968) drew a compelling picture of these restless Americans in his novel The Red Pony. In describing his journeys, the Grandfather in the story says:

> It wasn't Indians that were important, nor adventures, nor even getting out here. It was a whole bunch of people made into one big crawling beast. And I was the head. It was westering and westering. Every man wanted something for himself, but the big beast that was all of them wanted only westering. I was the leader, but if I hadn't been there, someone else would have been the head. The thing had to have a head....

> The westering was as big as God, and the slow steps that made the movement piled up and piled up until the continent was crossed.

Then we came down to the sea, and it was done.... There's a line of old men along the shore hating the ocean because it stopped them.

These "men with the West in their eyes" personified the call of the frontier. For these Americans, "ahead of them, always ahead, danced the will-o'-the-wisp of illusive fortune: the untrapped beaver stream, the vein of gold ore, the fortunate land speculation. 'If hell lay to the west,' wrote one observer, 'they would cross heaven to reach it,'" according to Billington. Americans as a whole were constantly searching for a utopia they were certain existed on the frontier.

The Half Dome in Yosemite Valley, California, a glacial gorge about 7 miles long and 1 mile wide. Many easterners couldn't believe the stories of fur traders and mountain men who first described the beautiful and amazing geography of the West. (© Hilton Getty/Liaison Agency. Reproduced by permission.)

Manifest destiny

By 1845, the fervor for westward expansion had become a national obsession. In an article written in the *United States Magazine and Democratic Review* in 1845, newspaperman

John O'Sullivan coined the phrase "manifest destiny," which captured Americans' thoughts about the frontier and their rights to it (see Chapter 4). O'Sullivan wrote:

> The American claim is by the right of our manifest destiny to overspread and to possess the whole of the continent which Providence has given us for the development of the great experiment of liberty and federative self-government entrusted to us. It is a right such as that of the tree to the space of air and earth suitable for the full expansion of its principle and destiny of growth.... It is in our future far more than in our past or in the past history of Spanish exploration or French colonial rights, that our True Title is to be found.

O'Sullivan's description crystallized what many Americans had already said or thought about the frontier. A year before O'Sullivan's article, Senator David R. Atchinson of Missouri declared that the American "march of empire is westward; nothing will, nothing can check it." By 1848, America had already won the continent from the British, the French, and the Mexicans. The remaining Native American cultures bore the brunt of the drive to civilize the West. Belief in manifest destiny allowed the American government to declare Native American cultures "uncivilized" because they did not use the land in ways Americans perceived to be "productive" or "efficient." Believing themselves entitled to the land, Americans assumed the authority to dismiss other cultures' claims to the continent Americans desired. The government would enforce these beliefs during the Indian wars that dragged on until the 1890s (see Chapter 3).

The American character

America is a young nation compared to European countries and certainly an infant when measured against the ancient cultures of China and Japan. The immigrants (mostly European) who raced to America's shores during its first century brought with them their own traditions and histories. Though the cultures these immigrants brought with them were centuries old, the American continent transformed the immigrants' way of life so dramatically that a new American culture came to dominate their lives.

The frontier was the force that changed the lives of many Americans. Historian Frederick Jackson Turner (1861–

1932) first described how the American frontier transformed these immigrants to make the American character and culture unique. On July 12, 1893, Turner asserted that the call of the West played a bigger part than the cultural legacies of Europe in forming American culture. The trials and tribulations suffered by people who dared to enter an unknown wilderness made them stronger, more self-reliant, and more inventive. Turner maintained that the experience of picking up their belongings to forge a new life in a new place made Americans uniquely American. Turner credited the frontier with giving Americans a "coarseness and strength combined with acuteness and inquisitiveness; that practical, inventive turn of mind, quick to find expedients; that masterful grasp of material things, lacking in the artistic but powerful to effect great ends; that restless, nervous energy; that dominant individualism working for good and for evil; and withal that buoyancy and exuberance which comes from freedom." Each of these adventurous and self-reliant traits continues to be associated with the American character.

Turner's thesis revolutionized the way Americans thought of themselves. Between 1830 and 1870, a little more than 2 percent of history textbooks cited the importance of the West in shaping the American character, while the majority explained it in terms of European ancestry. After Turner's thesis became widely accepted, the Western experience became a rich source that historians could mine for clues about the American character. Between 1900 and 1925, 93 percent of published student textbooks named the frontier as the most influential force in the nation's development, according to Paul O'Neil in *The End and the Myth*.

Democracy and the frontier

Further study into the West and how frontiering reshaped men and women revealed more commonalities among Americans. In his book *America's Frontier Heritage,* Ray Allen Billington elaborated on Turner's description of Americans' unique qualities:

> Their faith in democratic institutions, their belief in equality, their insistence that class lines shall never hinder social mobility, their wasteful economy, their unwillingness to admit that automation has lessened the need for hard work,

their lack of attachment to place, their eagerness to experiment and to favor the new over the old, all mark the people of the United States as unique. To say that these characteristics and attitudes were solely the result of a pioneering past is to ignore many other forces that have helped shape the American character. But to deny that three centuries of frontiering endowed the people with some of their most distinctive traits is to neglect a basic molding force that has been the source of the nation's greatest strength—and some of its most regrettable weaknesses.

Billington's description concurred with much that Turner had described, but he added insight into America's brand of governance. The idea that class lines would not condemn men to certain positions in life, Americans' desire for equality, and a trust in democracy shaped by the governments on the frontier have come to define some of the most vital American institutions. The rugged individualists who forged the new frontier did not want the government to tell them what to do. Instead, they favored governance by many. As new governments formed in the West, these pioneers established more relaxed voting requirements than those found in the East, granting more men the right to vote—and extending the vote to women well before eastern states. Indeed, once settlers stopped and founded their own communities, they demanded certain protections from the federal government. Senator Thomas Hart Benton (1782–1858) noted that westward expansion "was not an act of government leading the people and protecting them, but ... it was the act of the people going forward without government aid or countenance [approval], establishing their possession and compelling the Government to follow with its shield and spread it over them," according to Richard White in *"It's Your Misfortune and None of My Own": A New History of the American West.*

Settlers demanded protection, and the U.S. government responded to their needs. The national legislature passed two laws that were crucial to the history of westward expansion: the Ordinance of 1785 and the Northwest Ordinance. The Ordinance of 1785 established a pattern for the surveying and division of all territories west of the point where the Ohio River leaves the state of Pennsylvania. "That first square inch of the first surveyor's stake," writes Elliot West in *The Oxford History of the American West,* "was

a kind of polestar of national development, the anchored point of reckoning for more than a billion acres. Nowhere else in the world would an area of such size be laid out in a uniform land system." While the Ordinance of 1785 provided for the orderly arrangement of the land, the Northwest Ordinance, also known as the Ordinance of 1787, provided for the orderly establishment of future states. The Northwest Ordinance guaranteed that new states would enjoy all the rights and privileges of existing states. It established a system of laws in the territories, forbade slavery, and guaranteed certain civil rights. These two ordinances attempted to impose order on the growth of the United States, and in so doing they established the power of the federal government over the country. The frontier thus shaped the balance of power between the states and the federal government. In fact, Turner felt that the "most important effect of the frontier has been in the promotion of democracy here and in Europe."

Ferdinand Vandiveer Hayden's survey camp, part of the United States Army's Corps of Topographical Engineers in 1870, near Pelican Creek, fifteen miles east of Yellowstone Lake, Wyoming. The Corps of Topographical Engineers was formed in 1838 to make maps and surveys that would help settlers move into the frontier. (© Hulton Getty/Liaison Agency. Reproduced by permission.)

The Frontier and American Character | 239

Spreading the myth

Some of the best evidence of the frontier's influence on the American character comes from popular culture. In paintings and sculpture, literature, dime novels, pulp magazines, live performances, film, and television, western life was exaggerated and glamorized. These retellings formed a western myth. The heroes and villains who conquered the West lived such extraordinary lives that their legends still thrive more than a century after their deaths.

In 1823, novelist James Fenimore Cooper (1789–1851) introduced his fictional frontier hero, Natty Bumppo, in *The Pioneers*. In the first of Cooper's four Leatherstocking tales, the frontiersman Natty Bumppo, also known as Leatherstocking, is pitted against the forces of a developing, westward-moving American society. The stories explore the conflicts between civilization and freedom and between law and nature. Cooper's protagonist was modeled after the famed backwoodsman and settler of the state of Kentucky, Daniel Boone (1734–1820). Both wore buckskins, lived alone in the wilderness, befriended some Indians and killed others, fought wild animals, and remained modest throughout their exploits. Although Cooper never visited the West, his character Leatherstocking became one of the most influential and enduring characters in American literature.

In the 1860s, novels sold for a dime apiece and reached a mass market. In these "dime novels" the western developed as a distinct form of writing, one that relied on moral heroes, a great deal of action, and sentimental descriptions of the western landscape. The heroes and outlaws of the real West inspired many of the writers, who wrote about both real and imaginary westerners. The novels did much to establish the western legend in the public's mind with stories about circling wagons, U.S. Cavalry battles, rustlers, cowboys, and strong (and beautiful) pioneer women. The Street and Smith publishing house dedicated its dime novels to stories about Buffalo Bill Cody (1846–1917). Other publishers turned out novels about the real and exaggerated exploits of scouts Kit Carson (1809–1868), Wild Bill Hickok (1837–1876), and General George Armstrong Custer (1839–1876), among others. By 1919, *Western Story Magazine* offered these epic themes to a mass audience. Similar western pulp magazines soon circulated.

One of the most famous writers of westerns during the early twentieth century was Max Brand (1892–1944), who wrote hundreds of western stories as well as some of the first western films. Perhaps the most influential western story was Owen Wister's *The Virginian*. Published in 1902, the book went through sixteen printings in its first year and remained in print at the end of the twentieth century. The book's hero is "a horseman of the plains" who ably handles horses, whose character is tested in battles with cattle rustlers, and who wins the heart of a cultured schoolteacher. *The Virginian* "draws all the elements of the mythic West together into an artistic whole, which in turn became definitive for the westerns of the new century," according to *The Oxford History of the American West*.

The Wild West show

In 1883, Buffalo Bill Cody became the first real westerner to try to cash in on the western myth. In his three-hour Wild West show, Buffalo Bill, dressed in buckskin, offered audiences displays of marksmanship and horsemanship. He hired real Native Americans to wear warbonnets and reenact battles with sharpshooting scouts or cowboys. At one time Cody hired the Sioux chief Sitting Bull (c. 1831–1890) and later the Apache chief Geronimo (1829–1909) to tour with his show. Audiences flocked to the shows to get a glimpse of what they thought were accurate slices of frontier life. Although Cody did hire "real" cowboys and Indians, the show did not realistically depict western life. The cowboys wore furry chaps, ten-gallon hats, and shining spurs; they were not the sweat-stained cow-

James Fenimore Cooper

James Fenimore Cooper (1789–1851) became a novelist by chance. Born in Burlington, New Jersey, he grew up in Cooperstown, New York, a settlement founded on Otsego Lake by his father, William, a prominent land speculator, judge, and Federalist politician. Entering Yale at age thirteen, Cooper was expelled in his third year for playing a prank. He enlisted in the U.S. Navy for many years, leaving in 1811 to marry Susan DeLancey, heiress to what Cooper called "a handsome fortune." Cooper then prepared to spend his life as a gentleman farmer.

But while Cooper was reading aloud to his wife in 1820, he suddenly threw down the novel and declared, "I can write you a better novel than that, myself!" His wife challenged him to do so, and he quickly wrote and published *Precaution* that same year. He wrote another novel the following year and in 1823, published *The Pioneers,* the book that established him as a successful American author. His tales of Leatherstocking explored the moral implications of westward expansion and made Cooper one of the first to depict the West in fiction.

boys of the range. Indians appeared in flamboyant war paint and feathered warbonnets rather than their drab everyday dress. The public lapped up the Wild West show, and imitators scrambled to put on similar extravaganzas. These shows live on in the public rodeos that started in the mid-1800s as relaxing festivals for real cowboys. Today, rodeo continues as a sport that is far removed from the task of bringing beef to market. Nevertheless, the public still thrills to see displays of western skill.

Film and art

More than any history or novel or live performance about the western experience, however, movies have shaped the public's image of the West. The first western film was *The Great Train Robbery* in 1903. For the first time, audiences could see a holdup, a pursuit on horseback, a saloon scene, and a showdown between criminals and lawmen. By 1910, the Old West was regularly depicted in film. The cowboy hero remained tough, resolute, and always masculine. Tom Mix (1880–1940) became the most popular western film hero of the silent era with his white hat and his sidekick horse. He appeared in more than three hundred films in which he wore fancy western costumes and performed fantastic stunts that engendered decades of imitation. With his performance in *Stagecoach* in 1939, John Wayne (1907–1979) took Mix's place as the embodiment of the western hero in film. Wayne, Mix, and hundreds of other Hollywood cowboys shaped the public's perceptions of the West. "The myths they wove and those woven about them were in themselves a force that shaped the history of the West and of the country as a whole," according to O'Neil in *The End of the Myth*. These myths were reinforced later in television shows like *Bonanza* and *The Lone Ranger.*

Paintings and sculptures also shaped Americans' image of the frontier. George Catlin (1796–1872) was the first painter to devote his career to the West. Intrigued by a delegation of Indians he saw passing through Philadelphia, Catlin resolved to document them as a historian. Starting in 1832 he began an eight-year study to document what he called a "doomed" race. By the end of his study he had painted members of 146 different Indian nations. With his portraits, in-

cluding his 1832 *Buffalo Bull's Back Fat, Head Chief of the Blood Tribe of Blackfeet,* he became the first American to portray Indians with individual identities. Catlin, Samuel Seymour (who was the first to provide pictorial accounts of the Rocky Mountains), and John Mix Stanley were the first to document the landscape and the people of the West.

Though earlier artists created hundreds of pictures of the West, later painters, especially Frederic Remington (1861–1909) and Charles M. Russell (1864–1926), would define western art. Remington and Russell began to glamorize the West in their art even as the frontier was closing. Between 1889 and 1909 Remington created more than twenty-seven hundred paintings and drawings and twenty-four editions of bronze sculptures that captured the winning of the West. He made a career of painting the white–Indian conflict, especially the white man's triumph in those conflicts. Russell, called the "cowboy artist," spent his career depicting the loss of the

Utes Watching for the Relief Column, **by Frederic Remington.** *(Reproduced by permission of North Wind Picture Archives.)*

frontier in his paintings. The sixteen-year-old Russell wrangled horses in Montana starting in 1880, but within a decade the roving Indians, the cowboys, and the roundups of open-range cattle he cherished were disappearing. Russell vowed to become the Old West's main chronicler. His paintings commemorated the Old West of his memories and imagination. His subjects were heroes of the open range, men who roamed the prairies before barbed wire fenced in their cattle. From memory he drew prairie schooners (covered wagons), buffalo stampedes, longhorn herds, cow camps, and saloons.

Conclusion

The frontier and its effect on the American character remain central to understanding what makes Americans unique. Though the frontier has been gone for more than a century, Americans continue to identify with the trials and tribulations of those who conquered the West. Presidential nominee John F. Kennedy (1917–1963) tapped into Americans' love of the frontier to call Americans to new action. At the Democratic Party's national convention in 1960, Kennedy implored Americans to look to the new frontiers of "science and space, unsolved problems of peace and war, unconquered pockets of ignorance and prejudice, unanswered questions of poverty and surplus." At the end of the twentieth century, Americans continued to look to these new frontiers.

For More Information

Barr, Roger. *The American Frontier.* World History Series. San Diego, CA: Lucent Books, 1996.

Billington, Ray Allen. *America's Frontier Heritage.* New York: Holt, Rinehart & Winston, 1966.

Billington, Ray Allen. *Westward to the Pacific: An Overview of Westward Expansion.* St. Louis, MO: Jefferson National Expansion Historical Association, 1979.

Folsom, James K. *The American Western Novel.* New Haven, CT: College & University Press, 1966.

Mancall, Peter C., ed. *American Eras: Westward Expansion 1800–1886.* Detroit: Gale Research, 1999.

Milner, Clyde A., II, Carol A. O'Connor, and Martha A. Sandweiss, eds. *The Oxford History of the American West.* New York: Oxford University Press, 1994.

O'Neil, Paul. *The End of the Myth*. Alexandria, VA: Time-Life Books, 1979.

Schlissel, Lillian, ed. *Women's Diaries of the Westward Journey*. New York: Schocken Books, 1982.

Smith, Carter, ed. *The Conquest of the West: A Sourcebook on the American West*. Brookfield, CT: Millbrook Press, 1992.

Steckmesser, Kent Ladd. *The Western Hero in History and Legend*. Norman: University of Oklahoma Press, 1965.

Steinbeck, John. *The Red Pony*. New York: Viking, 1945.

Turner, Frederick Jackson. *The Frontier in American History*. New York: Henry Holt and Co., 1950.

White, Richard. *"It's Your Misfortune and None of My Own": A New History of the American West*. Norman: University of Oklahoma Press, 1991.

Where to Learn More

The following list of resources focuses on works appropriate for middle school or high school students. These sources offer broad coverage of the history of westward expansion. For additional resources on specific topics please see individual chapters. Please note that the web site addresses, though verified prior to publication, are subject to change.

Books

Billington, Ray Allen. *Westward to the Pacific: An Overview of Westward Expansion.* St. Louis, MO: Jefferson National Expansion Historical Association, 1979.

Collins, James L. *Exploring the American West.* New York: Franklin Watts, 1989.

Edwards, Cheryl, ed. *Westward Expansion: Exploration and Settlement.* Lowell, MA: Discovery Enterprises, 1995.

Erdosh, George. *Food and Recipes of the Westward Expansion.* New York: PowerKids Press, 1997.

Faber, Harold. *From Sea to Sea: The Growth of the United States.* New York: Charles Scribner's Sons, 1967, 1992.

Mancall, Peter C., ed. *Westward Expansion, 1800–1860.* Detroit: Gale, 1999.

Milner, Clyde A., II, Carol A. O'Connor, and Martha A. Sandweiss, eds. *The Oxford*

History of the American West. New York and Oxford: Oxford University Press, 1994.

Penner, Lucille Recht. *Westward Ho!: The Story of the Pioneers.* New York: Random House, 1997.

Smith, Carter, ed. *The Conquest of the West: A Sourcebook on the American West.* Brookfield, CT: Millbrook Press, 1992.

Utley, Robert M., and Wilcomb E. Washburn. *Indian Wars.* Boston: Houghton Mifflin, 1987.

Waldman, Carl. *Atlas of the North American Indian.* New York: Facts on File, 1985.

Wexler, Alan, ed. *Atlas of Westward Expansion.* New York: Facts On File, 1995.

White, Richard. *"It's Your Misfortune and None of My Own": A New History of the American West.* Norman: University of Oklahoma Press, 1991.

Web sites

"American History Sources for Students: The Westward Movement." *Global Access to Educational Sources: A Cybrary for Middle School and Beyond.* [Online] http://www.geocities.com/Athens/Academy/6617/west.html (accessed June 5, 2000).

The American West [Online] http://www.americanwest.com (accessed April 4, 2000).

Georgia College and State University. *Ina Dillard Russel Library Special Collections: Native American Resources.* [Online] http://library.gcsu.edu/~sc/resna.html (accessed April 6, 2000).

Internet Resources about Black Cowboys and Pioneers. [Online] http://danenent.wicip.org/lms/themes/cowboys.html (accessed April 14, 2000).

The West [Online] http://www.pbs.org/weta/thewest/ (accessed April 4, 2000).

"Which 'Old West' and Whose?" *American History 102: Civil War to the Present.* [Online] http://us.history.wisc.edu/hist102/lectures/lecture03.html (accessed June 5, 2000).

Index

A

Abbott, Teddy Blue 178
Abilene, Kansas 74, 176
Adams, John Quincy 64
Alamo Mission 64–65
American River 71, 106, 110
Annexation 66
Apache Indians 100, 133, 135
Argonauts 119
Astor, John Jacob 33, 34 (ill.), 84
Astoria 33, 34

B

Barbed wire 72, 183, 225
Barboncito 134, 156
Battle of Chapultepec 70
Battle of Little Bighorn 142–43, 166
Battle of New Orleans 17
Battle of the Thames 17
Battle of Tippecanoe 50–51, 51 (ill.), 192

Battle of Wounded Knee 143 (ill.), 144, 167
Bear Flag Revolt 69
Becknell, William 79
Black Bart 211, 212–13, 213 (ill.)
Black Hills, South Dakota 141, 164
Black Kettle 139, 162
Blackfeet Indians 27
Bloody Island Massacre of 1850 125
Boone, Daniel 5, 23
Bonaparte, Napoleon 14
Bosque Redondo 135, 157
Bowie, Jim 65
Bozeman, John 100
Bozeman Trail 100–2, 163
Brand, Max 241
Brannan, Sam 110
Brant, Joseph 6, 154, 154 (ill.)
Bridger, Jim 34
British colonies 1–6
Buffalo 159, 161 (ill.), 162, 163
Buffalo Bill *see* William Cody
Butterfield, John 100, 210

Illustrations are marked by (ill.).

C

California 106–9, 124–26
California Trail 90–92
Californios 109–10, 126
Camino Real 82
Canals 206–9
Canby, Edward 134
Canyon de Chelly 135, 157, 157 (ill.)
Carleton, James 134, 136, 156
Carrington, Henry B. 101
Carson, Kit 135, 156, 220
Cartwright, Peter 196 (ill.), 197
Catlin, George 242
Cattle drive 172–78
Cattle Kingdom 179 (ill.)
Cattle ranching 74, 225–27
Cayuga Indians 152
Chapultepec, Battle of 70
Cherokee Indians 6, 54
Cheyenne Indians 101, 140
Chinese immigrants in California 124, 127 (ill.)
Chippewa Indians 48
Chivington, John M. 139
Cholera 98, 117, 190
Church of Jesus Christ of Latter-day Saints 197
Cimarron Cutoff 80–81, 81 (ill.)
Cincinnati, Ohio 12
Civil War 40–41, 174, 214–16
Clark, William 24–28, 25 (ill.), 60
Cochise 100, 136, 137 (ill.)
Cody, William 222, 241
Colonies see British colonies
Colorado Valley 40 (ill.)
Colt revolver 218–20
Columbia River 62
Commerce in the West 82
Compromise of 1850 125
Cooper, James Fenimore 240, 241
Cornplanter 154
"Corps of Discovery" 25–28
Corps of Topographical Engineers 35–37, 40, 239 (ill.)
Covered wagons 67(ill.), 71 (ill.), 92–96, 96 (ill.), 116–19
Cowboys 74, 172–81, 175 (ill.), 225 see also Vaqueros
Crazy Horse 140, 142–44, 166, 166 (ill.)
Creek Indians 52
Crockett, Davy 65
Crook, George 137
Crow Indians 101
Custer, George Armstrong 141–42, 166

D

Davis, Jacob 118
Deadwood, South Dakota 171 (ill.)
Deere, John 72
Diggers 107
Dime novels 240
Dodge City, Kansas 180
Donner Party 92, 93 (ill.), 94–95

E

Early expansion 1, 13 (ill.), 21
Emigrants 10, 11 (ill.), 71 (ill.), 96 (ill.), 116
Erie Canal 206–9, 206 (ill.)
European claims in the United States 3 (ill.)
Evans, John 139

F

Fallen Timbers 9, 49
Far West 29–33, 35–39, 59
Farmers 72–74
Fence Cutter's War 183–84, 227
Fetterman, William J. 101
Fields, Mary 214
Fort Astoria 33–34
Fort Defiance 134, 156
Fort Duquesne 3, 5, 23
Fort Kearny 88
Fort Laramie 88
Fort Pitt 5
Forty-Mile Desert 92, 119
Frémont, John C. 37–39, 39 (ill.), 125
French and Indian War 3–4, 47, 151, 153
French influence in North America 2, 47, 150

Frontier 13 (ill.), 23–24, 231
Fur trade 22, 33–36, 60, 66, 86

G

Gadsden, James B. 70
Gadsden Purchase 70
Geronimo 137–39, 138 (ill.), 145 (ill.), 241
Ghost Dance 144, 167, 192–93, 194 (ill.)
Gila Trail 98–100
Glorieta Pass, New Mexico 83
Gold fever 114–15
Gold rush 56, 70–72, 73 (ill.), 87, 100, 105–28, 115 (ill.), 123 (ill.), 124 (ill.), 131, 170, 195
Great Migration 71, 84, 87
Great Northern Railroad 216
Great Plains 13–39, 72–74, 159
Great Surveys 35, 41, 239 (ill.)
Gunfighting 183
Guns 170, 217–20, 219 (ill.)

H

Hall, John 220
Hardin, Wes 181
Harmer, Josiah 49
Harrison, William Henry 17, 50, 50 (ill.)
Harrison Land Act of 1800 10
Harrod, James 23
Hayden, Ferdinand Vandiveer 41
Henderson, Richard 5, 23
Herrera, Jose Joaquin 68
Hill, James J. 216
Holladay, Benjamin F. 211
Homestead Act of 1862 73
Horses, as part of Indian culture 160
Houston, Sam 64, 65
Howard, Oliver O. 137

I

Independence, Missouri 88
Independence Rock 90, 91 (ill.)

Indian attacks
    on railway workers 215
    on settlers 170
    on wagon trains 82, 96, 97, 117
Indian population decline 109
Indian Removal 43–58
Indian Removal Act of 1830 54
Indian Territory 54, 174
Indian Wars 9, 16–18, 46–54, 59, 131–46
Indians, European attitudes toward 44
Indians, religious practices 45, 188–93
Indians, trade with 150
Indians in California 106–9
Iroquois Indians 6, 152–54

J

Jackson, Andrew 17, 52, 53 (ill.), 65
Jefferson, Thomas 14, 24, 48, 60

K

Kearny, Stephen Watts 83
King, Clarence 41
King Philip's War 46

L

Lame White Man 142
Land sales 10
Land speculation 2
Land speculators 8, 10, 74
Lawlessness 170–72, 173 (ill.)
Levi Strauss 118, 127
Lewis, Meriwether 24–28, 26 (ill.), 60–61
Lewis and Clark expedition 24–28, 30 (ill.), 60–61, 61 (ill.), 78
Lexington, Kentucky 12
Little Bighorn, Battle of 142–43, 166
Little Turtle 9

Little Turtle's War 49–50
Livingston, Robert 14
The Long Walk 158
Longhorn cattle 173
Louisiana Purchase 14–15, 15
(ill.), 60
Louisiana Territory 14, 59

M

McCoy, Joseph M. 74
Magoffin, Samuel 80
Magoffin, Susan Shelby 80
Mandan Indians 28, 29, 61, 162,
190
Manifest Destiny 38, 55, 56, 63,
67, 68, 87, 132, 236
Manuelito 134, 156
Marshall, James 71, 105, 111
Mexican independence (1821) 79
Mexican-American War 56, 69,
70, 100, 156
Mining booms 72
Mining camps 73 (ill.), 122–23,
171
Mining claims 122
Minniconjou Sioux Indians 144
Missionaries 29–31, 193–96
Missions 107–9
Mix, Tom 242
Mohawk Indians 152
Monroe, James 14
Mormon Trail 91, 118, 199
Mormons 196–202, 199 (ill.)
Morse, Samuel F. B. 223
Murieta, Joaquin 126

N

Native Americans 9–10, 43–56,
45 (ill.), 82–83, 96–97, 97
(ill.), 100–2, 106–8, 131–46,
145 (ill.), 149–68, 188–93 see
also Indian
Nauvoo, Illinois 198
Navajo Indians 133, 155–59
New Orleans 12, 14
New Orleans, Battle of 17
Northwest Ordinance 8, 9, 48,
238

Northwest Passage 78
Northwest Territory 6, 8, 47, 48

O

O'Sullivan, John 63, 236
Ohio Valley 2, 5, 23, 49
Oklahoma land rush 74
Old Northwest 6, 14, 47, 48
Old Spanish Trail 91
Onate, Juan de 188
Oneida Indians 152
Onondaga Indians 152
Ordinance of 1785 7–8, 48, 238
Ordinance of 1787 8
Oregon Country 62, 66, 87
Oregon Trail 66, 67 (ill.), 71,
84–86, 85 (ill.), 89 (ill.), 138
Oregon-California Trail 84–92, 85
(ill.), 116–19
Ottawa Indians 48
Outlaws 181–82
Overland Mail Company 211
Overland mail service 100

P

Pacific Fur Company 33
Pacific Railroad Act 214
Pakenham, Sir Edward 17
Pantheism 189
Parker, Samuel 66
"The Pathfinder" see John C. Fré-
mont
Perry, Oliver 18
Pike, Zebulon Montgomery 31,
31 (ill.), 78
Pikes Peak 31, 32 (ill.)
Pioneer cabin 233 (ill.)
Pitt, William 4
Pittsburgh, Pennsylvania 12
Plains Indians 138, 159–67
Platte River 88
Polk, James K. 66, 67, 114
Pontiac 4, 47
Pony Express 72, 221–23, 222
(ill.)
Pope, John 163
Population growth 62
Potawatomi Indians 48

Powell, John Wesley 41
Prairie Schooners 93
Proclamation of 1763 4
Prostitutes 122
Pueblo Indians 156, 188

R

Railroads 84, 102, 176, 213–17,
    215 (ill.), 217 (ill.)
Ranchos 109
Raton Pass 79
Red Cloud 101, 140, 163, 164
    (ill.)
Religion and the West 187–202
Remington, Frederic 243, 243
    (ill.)
Rendezvous, mountain man 35,
    36, 37 (ill.), 86
Reno, Marcus 142
Republic of Texas 63–66
Revolutionary War 5–6, 151
Root, Elisha K. 219
Russell, Charles M. 243
Russell, William 221

S

Sacajawea 26, 28–29, 61, 61 (ill.)
Sacramento Valley 110
St. Clair, Arthur 9, 49
Salt Lake City 118, 200
San Diego Mission 108 (ill.)
San Francisco, California 107,
    114, 120, 121 (ill.), 123, 171
Sand Creek Massacre 139, 141
    (ill.), 162
Santa Anna, Antonio Lopez de
    64, 70, 143
Santa Fe, New Mexico 34
Santa Fe Trail 69, 71, 79, 81 (ill.),
    116
Scott, Winfield 55, 69
Selman, John 182
Seminole wars 52, 53 (ill.)
Seneca Indians 152
Serra, Junipero 188
Shawnee Indians 16, 48, 192
Sheridan, Philip 141
Sibley, Hiram 224

Sierra Nevada mountain range 71
    (ill.), 121
Sioux Indians 101, 140, 159
Sitting Bull 140, 142, 164, 165
    (ill.), 241
Slavery 65
Slidell, John 68
Smallpox 190
Smith, Joseph 197
Smith, Tom "Bear River" 182
Snake River 90
South Pass 85, 90, 118
Southwest 29–33
Spalding, Eliza 86
Spalding, Henry 86
Spanish control of the Louisiana
    Territory 14
Spanish influence in America 78
Spanish influence in California
    29–33, 107
Spanish influence on Navajo In-
    dians 155
Spanish missionaries 29–31, 107
Squatters 10
Stagecoaches 207 (ill.), 209–13,
    210 (ill.)
Strauss, Levi 118, 127
Stuart, Robert 85
Sutter, John Augustus 110–11,
    112 (ill.), 113
Sutter's Mill 111 (ill.)

T

Taylor, Zachary 69
Technology 205–28
Tecumseh 16–18, 17 (ill.), 48–51,
    191–92
Telegraph 223–25
Telegraph Act of 1860 224
Tenskwatawa 16, 50, 191
Texas 64–66, 172
Thames, battle of the 17
Timber Culture Act of 1873 73
Tippecanoe, Battle of 50–51, 51
    (ill.), 192
Topographical engineers 35, 40
Trade with Indians 150
Trail of Tears 54
Trails west 77–102, 87 (ill.), 99 (ill.)
Trans-Appalachian frontier 2,
    21–24

Trans-Appalachian region 152
Trans-Mississippi frontier 132
Transcontinental railroad 71–72,
    84, 213–17
Trappers 34–36
Travis, William Barret 64
Treaty of Ghent 18
Treaty of Guadalupe Hidalgo 70
Treaty of Paris (1763) 4
Treaty of Paris (1783) 6
Treaty of San Ildefonso 14
Trist, Nicholas 70
Turner, Frederick Jackson 74, 236
Tyler, John 66

V

Van Buren, Martin 55
Vaqueros 108–10
Vigilantes 171
Violence 123–24, 184–85
The Virginian 241

W

Wagon trains 71 (ill.), 88–98, 97
    (ill.), 99 (ill.), 115–19

War Hawks 16
War of 1812 2, 16–18, 34, 50–51,
    152
Warren, Kemble 40
Washington, George 3, 9, 49
Wayne, Anthony 9, 49, 191
Wayne, John 242
Weatherford, Bill 52
Webner, Frank E. 222 (ill.)
Wells Fargo 212
Western Union Telegraph Com-
    pany 224
Wheeler, George Montague 41
Whitman, Marcus 67, 86, 195,
    195 (ill.)
Whitman, Narcissa Prentiss 67,
    86, 195, 195 (ill.)
Whitman Mission 90, 195
Wild West 169–85
Wister, Owen 241
Wounded Knee, Battle of 143
    (ill.), 144, 167
Wovoka 193 (ill.)

Y

Yosemite Valley, California 233
    (ill.), 235 (ill.)
Young, Brigham 198